Reframing the House

Reframing the House

Constructive Feminist Global Ecclesiology
for the Western Evangelical Church

Jennifer M. Buck

☙PICKWICK *Publications* · Eugene, Oregon

REFRAMING THE HOUSE
Constructive Feminist Global Ecclesiology for the Western Evangelical Church

Pickwick Publications
An Imprint of Wipf and Stock Publishers
199 W. 8th Ave., Suite 3
Eugene, OR 97401

www.wipfandstock.com

PAPERBACK ISBN: 978-1-4982-7882-9
HARDBACK ISBN: 978-1-4982-7884-3
EBOOK ISBN: 978-1-4982-7883-6

Cataloguing-in-Publication data:

    Names: Buck, Jennifer M.
    Title: Reframing the house : constructive feminist global ecclesiology for the western evangelical church / Jennifer M. Buck.
    Description: Eugene, OR: Pickwick Publications, 2016 | Includes bibliographical references.
    Identifiers: ISBN 978-1-4982-7882-9 (paperback) | ISBN 978-1-4982-7884-3 (hardcover) | ISBN 978-1-4982-7883-6 (ebook)
    Subjects: LCSH: Church | Feminist theology | Oduyoye, Mercy Amba | Kwok, Pui-lan | Aquino, Maria Pilar | Title.
    Classification: BV600.3 B84 2016 (PRINT) | BV600.3 B84 2016 (EBOOK)

Manufactured in the U.S.A.   05/23/16

To Adam, my bookshelf-builder, animal caregiver, and life partner, for all the faith, encouragement and joy you bring my life. I could not have survived this last year without you by my side. There aren't enough words in all the books to express that no one's gonna love you more than I do.

To my parents and grandparents, for their legacy, for supporting every step of my academic journey, and for always believing in me. Especially my grandma, Virginia Prickett, the first great feminist thinker and reader I ever knew. You are why I'm here today.

To everyone at Rose Drive Friends Church: you all continue to motivate me to think critically about the future of the Church. It's because of the faithfulness of so many of you that I have seen Christianity modeled well and I've been able to encounter it in other cultures.

For the many edits of my doctoral work by Chris Conway, the editing of Amy Leonardt, and the incomparable legacy and insights of Rosemary Radford Ruether. Thank you.

Contents

Introduction

To BEGIN THIS PROJECT, the question that drove my academic curiosities centered on why the Christian church is growing in non-Western parts of the world and on the decline in the West. Will this trend ever be reversed? Does globalization present a possibility where both the dichotomy between the West and the non-Western world will one day disappear? And most significantly for this work here, is it possible that the non-Western church understands key aspects to the Gospel that the Western church has overlooked, misunderstood, or never accurately interpreted because of cultural barriers? These questions will in no way be answered in definitive manners, but they press forward the research and observations presented here.[1]

This work intends to be a critique of the incomplete and often one-dimensional ecclesiological frameworks presented by Western theologians.[2] Such a critique will occur using the works of Majority world (third—world) feminist theologians with their approaches as to how to speak of the church.[3] One feminist voice from Asia, the Americas, and Africa, respectively, will be thoroughly assessed to highlight the manner in which the Western church has systemically and systematically ignored the realities of much of the world in forming its limited ecclesiology. The future of theology, particularly in regard to forming the marks of the Christian church, must come with deep reflection from the margins of globalized society. The

1. I am aware that the dichotomy of Western and non-Western is not completely black and white and the specificity of this duality and its dimensions will be unpacked further in subsequent chapters.

2. "Western" here does not speak of the eastern—western theological distinction, but instead the geographic separation of hemispheres.

3. As will be discussed in the section on Kwok Pui-Lan, these authors prefer the term "Third World" as opposed to the more politically correct "Majority" world because it speaks to the injustice and disparity still existing in our context today.

lived experiences of Christians in growing corners of the globe must be invited to the table and asked to become our teachers.

Let us be abundantly clear: this paper seeks to prove the thesis that Third World feminist ecclesiology forms a relevant critique of Western evangelical ecclesiology. These voices form a global ecclesiology, with differing and distinctive marks of the church and wrestles with the challenge of globalization. I believe they form a "global" ecclesiology because these theological voices come from all over the world and the theology created can now be applied to the evangelical church worldwide. This theology takes seriously the manner in which the Holy Spirit is shaping and forming the Church worldwide, which contains implications for the Western church. This project speaks to Third World feminist descriptors of Church and believes that their attributes extend to the entire theological enterprise of ecclesiology and applies across geopolitical contexts and spaces. Likewise, this paper will address how the Western church has found itself held captive by cultural hindrances or structures of sin that limit the breadth and consistency of Christianity. Such a thesis involves a criticism of aspects such as individualism, racism, sexism, hegemonic nationalistic agendas and violence, and other institutions that marginalize and oppress the weakest in society. I am well aware that the task at hand is to avoid colonizing them, and instead be cautious to use their voices to critique something I as an author come from within, namely the Western evangelical church.

This work will be creating an ecclesiology to further both the evangelical and the low church/free church tradition.[4] To represent the evangelical tradition, I will assess the writings of Karl Barth, John Howard Yoder and Jürgen Moltmann as evangelical predecessors to the liberationist movement and voices that began the launch of ecclesiology from a political perspective. From the Quaker writings, I will look at the journal of George Fox as well as the writings of Robert Barclay and Margaret Fell. After such a discussion, the bulk of the project will focus on third—world feminist theologians in order to propose a new direction for Western ecclesiology. Three voices will be given prominence in this work from the Majority world: Mercy Oduyoye, a Ghanaian feminist theologian as representative of Africa; Kwok Pui-Lan, a Chinese feminist theologian as representative

4. Even my usage of the term *church* comes with an understanding that there is still a distinction between the universal and localized church as well as a difference between the visible and invisible nature of the church. This will be discussed further in the chapter on ecclesiology. *Evangelical* refers to those who value Scripture as a central norm for Christianity.

2

of Asia; and Maria Pilar Aquino, a Mexican feminist theologian representative of the Americas. The process of choosing each of them considered the following criteria:

- each woman represented a differing continent, including their voices as representative in a global conversation,

- each of these women has given some time and thought into the enterprise of the Christian church in this era in time, and

- each woman has compiled a introduction to feminist theology from their particular continent, so they are familiar with the other voices surrounding theirs and serve as the best representatives possible

Other female theologians would represent these claims as well, yet in particular these three represent each continent and have written the most primary texts on ecclesiology. These women are versant in the theology of women on their continent, though no sole voice can speak for all. Each of them serve as representatives of their continents, with their writings on ecclesiology particularly helpful in forming a global vision of the Church. They each serve as one of many who present an alternative ecclesiology to the traditional, orthodox models generally accepted in Western theology. Though my focus is narrowed within a particular ecumenical vein, the hope would be that one tradition can highlight the potential strength of such a globalized ecclesiology and also demonstrate how such progress can naturally further the development of particular denominations.

Lastly, each of the concerns of the Third—World feminist theologians will form a critique that I will title a "constructive global ecclesiology." I will address a number of specific areas for concern that I believe will give some distinct differences between the current Western church and the vision for a globalized church. These areas will be salvation, sin, peacemaking, women in ministry and multiethnic churches. Globalization may serve in the role of helping to abolish distinctions between the West and the non-West, but in the current time, the separation requires greater conversation and a reflection on what is working and developing in the Third World. The specific criticism from these three Third—World feminist theologians is that the Western church misses and misunderstands so much of what the church is intended to be about. It is worth noting that the goal of this work is not necessarily to highlight where Christianity is growing in number, as though size growth is the only factor of significance. Christianity in our post-modern culture has found a unique type of effectiveness in the developing world, within a globalized impoverished context. Yet there is an awareness within the tradition of Christianity that the Holy Spirit is working in these areas of the world where the church is growing in size. Each of our authors (Aquino, Oduyoye and Pui-Lan) speaks out of an experience of struggle and tells of the significance of Christianity for those on the margins. Here Christianity was able to present and provide something of significance in supplement to or in stark contrast to their local culture. In this manner, their vision of ecclesiology offers an alternative proposal, presenting entirely different ideas and critiquing our Western culture today. The hope is not necessarily for church growth as much as it is for an accurate, holistic understanding of the Gospel in order for it to be most effective in our globalized world today. The most holistic theology integrates as many voices into the theological conversation as possible and looks to learn from places where the church is growing despite being on the margins.

Significance: Globalization, Evangelicalism, and Quakers

A brief discussion of globalization is worthwhile in this introduction. The intent is that such a work will continue to further the idea proposed by Anselm Min in his *A Solidarity of Others in a Divided World* in working to construct an ecclesiology for the globalized world. Globalization speaks to "the context of all contexts," a context broader than one particular social location, and this involves not retrieving a context but better addressing the globalized nature of ecclesiology in the West. This is the methodology that will later be discussed as "contextual theology" and will demonstrate its characteristics and connection with the globalization of the West. This intricately involves an engagement with the political and liberatory framework, while also addressing the current inadequacies, such as injustice and oppression, of such limitations for the postmodern, globalized era.[5] A critique from those frameworks is intended to be an expansion upon their shared foundation of theology. Political and liberation theologians view their enterprise as a transforming power in the world to critique unjust social structures as a part of its ecclesial faithfulness. A significant portion will be given to addressing the globalized nature and future of the current

---

5. "Political" and "Liberation" ecclesiologies will be differentiated further in subsequent chapters. These terms are not intended to be used interchangeably, though much of liberation theology builds upon a framework of political theology and political theology, finds a good example of its methodology in liberation theology.

Christian church. Some topics to be addressed in greater depth in this ecclesiology are the church's role in peacemaking, taking a liberatory rather than charitable stance towards injustice, the place of women in church leadership, and the need for multicultural congregations in our globalized world. This will include a broader approach to sin and salvation that address entire personhood as well as structures of sin embedded in corporate entities.

Working from both an Evangelical and a Quaker perspective myself, I intend to briefly survey Christian ecclesiology from such a vantage point before engaging with contemporary, majority world scholarship. A natural question is why limit this work to the Evangelical and Quaker streams of Christianity. On the one hand, these are the two communities I as an author identify with most (as a recorded Evangelical Quaker pastor) and the two contexts with which I am most familiar. On the other hand, this topic is so broad and in some ways so significant that I believe each faith community must wrestle with it within its own context. For the Catholic Church, global ecclesiology and non-Western critiques has an entirely different meaning than for the Evangelical community. In particular, the three non-Western voices I have selected also come from outside of the Evangelical church. I also believe that Quaker history contains valuable examples to teach us today regarding the role of women in positions that critique traditional ecclesial structures. The Evangelical community centers itself strongly on Scripture and on ecclesial communities as the spaces where Scripture is interpreted and lived out. Since this is my framework, the language of biblical theology will be contained within evangelicalism as a part of my methodology. This will involve a conversation about the difference between what is authoritative versus normative when examining Scripture, and uses the methodology of the Prophets and Midrash as an interpretation of the Torah to examine how the Bible is intended to be reinterpreted in new contexts.

As a peculiar people, the Friends movement saw their communal ethos and faithful witness in the public square as an apologetic tool. In the context of Christian history, the Quakers, like others who emerged from the Reformation with their own revisions, have often had a quiet voice yet nevertheless they provide a unique contribution into alternative approaches to ecclesiology. Quakers looked to identify the "light of Christ" living in all people, as George Fox so aptly identified in his conversion, and use this as an impetus for missions work worldwide. Human flourishing, for Quakers, involves all peoples understanding the light within them as God working and this provides a valuable framework for the conversation of reacting to globalization through ecclesial communities. Fox went on to be known for public preaching in various unorthodox places and gathered other preachers to roam the English countryside and teach the Scriptures. This led to suffering and persecution, and, for many, imprisonment in the early movement, yet this only encouraged its growth and expansion to the Americas and West Indies. With the emphasis on the personal and corporate guidance of the Holy Spirit, Quaker spirituality began to form, and with it concerns for specific testimonies such as simplicity and integrity that served as signposts to continue to guide the movement. When all around them the Quakers observed complex ecclesial structures, the Friends arose as gatherings marked by plainness and quietude. Such an opening serves as simply a brief sketch of the origins of the Quaker movement. As the denomination grew, many splits and branches emerged, and I am speaking from the Evangelical Friends International strand, looking in particular at the emphasis on Scripture as a norm for theology and on the missions focus of its tradition as it relates to global theology.

Previous Work

One attempt at such dialogue has been movements such as the World Council of Churches or other bodies and writings that reflect an emphasis on ecumenicism. These types of movements fail to go far enough in engaging the tension between the globalized and the contextual. Too often, a watered-down statement is agreed upon, without the voices from the West acknowledging their sin and taking a posture of learning from the non-Western voices.[6]

Until now, theological scholarship critiquing the Western church has primarily located itself solely in the Majority/Third World or in the Western world, with little crossover. Rarely has the emergence of non-Western theology been viewed through the lens of criticism and assessment of the incomplete nature of Western Christian ecclesiology. One great example of this crossover has been Philip Jenkins's trilogy on global Christianity. As Philip Jenkins highlights in his thesis on the current state of Christendom, the central point of the church has migrated to the Global South, highlighting the recent movement of growing churches in the Southern Hemisphere. In 2050, 72 percent of the world's Christians will live in Africa, Asia and

---

6. See Faith and Order paper 214 from the World Council of Churches as an example of this.

Latin America and a sizeable share of the remainder will be an immigrant from one or more of those continents.[7] Likewise, the recent trend has been that, in growing hubs of Christianity, such as Korea and Nigeria, missionaries are being sent to the United States and Europe in hopes of reinvigorating and reforming dwindling areas of former Christendom. Because of this, the Western church must be honest with the reality that Christianity is now a globalized religion, and its Euro-American roots have ceased to be the solely relevant voices. Jenkins's project limited itself to sociological and religious observations, thus making it not a perfect fit for this project here, yet his thesis demands broader explications from the enterprise of Christian theology. Voices not unlike my own, from vantage points of privilege and power must humbly learn and listen to the teachings of emerging theologians in order to form broad and accurate ecclesiological reflections.

Other authors have attempted to reconcile the wealth and status of the West through Scripture rather than through balanced assessment of global economic injustice. Far too many concepts from Scripture have been misconstrued by evangelical Christians today to justify the inaction of the church. "You will always have the poor with you," for example, from Matthew 26:11, is oddly used by some Christians to justify doing nothing, even though Jesus casts a vision for his disciples to always be among the poor based on other teachings and the broader lifestyle of Christ. This idea is proponed in works like *The Good of Affluence* by John R. Schneider, a book that speaks to a Scriptural basis of supporting a wealthy, affluent lifestyle in our modern economic world.[8] This project intends to critique works like that of Schneider.

Yet other works, such as the collection of essays entitled *Evangelicals and Empire* would have to present a radical critique. "To dismiss concern for the poor at a time when the gap between the wealthy and the poor is growing across the globe is not just a result of the personalizing of sin and redemption. It is also the triumphalism of empire. The structural causes of poverty tend not to be acknowledged in the United States, because to do so would undermine the triumphal notion of America as a nation anointed by God."[9] As valuable as works like *Evangelicals and Empire* are, they find themselves primarily authored by white, Western voices giving a critique of Empire, rather than as those from the overlooked corners of Empire them-

7. Jenkins. *The Next Christendom*, xi.

8. Schneider, *The Good of Affluence*.

9. Benson and Heltzel, eds., *Evangelicals and Empire*, 41.

selves. A similar example with similar shortcomings is that of David Fitch's *The End of Evangelicalism?*[10] Likewise, when the teachings of the atonement and salvation in Christian theology relate only to personal morality and individual choices, the church incorrectly accepts its ecclesiology as ill-equipped and unable to work against larger forces of injustice battling in the world. The Church needs to expand its theological teachings in order to find itself better equipped to address the struggle against the structures of sin. The church's hope wrongly becomes in leaving this world one day to spend eternity with God separated from earth rather than to envision a renewed creation. If salvation for all of creation is something Christians participate in alongside God, then the consequences of empire for those in poverty must become of utmost importance for the community of faith.

A final example is the post-Marxist or continental philosophy movement that attempts to critique imperialism and modern nation—states. One example is *Empire* by Antonio Negri and Michael Hardt.[11] Their work does engage the prophetic role of the church by affirming how it ought to engage the prophetic, apocalyptic imagery from Scripture to support the necessity of its witness in the world as subverting empire.[12] Using Revelation 7:9–17 and its vision of the war of the Lamb, the church is called to speak against the structures of globalization like the "headed" one. The Lamb will be the agent both of cleansing and conferring of a new identity that inverts the categories of "being against" and "being for," and of leading the faithful to paradise. John's vision bespeaks a new empire of peace, purchased precisely through "the blood of the Lamb," which thus takes seriously the prevalent reality and nature of violence yet proposes the reality of a Christocentric transcendent solution through the vision of the new city and new earth. John serves as a metacritique for Hardt and Negri; though they target a critique of market-driven capitalism, it isn't sufficient for a new global order.[13] Hardt and Negri are the first to point out that early Christians were generally an anti-imperial force and created a movement to oppose or escape from power.[14] Christianity today can serve similarly to protest and resist the domination of U.S. power. Their challenge is for the church to better understand love as a political concept. "To love God,

10. Fitch, *The End of Evangelicalism?*
11. Hardt and Negri, *Empire.*
12. Ibid, 396.
13. Ibid., 298.
14. Ibid., 373.

therefore, cannot be separated from a love of God's gifts, for to love the gift is to love the giver, just as to love the giver necessarily entails loving the gift. To destroy life and the conditions of life—be it through murder, war, or ecological destruction—is to demonstrate ingratitude towards God; it is to reject the abundant gifts of the Creator."[15] Standing with Hardt and Negri, this work will critique assumptions that globalization was a natural byproduct of capitalism and only present alternatives for how the forces of globalization can be redirected by the church.

Voices like William Cavanaugh, in his many works on political theology, remind Christians that "the modern state . . . is best understood as an alternative soteriology to that of the church . . . a false copy of the Body of Christ."[16] These words of Cavenaugh's pose a challenge to the church that through the Eucharist we birth a new political presence that engages society for redemption and renewal. "Christ's reign becomes visible as we embody the infinite gifting of forgiveness, faithfulness and love. This way of being together births the Kingdom not only among 'us.' It enables us to resist alternative politics of violence and isolation, to subvert them, and indeed to draw the world into the restoration of all things."[17] How this idea challenges globalization plays into the challenge of knowing and understanding consumption. Our products and economic purchasing power can be a force used by the Spirit of God to bring the Kingdom or it can continue to support systems of violence and isolation. Countercultural Christians must practice and not just preach alternative life modes of consumption and signify new and alternative forms of "being" in and through their entire lifestyles.

All of these authors take steps in a direction towards a critique of the evangelical church in its role in globalization, but none are Third-World women providing the critiques out of lived experiences. In speaking of globalization, Pope John Paul II challenges the church: "Even more in the era of globalization, the Church has a precise message: to work so that this world of ours, which is often described as a 'global village,' may truly be more united, more fraternal, more welcoming . . . In the church there are no strangers or sojourners, but fellow citizens with the saints and members of the household of God."[18] This calls the Church to realize the indwelling

---

15. Ibid., 351.

16. Cavenaugh, *Torture and Eucharist*.

17. Benson and Heltzel, eds., *Evangelicals and Empire*, 299.

18. Cheah, *Inhuman Conditions*, 244.

God as subversive moral agency constantly giving life and it involves continually seeing and naming the ways in which globalization damages life. The people of God must resist those ways, and courageously acting towards alternatives. And this conversation of globalization is all the more important when speaking of Third-World women.

> In the face of increasing global violence against women as well as the growing neocaptialist exploitation of the so-called two-thirds world and the explosion of an 'informatics of domination', feminist theory cannot stop with the postmodern 'subject-in-language' and its permanent destabilization, global dispersal and atomizing regionalization. It must develop a theoretical discourse and analytic framework that can account for the interaction between cultural-religious, economic, and political spheres of production.[19]

Elisabeth Schussler Fiorenza's assessment is accurate, as Kwok Pui-Lan understands it, regarding the challenge of Third-World feminist theology. The voices referred to in this summary of literature are helpful and lay the foundation for such a project of critique, but none are uniquely working with third-world, feminist voices to critique the Western world. Feminists worldwide must wrestle with violence and injustice brought from capitalism and globalization. Feminist theology is naturally contextually based, but those contexts are inseparably linked together in our modern era like never before.

Methodology

Before addressing the plan of argument, I want to give a brief amount of space to the methodology and the reason for working with the model of contextual theology. Methodologically, this work will expand on both the liberationist framework and the work of political theology, challenging the West to understand how our approach to ecclesiology served as a silencing and oppressive vehicle in and of itself. Both political theology and liberation theology serve as helpful predecessors because rather than calling for reform, each approach sees the most effective use of the church's resources as calling for radical structural change of the entire theological system. Both share the framework that the church provides an alternative ethic to confront unjust systems that demands a starting point at the margins

---

19. Schüssler Fiorenza in Kwok, "Feminist Theology as Intercultural Discourse," 33.

of society. When the oppressed and the disenfranchised are invited to be the cornerstones for rebuilding the system of theology, then the church is forced to reflect on itself and the manner in which it has perpetuated and, in many aspects, enforced such systems of injustice. The direction of liberation theology has shifted since its heyday and its significance at this point in history relates more toward particularized struggles for justice rather than entire government revolutions, which I believe positions it well as a methodology for this project. The hope is that through deep ecclesiological critique, the enterprise of theology can properly construct a liberatory, political presentation of the church.

A re-envisioning of the work of the Church calls for conversation with politically minded theologians. The task of such theology is to continue to challenge evangelical Christianity, which finds itself lacking in holding to a robust enough ecclesiology so as to engage injustices with the Gospel, so that our politic "embodies the integrity of our existence 'in Christ' incarnationally for God's mission in the world. Christianity must restore the ontological core of its political existence in the life of the triune God for its own integrity in the globalized world today. This is the path towards our political life in the world becoming evangelical again."[20] We must create a Christian critique that radically exposes the hypocrisies and double standards of powerful nations with economic policies that run counter to their lip service to universal norms and human rights. This involves listening to the voices of Third-World women and allowing their realities to shape the conversation. The church must ask: "What might it mean, in the Western context of economic globalization, to practice the morally transformative consequences of God indwelling creation? What might our being communal and communing body of God contribute to the transformation of economic structures that violate the body and its members—human and other . . . for the presence and power of God, living in and loving in creation, will lead those who dare to know that presence more intimately and to see the realities of globalization more clearly, along unknown paths."[21] These questions must drive our existence in the world as we consider how purchases and lifestyle choices either support or subvert the economic empire and challenge the dying Western church.

One major type of methodology that will be used is that of contextual theology. This work is build on the presupposition that the church is the

---

20. Fitch. *The End of Evangelicalism?*, 130.

21. Moe-Lobeda, *Healing A Broken World*, 149.

space in which theological reflection is lived out, where questions of God find lived answers in the experiences of the community. Such a methodology values the role of doing contextual theology and at the same time recognizes the difficulty of it. Context is the space where theology is lived out, and yet particularities of context are fading away in our globalized world. We will look to our teachers who have attempted this project before with Trinitarian, Political, and Liberation Ecclesiologies—voices like Leonardo Boff, Jon Sobrino, Letty Russell, and so forth. Their works pivotally shaped the theological conversation of low church ecclesiologies by giving us new language and metaphors for the church: church as base communities, church in the round, and church as new ecclesial praxis in solidarity with the poor. Too often, the Western Christian church has failed to influence secular culture and has instead found itself existing in reaction to developments and progress in the secular state rather than proacting and leading culture. With its groundings in eschatological hope, the church must locate a manner in which it can better utilize its resources in order to stand in solidarity with its brothers and sisters around the globe. It is not surprising to learn that in our postmodern, globalized world, the Kingdom of God is growing in areas of deep injustice and suffering. Persecution and martyrdom have often served to refine and strengthen the Christian church, whereas apathy and stability have historically weakened its movement.

Speaking of ecclesiology is always best done as a reflection of contextual theology. Literature on ecclesiology in the West has, up until this point, found itself written by voices in the West. Likewise the conversations happening in the Global South have rarely translated to the Western context, or have been read as examples of contextual theology done somewhere else rather than as penetrating critiques of the church here. This is all the more significant when having conversations regarding a rethinking of contextual theology in the globalized context. No longer can any church community faithfully reflect merely one context, but must be open theologically to how the picture of the church in Ghana (Hong Kong, Mexico, etc.) affects what our communities of faith look like in the West. Separation is no longer a viable ecclesial option in the globalized context.

Maria Pilar Aquino, Kwok Pui-Lan, and Mercy Amba Oduyoye

Maria Pilar Aquino, Kwok Pui-Lan and Mercy Amba Oduyoye each hold significant merit in their own right, but a brief background should help frame the reasoning behind their selection for this work. Their visions will be developed at greater length in a chapter given to each of their ecclesiologies, but it is worth identifying that all three of them find a united vision in valuing indigenous cultures over colonialist representations of Christianity, placing women as equal voices and leaders with men in churches, and reinterpreting history, Scripture, and Christian tradition through new lenses that value women's interpretations. Since all three of these women come from marginalized contexts, their words on church also require a strong stance against globalization and the Western church's direct or indirect hand in such subjugation.

Maria Pilar Aquino is a Mexican woman whose focus on Catholic Hispanic Theology and Latin American Women in the church and theology has led her to become one of the most vocal members in the movement of Latina Feminist Theology. Methodologically, she believes that theology must represent a shared perspective, which poses problems for Latino theology because of the weight of Western theological tradition and the need for theological diversity. She understands *mestizaje* as its theological method and *lo cotidiano*, or "daily life" as a category for analysis.[22] Feminine spiritualties are invited to engender a new world by standing up to the homogenizing avalanche of kyriarchal ecclesiology and dismantle the spiritual mechanisms that support it in order to provide new visions of transformed spiritual community.[23] The concern for eliminating all oppression, but especially that of women, must be at the center. Her focus is one on the realities of globalization being a part of everyday life rather than an abstract concept, and this presses her to believe that ecumenical discussions must come from the base. Theology must be connected to pas-

22. *Mestizaje* refers to the new hybrid race, Mexicans who are the mixed people born of Indian and Spanish blood in the sixteenth century. She co-opts this term into theological language, speaking of a hybridity and the syncretic nature of theology and culture. This definition comes from Maria Pilar Aquino's definition in *A Reader in Latina Feminist Theology*.

23. I credit Rosemary Radford Ruether to introducing me to Elisabeth Schüssler Fiorenza's term "kyriarchal." The preference of this term over patriarchal is because it involves structures of domination working together as a network—including but not limited to racism, sexism, heterosexism, ageism, and ableism.

toral action on behalf of the poor, with a re-reading of history in order to create an alternative ethical—political project for advancing Christianity. "From my own experiential position in the Americas, I can see clearly that this kyriarchal Christian tradition not only has not contributed to forging systems that engender social justice, but that it also is still failing in its mission to provide people reasons to assert their hope that another world is possible."[24] For Aquino, the role of women who understand suffering and hope is to carry on the faithful work of keeping the gospel message together with the best elements in their own ancestral cultural symbolic world. She uses the metaphor of women as actors/subjects in the church so that they can best integrate culture and community into the gospel work of proclamation, witness, celebration and unity. Women in Latin America see their fate as closely linked to the church and likewise understand the church as the mechanism for which socio-political transformations can happen (*ecclesiogenesis*) to create a new society.[25] Her vision of theology as an intercultural activity connects well with a global ecclesiology.

Kwok Pui-Lan, from Hong Kong, has published extensively on Asian feminist theology and postcolonial theology. Her belief is that women in Third-World churches "bear witness to a faith that empowers people to break through silence and move to action."[26] The problem with being caught between two identities, like Christian and Chinese, becomes all the more complicated in a globalized context when Pui-Lan understands the struggle of being torn between her identity as being from Hong Kong but also from China, and being a woman but also being from the Christian tradition. Her stress is on an inclusive theology that moves away from a unified theological discourse to a plurality of voices and a genuine catholicity. In the missionary movement in China, women were not just onlookers but integral members in the church—participating and leading, as well as working against injustices, alongside those who campaign for the anti-footbinding movement, temperance unions, and so forth. Christianity offered women new symbolic resources and thus she advocates the demythologizing and demystifying of theology. Pui-Lan herself even values continuing to use the term "Third World" because it connotes not simply a geographical area but the tremendous power imbalance between the powerful and the

24. Aquino, ed., *Feminist Intercultural Theology*, 10.

25. Leonardo Boff's use of the term *ecclesiogenesis* is borrowed by Aquino and involves lengthy unpacking later.

26. Kwok, "Mothers and Daughters, Writers and Fighters," 24.

disenfranchised. It also metaphorically reminds us that theology, for Asian women and others, exists in a third space outside of the binary, dualistic, or hierarchical constructions thus far. Women may be the majority in Asian churches but too often they are still marginalized in the power structure of the life of the church. She wants to move the conversation away from being "missiological objects" or "theological subjects" to ecclesial creators themselves. She rejects the myth of the uniqueness of Jesus Christ when used by Christian missionaries to fuel triumphalism and exclusivity. The value for Pui-Lan is in localized networks and collaborative communities to affirm her "power-with-others" rather than "power-over-others" model.

Mercy Amba Oduyoye is one of the pioneers of African women's theology and ecumenical work. She is a third-generation Ghanaian Methodist Christian and has seen her homeland struggle against colonial domination but she herself never experienced the subjugation of women until leaving her matriarchal home for academia. Her work focuses on postcolonial Christianity in Africa, women in the gospel tradition, and theological issues from an African perspective. She believes in a postcolonial trajectory for a future history of Christian theology that is dialogical, uses narrative genres, respects all cultures, and addresses gender dynamics in complex ways.[27] Oduyoye believes that they are many churches, divided and "being church" in a number of ways all throughout Africa. One unified church can emerge only if all expressions of church are validated in their representation of African Christianity based out of African culture. Each of these spirit-led representations of God must be acknowledged and vindicated in order to bring women into full personhood. African Christianity cannot resort to a nativist mode of returning to traditional culture, nor can it simply mimic Western colonial forms. Instead, Oduyoye values intercultural theological dialogue without allowing it to devolve into cultural pluralism in what she calls "crossroads Christianity," a Christianity that takes cultural dialogue seriously while still remaining faithful to its theological core.[28]

Conclusion

As a collective vision, the church is invited to stand faithfully to the calling of the gospel. There are deep ethical and theological implications of the

27. Kwok, "Mercy Amba Oduyoye" in Kwok and Rieger eds., *Empire and the Christian Tradition*, 485.

28. Odyoyoe, "Christianity and African Culture," 80–81.

violence inflicted on humanity as a result of globalization within the majority world as well as with those on the margins in the minority world. As a result of globalization, our collective humanity became marred through economic structures used for sin, structures that consumed the wealthy and exploited the poor. The church, in countering globalization, is invited to imagine how God's Kingdom can exist here on earth in our globalized world. Our task is now one to let the voices from the Third World teach us and construct a new framework of distinct markings of the church. The saints who have gone before us have fought the good fight and challenged the same demons in different forms—those of greed, injustice and everything that dehumanizes—and the church today can be inspired by their example but must construct a broader ecclesiology moving forward. As the church moves toward greater solidarity with our brothers and sisters abroad and at home, we can together with them reclaim the lost ground of human equality and witness the power of God working among us to, in the prophetic words of Isaiah, "loose the bonds of injustice, undo the thongs of the yoke, to let the oppressed go free, and to break every yoke."

Ecclesiology is intended to be a project that serves as a way of unifying ecumenically without undermining diversity. The significance of cultures and traditions still exists even within a globalized context. After a deep assessment of the (politically oriented) evangelical, Quaker, and Third World feminist theologies, this work will attempt to theologically construct an ecclesiology of globalization. It intends to present the case for how such development in theology is desperately needed in order to enrich the growth of the Western church and its theology. By forming entirely new marks of the globalized church, the hope would be that now the gospel is better represented in the majority world in regards to the practical, lived-out nature of the Christian community. Truths of Christianity and "respectable" sins that have for years been ignored in postindustrialized nations will now be assessed in terms of their impact on the poorest and most marginalized members of the Christian church. Women in Third-World communities' have borne disproportionally the burden of globalization; the hope is that their voices can articulate a globalized, transnational, or intercultural feminist theology of solidarity. I believe their theology holds to impact the entire landscape of theology and should not be limited to only apply in their Third World context. The critiques of Odoyuye, Pui-Lan, and Aquino will provide the framework for the construction of a more robust ecclesiology, one that takes into account the gaping holes in the gospel as presented in the

West and forces the church to be accountable for the manner in which its nature has perpetuated structures of oppression and disparity. Their major themes will be compiled to help form the second half of this dissertation, a type of constructive global ecclesiology. Some of the areas this theology will address are salvation of whole persons, structures of sin, peacemaking, women in leadership and multiethnic church communities. This outlined structure comes with the hope of a vision of a more adequate ecclesiology, one attempt that better reflects the many dimensions of Christ's vision for his people in the world. This is the church as envisioned in Matthew, one that the gates of Hades itself cannot even overcome. This is a Kingdom of God as envisioned by Jesus of a shared community of healing and eating, with spiritual and physical resources available to each and all without distinctions, discriminations, or hierarchies.

Table of Contents

After this introduction, this paper intends to lay out a foundation for aspects of constructive global feminist ecclesiology by discussing the significance of Christian ecclesiology and the background of the evangelical ecclesial tradition, where doctrines such as Christology and the role of Scripture will be presented. Contained in that will be a conversation around globalization and the context of the Western Christian church today (chap. 1). Then some space will be given to the methodology from which the author understands ecclesiology: the Quaker ecclesiological tradition, political and Feminist ecclesiology (chap. 2). This chapter will also give a brief treatment of Trinitarian theology and its influence on ecclesiology as well as discussion on liberation theology and the place of base communities. From here, our three Third-World feminist theologians will be given a chapter of space: Mercy Amba Oduyoye, Kwok Pui-Lan, and Maria Pilar Aquino (chap. 3). Then those conclusions will be presented as a constructive global ecclesiology, with attention given to the following subsections: salvation of whole persons and structures of sin as theological treatments (chap. 4). And lastly, constructive practical theology will explore these three ecclesiological tenets: peacemaking, women in leadership, and multiethnic churches (chap. 5). This intends to cover the project of a constructive Christian global ecclesiology for Western evangelical churches.

1

The Significance of Christian Ecclesiology

The Evangelical Ecclesiological Tradition, Globalization, and the Context of the Western Christian Church

Introduction

WITHIN THE FIELD OF theological reflection, ecclesiology both contains the theological embodiment of the Church and serves as the aspect that grounds the lived experience of the present historical era within the tradition of Church history. Theological embodiment speaks to the manner in which the historical nature, theological convictions, and globalized context unite together to form the church in this particular instance in time. Ecclesiology should never be stagnant, but instead viewed as an area of theology that is always in progress as the Holy Spirit continues to guide and refine the community of believers toward greater faithfulness. In each era in history, the Church must confront the great needs in broader society with the resources provided by God. Ecclesiology serves the Spirit-formed and Spirit-sustained community, modeled after the perichoretic community of the Trinitarian persons. Only through the Kingdom of God does the Church possess the tools to disarm the powers of sin and contain the ability to adequately provide an alternative politic.[1] Similarly, biblical scholar

---

1. My use of the term "politic" borrows from John Howard Yoder in *The Politics of Jesus*. This will be explained at greater length in the chapter on political ecclesiology.

N.T. Wright speaks of the Church as the fifth act of a play, with the prior four acts being represented in Creation, Fall, Israel and Jesus.[2] The Church continues to live out the biblical story, embodying Scripture and modeling redemption in the world until the eschaton. Such a presentation is found when the enterprise of theology appropriately reflects on what should be the true marks of the Church and how its ethos sufficiently embodies all tenets of the Gospel.[3] This challenge becomes all the more relevant in the twenty-first century, as the pluralized society is forced to confront the realities of the ever-changing and diversifying nation—state.

The methodology to be harnessed in this chapter will examine specific models of churches used by various Christian denominations within the Evangelical tradition as well as an unpacking of Scripture's role in forming communities. I will also work with Avery Dulles's seminal work, *Models of the Church*, for a framework for the various types of Western church models that influence our modern context, as well as a few other authors who have given time to the conversation of the current or future state of evangelicalism. Ecclesiology finds itself formed by an unpacking of prophetic visions in the Hebrew Bible as well as replications of the early Church communities in the New Testament. Likewise this chapter will flesh out the understanding of Christology that informs and underpins Christian ecclesiology. Trinitarian theology, which is also essential in understanding ecclesiology and is deeply connected to Christology, will be addressed at greater length in the chapter on political theology.

It is worth briefly discussing why an understanding of Christian ecclesiology can be identified as "significant." This work builds upon the premise that how we form, define, and embody ecclesial communities shapes the growth and effectiveness of the Christian Church. This task holds significance, not necessarily over any other theological work, but especially because of the importance it maintains in the future of the Christian Church and the effectiveness of the Gospel going forth. Sociologically, the term "church" would speak to a group of people who consider themselves to be followers of Jesus of Nazareth and exist in community. This lowercase church reflects every local, particularized representation of

2. Wright, "How Can the Bible Be Authoritative?"

3. The term "gospel" is a reflection of the biblical theology language that will serve as a part of my methodology. One of the dimensions I intend to explore is how culturally embedded even the term "gospel" is, implying very different contextual definitions of the Gospel and the nature of salvation. I am choosing to capitalize the term "Gospel" with respect to the Evangelical understanding of the term.

the Church worldwide. In contrast, theologically, each of these localized expressions of the Church tells of mystery of the Body of Christ, the Christ of Faith, made known in the world and in the communion of saints across the ages. This uppercase Church stands throughout history and universally worldwide. Theologically, the Church is both present and otherworldly, a spiritual communion with the Divine and other believers. This Church, as spoken of in the creeds, is one, holy, apostolic, and catholic. Martin Luther identified the "true" Church as the space where the proper preaching of the Gospel and the proper administration of the sacraments occurs, but it is worth mentioning that harmonious agreement of what the true Church is or how it should be recognized does not exist. There is a reality that the perfect Church will never be completely realized on earth, and all ecclesial bodies will be flawed representations. This reality, taken with the vision of church unity, allows for local congregations, each with particularized contexts and doctrinal representations. The challenge emerges when such representations present in conflict with one another. True ecclesiology intends to present the most faithful representation of the scriptural vision of the Church possible while still including the truths of God at work as made present in culture. This is no small task, but it does require a thorough discussion of Christian ecclesiology before proceeding.

In assessing the evangelical ecclesiological tradition, one must begin with a hearty definition of the term "evangelical," as best it can be divorced from its current Western cultural baggage. Primarily, my usage of this term centers on specific Christians who identify the Bible as their central norm for Christianity. For the sake of our in-depth analysis here, added qualifiers will be helpful. Four attributes appear to be present in the communities that identify as evangelical: biblicism, crucicentrism, conversionism, and activism.[4] Biblicism emphasizes the centrality of Christian Scriptures as normative for theology, crucicentrism stresses the cross of Christ as necessary for salvation and discipleship, conversionism emphasizes life transformation and the process of being born again, and lastly, activism focuses on evangelism, outreach, and the preaching of the Gospel. This focus should, in an ideal sense, separate the evangelical churches from those of the Roman Catholics, the mainline Protestants, and for use in later portions of this work, Third—World "Initiated" churches. Evangelical churches,

---

4. I borrow this from David Bebbington's widely used definition. McGrath, "The Future Configuration of a Global and Local Tradition," in O'Mahony and Kirwan, eds. *World Christianity*, 172.

since the Reformation in the sixteenth century, have acknowledged *sola scriptura* ("Scripture alone"), using acknowledged canonical Scripture as the primary source for revelation and theology. Evangelicalism traces its origins back to medieval Europe, yet the eighteenth-century revivals in England and figures such as John and Charles Wesley are thought to be its foundations. In the United States, the growth of Evangelicalism came in connection with the Protestant Reformation and American revivalism. State churches and free churches spawned missionary movements, historic documents to protect the Christian faith such as the Barmen Declaration in 1934, and theological education schools worldwide. The twentieth century saw a rise in "neo-evangelicalism" and a division between the fundamentalist movement and a more moderate, culturally engaged and intellectually developed evangelicalism. The latter will be the focus of this background chapter. This movement arose in the United States in the late 1940s and reacted to fundamentalism, with a greater emphasis on addressing social issues. The denomination and the term "Evangelical" are best understood as a fluid and changing concept even throughout history, and this will be explored here.

The Ekklesia of God

Ecclesiology concerns itself with the *ekklesia* of God. The *ekklesia* speaks of the assembly of the people—the coming together as a public demonstration of diverse peoples united only by God. As Gerhard Lofink teaches, "The Christian community was not a *thiasos* or an *eranos* or a *koinon* or a *collegium*. It was not a segment or part of a larger whole . . . or a group, or a faction or a club nor was it a sect."[5] This is distinct because the early Church was distinctly a public assembly of the whole. The "whole" speaks to the idea of the people of God, not being merely another gathering of people but centered on the idea that its people are incapable of resembling a community without the centrality of the Holy Spirit. The unity given by the Spirit of God is the only means that a gathering or an assembly moves into an *ekklesia*. Paul speaks of this in Philippians 2:1—5, describing the believers as "sharing in the Spirit" and "being in Christ."

Lofink also reminds that the Church as a distinct body of believers must be a body that cannot forget and works to remember correctly in order to truly worship. "The Church therefore needs a place in which it

5. Lofink. *Does God Need the Church?*, 218.

can not only hand on its own memories but continually subject them to critical examination . . . its narratives and confessions, its laws and commandments, its exhortations and promises, prayers and songs, symbols and symbolic actions are its life-giving memory."[6] Others speak of this as the "memory of the future," or the idea of endless eternal time disrupting our temporal lives.[7] The Holy Spirit allows the eschaton to enter into history through the liturgical event, calling all persons into communion. In the gathering of believers, the Church's memory is kept alive and it embodies its sacraments and liturgy, so as not to erode its memory. This makes present the past action of God and allows the believers to participate in the ongoing life of Jesus.

The *ekklesia* also understands itself as the Body of Christ in the world. The *ekklesia* is distinctly not Christ and paradoxically the *ekklesia* distinctly is the real presence of Christ in history. This is the paradox of the *ekklesia* as saints and sinners, baptized "in Christ" and yet also still very much the earthly, incomplete gathering of human beings. Galatians 2:19–20 and 1 Corinthians 12:24—27 speak of the death to self and the rebirth to life in Christ that comes with becoming a part of the Body. There is a freedom and a voluntariness to this Body, and still a weaving together, assembling, and an incorporating into the Body of Christ. The communion of believers must be an embodied place where it can take shape so that our lives are not lived in isolation but woven together into one single body. The *ekklesia* is the visible community of reconciliation to the world as the Body of Christ, the different members brought together to serve in unity through the power of the Spirit of Jesus Christ.

Models of the Church

The Church as a theological embodied reality is one of mystery.[8] Models and imagery are intended to illuminate the mystery of the church without being overly limiting or inclusive. Though an institution, Christian churches are intended to be marked by catholicity at all costs to avoid falling into sectarian distinctives. One perspective we will work with quite extensively

6. Ibid., 251.

7. This term "memory of the future" I borrow from Zizioulas, *Being as Communion*, 96.

8. "Mystery" as taken from the Pauline epistles; see Eph 3:8 and 5:32; Col 1:12 and 3:9; and 1 Cor 2:12.

in this essay is that from Avery Cardinal Dulles's *Models of the Church*. His engagement with Protestant and Catholic ecclesiologies leads him to six models, or approaches, for local congregational formation. Those models are: Institution, Mystical Communion, Sacrament, Herald, Servant and Community of Disciples. Healthy ecclesiology, in Dulles's opinion, combines a balance of each of the six models and affirms the strengths of each.

As an institution, the church takes on aspects of political society by being as visible and palpable as any other community. Institutional ecclesiology divides the powers of the church into teaching, sanctifying and governing. This model gives emphasis to the doctrinal transmissions of the church and emphasizes the hierarchical conception of authority. Vatican II echoed this schema with three notable terms: clericalism, juridicism and triumphalism.[9] The institutional model understands the ministry of the church as conceiving of the bonds that unify the Church, the beneficiaries that are served by the Church, and the nature of the benefits bestowed by the Church. For the Roman Catholic Church, for example, the Institutional model has given a strong sense of corporate identity while lacking in scriptural basis and underemphasizing certain Christian virtues. This model serves as the one that most Third World feminist theologians are writing against, working to create an ecclesiology that best balances the demands of the times with a living theology. As an institution, the church takes a privileged position in the world, uniquely teaching, sanctifying and ruling through the authority given by Christ.

The Church as mystical communion, Dulles writes, "is a communion which is at once inward and external, an inner communion of spiritual life (of faith, hope and charity) signified and engendered by an external communion in profession of the faith, discipline and the sacramental life."[10] The Church is an outward and visible society, but it also rests on a deeper spiritual dimension of grace. The invisible element that binds all believers together is a concept identified in Romans 12 and 1 Corinthians 12, as well as stressed by Augustine and other Church Fathers. This model stresses the divinization of the Church, possibly to an unhealthy fault and seems to be at odds with the ideas of the New Covenant and the Body of Christ. If the Holy Spirit is working amongst and in the people of God, this must include

---

9. Dulles, *Models of the Church*, 31. It is also important to note here than Vatican II more than just echoed these aspects of institution but tried to go beyond these tendencies as well.

10. Ibid., 42.

the visible and invisible, and cannot alienate those from this communion by seeming egotistical or monopolistic. The feminist critique of such language or model would be that too often this communion of the People of God has centered on white male church leadership and excluded the voices on the margins from such a communion. The strength of this model is the emphasis on the interior graces and gifts of the Holy Spirit, a gathering connected by the reconciling grace of God. The potential for this model comes in the mystical connection that binds believers across countries and continents, forcing the people of God to address the reality of connection with our brothers and sisters in this globalized era. This model attempts to move the church beyond mere institution, yet still grounds itself in the Catholic tradition and the biblical models of *koinonia* and the Body of Christ.

The Church as sacrament reconciles the divine and human aspects of church. Borrowing from Henri de Lubac, Karl Rahner, and others, the church becomes the space wherein the "socially constituted or communal symbol of the presence of grace comes to fulfillment."[11] The church becomes the space for the full and ancient meaning of the sacrament of Christ made present. Rahner himself believes this Sacrament finds itself demonstrated best in the Eucharist:

> The Church is most tangibly and intensively an 'event' where (through the words of consecration) Christ himself is present in his own congregation as the crucified and resurrected Savior, the found of salvation; where the Redemption makes itself felt in the congregation by becoming sacramentally visible; where the 'New and Eternal Testament' which he founded on the cross is most palpably and actually present in the holy remembrance of its first institution.[12]

The sacramental model calls for active participation, a visible signpost to the world through its spiritual unity as represented in witness and worship. Here we see a picture of the church as a means for purifying and intensifying our response to grace while still supporting the idea of church as institution and mystical communion. The difficulty can be in overcoming mere externals and rituals to whole life and community transformation. The space of service and engagement in external injustices must be fleshed out in order for this model to fully embody Christ's sacrament. Church as

---

11. Ibid., 59.

12. Rahner, "The Church and the Sacraments," 317, as referenced by Dulles in his chapter "The Church as Sacrament."

sacrament connects more with Catholic thought and teaching and finds little parallel in Protestant ecclesiology. The beauty of this model is the integration of other theological doctrines—Christology, ecclesiology, pneumatology, etc.—into unity when lived out in a dynamic fashion.

The Church as herald stresses the Word primarily and understands the mission of the Church as to hear, believe, gather around and preach the Word of God to the world. Following the vision of Paul, Martin Luther, Karl Barth, Rudolf Bultmann, and other figures, the Church is called to faithfully proclaim the Word to the entire world, and this event is the point of encounter with God. Barth stresses the Church as the herald of Christ's Lordship and the future Kingdom of God as it emerges from the epistle to the Romans with a vision of the called out *ekklesia*. This model resonates with the Protestant vision of the church as the event between the Lord and the hearer when evangelical preaching occurs. Here one finds a vision for mission, a charge to fulfill the great commission of Matthew 28:18–20, a clear picture of salvation as extended throughout the biblical narrative. This model is limited in its vision of the fellowship of believers and in the Word being made flesh in community. The Word must translate into action as well as contain a clear understanding of the authority of the Church in relation to the Scriptures.

The Church as servant counters positions of privilege by viewing the ecclesial body as a servant to the world. Dulles connects this model with the vision given by Pope John Paul XXIII and the Vatican II Council to give a vision of the Church as suffering servant as well as healer and reconciler, and this vision affirms the ecclesial theology of those such as Teilhard de Chardin and Dietrich Bonhoeffer. In Bonhoeffer's own words, "The Church is the Church only when it exists for others."[13] This ecclesiology takes serious the secular developments of humanity and how those can inform the church's identity. Such a position forces the church to discern God's presence in the midst of our modern world and keeps it as a relevant, influential institution. The servant church reminds the world of the hope of Christ and seeks to transform institutions through prophetic critique and tangible service. This model is evidenced less in actual Scriptural accounts for the entire Church and more instead in the descriptors of how Jesus's followers are called to live. The vision of the Kingdom of God, as well as that of the *kerygmata*, best inform this servant model.

13. Bonhoeffer, *Letters and Papers from Prison,* 203, as referenced by Dulles in his chapter "The Church as Servant."

Lastly, for Dulles the Church as a community of disciples embodies the strengths of the previous five models and for the vision of this project, best aligns with the vision of both Third World and feminist theology. A post-Constantinian church must stress a deeper ecclesiology that harmonizes outer religious commitments with inner discipleship and transformation. The bridge between the institutional and community models comes as the fellowship of disciples carries on the mission of Jesus and his original followers. This vision stands with the ideas of the church as an alternative society, a type of "peculiar people" who exist as pilgrims in the Way of Jesus. "Christ's presence in the community of disciples is dynamic and effective. He is constantly at work transforming the disciples into his image, claiming their lives for his service, empowering them for mission, and causing their labors to bear fruit."[14] This model opens up the omnisacramental nature of the presence of God in the world, allowing every follower to see Christ at work in his or her neighborhoods and vocations. Critiques of this model are that it is individualistic, demanding, and set-apart, yet these are countered with the living Jesus existing at the center, drawing the community around the reality of God found in Christ. The truest sense of this model seeks to embody the charge in Galatians 3:28 of all being made one in Christ. Similarly, 1 Corinthians 1:13 stresses the community as being unified, indivisible, as one flock, and with one shepherd from John 10. This model stresses God at work in all humanity and in every corner of the world, stressing the equality of persons and the challenge of following Christ.

Karl Barth's Ecclesiology

In order to create this understanding of what is uniquely Evangelical ecclesiology, my intent is to work with Karl Barth primarily. My assertion is that his thinking on ecclesiology shaped the contemporary state of Evangelical ecclesiology more than any other. Though Barth's evangelical work at the time shaped the Lutheran and Reformed churches in Europe, his treatise on Evangelical Theology gives theological background and Word-centered theology to the present-day Western Evangelical church. His work focused a great deal on the nature of the church and shaped the Evangelical understanding of ecclesiology for years to come. This comes largely because of his emphasis on exegesis and biblical theology. His small yet powerful work, *Evangelical Theology*, as well as his volume from *Church Dogmatics* IV/3.2,

14. Dulles, *Models of the Church*, 214–15.

serve as the basis for the evaluation of his thinking on Evangelical ecclesiology.[15] His volume of *Church Dogmatics* speaks to his ecclesiology proper, yet my inclusion and heavy work with *Evangelical Theology* speaks to the less systematic, more grassroots approach to Evangelical ecclesiology today which I believe Barth strongly influenced. Barth understood his theology as the struggle of the Christian faith against distorted Christian faith rather than a struggle against those who did not claim faith. This thinking influences his authorship of the Barmen Declaration and a call for the Church to stand robustly against the globalizing force of fascist ideology as manifest in Germany. His concepts of the community, or the local church as a community of faith, as well as the Word, or the Word of God as written, spoken, and lived, serve as central theological ideas when forming an ecclesiology.

Primarily, Barth speaks in *Evangelical Theology* on the value of the Christian community as central. He desires for the word "community" to replace the word "church" and emphasizes that theology's place is in the community rather than with God. By this, Barth affirms that Christianity will address its problematic elements and find itself free to break from isolation. The community can now position itself where it properly belongs in order to best address schism and unity as well as obedience and disobedience in its midst. On some occasions, Barth goes as far as to advocate that "church" should be replaced by "Christianity," understood as a nation rather than a system of beliefs. This nation is gathered, founded and ordered by the Word of God. This is the communion of saints, women and men encountered by the Word and so moved by its message that they could not withdraw themselves from its call. Each individual believer is invited to completely become a member of a body and exist within a particularized church all the while not completely at home within them. Instead, each believer is invited to become able, willing and ready to receive the Word as secondary witnesses, proclaiming the Word to the world so that their faith does not become an end in itself.

For Barth's ecclesiology, the whole community is to possess an attitude of "I believed, and so I spoke."[16] This community is confronted by and created by the Word, not speaking with words alone but by its very existence. The community speaks again by its attitude toward world problems, by its service to the weak, and by the simple fact that it prays for the world. Theology also serves as this means by which the community speaks with words

15. Barth, *Evangelical Theology*; and Barth, *Church Dogmatics* IV/3.2.

16. Barth, *Evangelical Theology*, 31.

both written and spoken. The community of Christianity is required to do such a work in order to be a true witness. This work is to best understand the Word in its purity as truth, and to best position itself to render its secondary testimony responsibly and with a good conscience. The community speaks through the position it takes on the political, social, and cultural problems of the world, praying and working so that its speech is not obstructive, warped, or devious of the Word going forth.

In *Evangelical Theology*, Barth takes the time to outline how the community embodies truth as it concerns order of worship, discipline, constitution, and administration. The community is never to forget how serious their situation and tasks are, in order to be best open for the way to freedom and joy in their service. The community's confession is to be rooted in the faithfulness of the past while still concerned with more recent tradition and taking both aspects into consideration in its confession of faith. Tasks such as preaching, teaching, and counseling are, to Barth, to give special thought and activity to theology so that all within the community understand themselves commissioned to do this work. For Barth, every Christian is called to be a theologian and understand themselves as responsible for the testing of the whole communal enterprise in light of the question of truth. This truth is to be represented in the individual and the community's witness and must embody a faith seeking understanding.

The task of theology, for Barth, is to search for proposals for improvement upon the witness of the community. Nothing is to be forced upon the community but instead proposed for consideration without allowing anything to hinder it from this important task. Theology must be critical of the current beliefs of the community but still founded upon them. Barth believes that the precise task is still "I believe in order to understand."[17] He describes theology as groping in the dark with only a gradual, variable, partial knowledge. The community can embody Truth as best it possibly can only if it takes on the challenging task of assessing its witness to the world.

As stated previously, the Word written, spoken and embodied takes a position of centrality in Barth's ecclesiology. Theology must still seek to understand the Holy Scriptures, ever aware of the limited knowledge, nevertheless eager to capture a glimpse of God's glory mirrored in the totality of the biblical testimony. Barth emphasizes the community's careful attention to the Old and New Testaments, with a respect for the tradition and an eagerness to learn from it. No teaching should go untested because it is

17. Ibid., 37.

tradition, but truth today cannot exist apart from the history of the faith informing the contemporary community.

Contemporary Evangelical Ecclesiology

The contemporary Evangelical movement recognizes its fragmentation over ecclesial concerns, doctrinal disputes and the realities of the church growth movement. In recent times, academic Evangelicalism works to separate itself with popular Evangelicalism, which blurs the lines between fundamentalism and evangelicalism. Academic Evangelical theology seeks to continue to emphasize the infallibility of Scripture, Trinitarian orthodoxy, high Christology, missional ecclesiology, and robust eschatology.[18] Similarly, the emphasis on biblical literacy outstripped dogma and found itself supplanted by a biblicist approach to theology.[19] This proved more adequate to address areas of conflict between academic and popular Evangelicalism, such as cessationism. Within this discussion of evangelicalism, the Gospel as understood here will serve as synonymous with Scripture and with the Word, all embodying the living reality of God's Word being central to this understanding of ecclesiology. Working with Evangelical ecclesiology also implicitly implies a distinctly non-Catholic theology, within the Protestant tradition, and operating from a low church or free church model.

Evangelical piety is often inherently wary of the Church as a medium of salvation. Overlappings with the catholic faith of historical Christianity, for example, occur for scriptural warranty as opposed to ecclesial authority. Ecclesial consensus differs in Evangelical communities over the centrality and the efficacy of the divine Word. Personal piety is often emphasized over corporate visions, no doubt a product in part to the individualistic nature of Western Christianity. Recent works have taken up these concerns. "A properly evangelical commitment to the task of seeking to live out the gospel requires a life of joyful and obedient participation in the church as the community of the Word."[20] The church serves as the concrete space

---

18. Richardson, "Evangelical Theology," in Dyrness and Kärkkäinen, eds. *Global Dictionary of Theology*, 295.

19. Ibid.

20. Husbands and Treier, eds., *The Community of the Word*, 17. This volume was the product of a conference at Wheaton College Graduate School in April 2004 with the express intent of taking of the concerns of a lacking Evangelical ecclesiology. Other works such as Stackhouse, ed., *Evangelical Ecclesiology* are similar examples taking up this task.

for divine reconciliation and because of this, the church also must serve as the space to articulate a doctrine of the Church. Creedal language and sacramental importance will continue to be points of division, but true reconciliation can exist over Christ-centeredness, the ministry of the Holy Spirit, personal conversion, and embodying a Word-centered community.

Evangelical ecclesiology appears to be more implied than articulated. The difficulty of this is the confusion that results so that we exist not as another voluntary association or institution but instead as a robust, relevant articulate body of believers with a clearly articulated understanding of convictions. Half of global Christianity is represented in Evangelicalism and with the large emphasis on lay leadership, lay theology takes precedence throughout the movement.[21] The strength of contemporary Evangelical ecclesiology is its ability to adapt as needed within its commitment to mission. The weakness of this is the uncertainty of a definitive Evangelical ecclesiology, yet the strengths is that this serves as a *missional* ecclesiology, an "improvisational" dimension of ecclesiology.[22] An accurate understanding of "one, holy, catholic and apostolic" church allows for the mission of God in the world as embodied in the church to creatively and imaginatively respond faithfully to changing cultures and places. Howard A. Snyder believes that the Evangelical church has reinterpreted one, holy, catholic and apostolic in the following ways:

- Many as well as one

- Charismatic as well as holy

- Universal as well as local

- Prophetic as well as apostolic[23]

Olsen speaks of this "missing half" as not necessarily the opposites but instead the attributes that speak to the organic model of the church, the "improvisational" aspect of a Spirit-led dynamic movement. Evangelical ecclesiology embodies the doctrine and social practices of the church, influenced in this movement by its Reformation heritage, the free church

---

21. One strong example of this is the prominence of author C.S. Lewis in forming the theological convictions in lay evangelicals.

22. Wilson, "Practicing Church," in Husbands and Treier, eds. *The Community of the Word*, 71.

23. Snyder, "The Marks of Evangelical Ecclesiology," in Stackhouse, *Evangelical Ecclesiology*, 85–87. Synder affirms the biblical foundation for these attributes through passages such as Gal 3:23–29; Acts 2:4–38 ; 1 Cor 3; Heb 3:1; Eph 2:20, and others.

tradition, the revivalist movement, and the Western context. Too often, other historical sources take prominence over the true centrality of Scripture in Evangelical ecclesiology. That said, at its core, the contemporary Evangelical ecclesiology finds itself at a crossroads for a renewed identity in the age of globalization. Examples such as the Lausanne Movement and Covenant, the World Evangelical Alliance, and other documents such as "Evangelicals and Catholics Together" serve as attempts by contemporary Evangelicalism to extend into the future and continue to wrestle with post-colonial theology and interdenominational dialogue.[24]

Christology

Now we will address two other areas that greatly influence Evangelical ecclesiology: Christology and Scripture. The role of Christology in shaping ecclesiology will be examined because of the reality that both subsets of theology inform each other. One's understanding of the person and work of Christ inevitably manifests itself in church communities and similarly church communities only find their centering in a full and adequate understanding of the uniqueness as being a Christ-centered and Christ-formed fellowship. The life of Jesus takes on a socio-historical exegesis in regards to how the Christ of faith is understood in culture. The church becomes that space where Christ is mediated and the life, death, and resurrection of Jesus is understood.

Evangelical Christology centers around a Gospel-centered Christ revealed primarily through the narrative of Scripture. Passages such as 1 Timothy 2:5 explain Christ as the mediator between God and man, thus making, for Evangelicals, Christ the basis for understanding both the Old and New Testaments. Christ makes knowledge of God possible for humanity and the Reformation distinctive of *Solus Christus* stresses the uniqueness of Christ as Savior and Lord. Evangelicals use Scripture to understand this role of Christ, through examples such as Johannine *Logos* Christology and his exaltation in Acts 2. Christ alone serves as the hermeneutic principle by which all events throughout history are interpreted as well as the only means by which humanity is reconciled to God.

Contextual Christologies understand Jesus through a combination of the themes of his teachings and the culture by which those themes are interpreted. This serves as a type of accommodation that functions as a

24. Dyrness and Kärkkäinen, eds., *Global Dictionary of Theology*, 296.

basis for identity. Christ's personhood serves as the saving means by which each believer inscribes their own identity and comes to know God. Jesus Christ serves as the hermeneutical key, acting in history, and becoming the theological foundation for the process of inculturation. This is particularly significant for the three women used as examples in this work. "Re-reading the story of Jesus against the background of experiences of poverty and oppression . . . breaks open the narrowness of the Western theological tradition."[25] This conversation deserves lengthier discussion elsewhere, but, without question, the Third World ecclesiology of Kwok, Oduyoye and Aquino is deeply shaped by their inculturation of the person and work of Jesus Christ.

The Role of Scripture

The last section this chapter will address is the use of Scripture in form-ing and determining ecclesiology. Evangelicals concern themselves with a theology of Scripture, or a biblical theology that concerns itself with using the canon of Scripture as the starting point for speaking of God. "Bibli-cal theology naturally appeals to the evangelical mindset because of the inherent confidence that the Bible is God's word written, and written so that ordinary mortals can understand it."[26] This relates biblical history with lived history, develops the narrative theology contained in the broader story of Scripture, attempts to unify the themes of the entire Bible, and attempts to reconcile the intents of the original author and the original message given to particular recipients with the living manner in which God speaks through this Scripture into our context today. Evangelicalism works to embody the principle of *sola scriptura,* and theologically, Scripture serves as the focal point of this Word-centered movement understanding its identity. The Bible is given a particular authority in guiding theology, with the implication of it being self-consistent and also Gospel-centered and therefore Christological.

Scripture serves as message within Evangelicalism. Scripture becomes the means by which the centrality of Jesus Christ is understood in the

25. Küster, *The Many Faces of Jesus Christ,* 185. Significant examples of inculturation and Christology models, such as Jesus the proto-ancestor (Africa), Jesus the poor (Latin America) and Jesus the suffering one (Asia), are included and expanded upon by Küster.

26. Graeme Goldsworthy, "Evangelicalism and Biblical Theology," in Bartholomew, Parry and West, eds., *The Future of Evangelicalism,* 124.

Christian faith. Scripture is a religious document, but with a theological purpose of being the self-revelation of God. Debates exist within evangelicalism on the appropriate term for the trustworthiness of Scripture, be it the conservative "inerrant" or the broader "infallible." Agreement extends to the guiding value of Scripture for making salvation known in Jesus Christ and guiding the Church in its ecclesial practices.

Scripture serves as the primary authority, the truthful, absolutely reliable, God-inspired normative guide for Christian doctrines; God as revealed in Christ through the work of the Holy Spirit becomes known through the Scriptures. For Evangelicals, "this unique status makes the Bible normative above any church's traditions or officials."[27] This provides the particular role of Scripture in Evangelical ecclesiology, placing it as upmost in significance above reason, tradition or experience. Scripture serves as the special revelation of God to humanity for Evangelicals and its Christocentricity, illumination, inspiration and authority. Christ is revealed through Scripture and faithfully expounded in the proclamation of the Church, as Evangelicals affirm in the threefold nature of the Word of God.[28] The Holy Spirit both inspires the writers of Scripture and illuminates the readers of Scripture, giving it a self-authenticating authority. The *euangelion*, the "good news" or "gospel" of Jesus Christ, serves as the basis for the Christian faith and becomes known only through God's special revelation in Scripture.

Globalization and Context

For Christians in particular, being a people has been enhanced and challenged by a keener awareness in the twenty-first century that the faith is global and is spoken and represented by a host of disparate voices. For Christians in Europe and North America, who had grown accustomed to being the center of gravity for all things Christian in the world, the global reality can be perceived as a shift, or even as something new. In truth, centuries of colonialism in various forms have obscured Christianity's long history in places like Japan, India, South America and Africa. For those in the global south, who live in those regions which are becoming Christianity's center of gravity, the urgent need to bring their faith

27. Phillips and Okholm, *A Family of Faith,* 16.
28. Ibid., 53.

to bear on their political and social realities often means doing theology as a stark counterpart to Christendom.[29]

In order to best understand the realities of a shrinking Western Christian church and a growing Third World church, our context must be adequately addressed. Globalization emphasizes the increase of a global culture, with local cultures minimized as a result of technological advancements, economic empires, and political powers. With that said, in the twenty-first century, any conversation that separates the globe into dualistic spheres, though distinctly different by many accounts, must thoroughly discuss the realities of globalization. Christianity finds itself at a crossroads in regards to how the multicultural shifts in culture impact ecclesiology. Globalization here is not seen as a positive reality, in fact the theologians worked with most extensively here support the values of the anti-globalization movement, but globalization is an inescapable reality. Working with David Held's definition, globalization is understood as a stretching of social, political and economic activities across political frontiers, the growing magnitude of interconnectedness, the accelerating pace of transborder interactions, and the growing extensity of global interactions associated with a deepening enmeshment of the local and global.[30] This portion will identify and discuss the realities of globalization, with particular respect to how globalization relates to both colonization and to the Church. This chapter will also attempt to give an assessment of the current context faced by the Western Christian church, with particular treatment to Philip Jenkins's *Future of Theology* trilogy.

Globalization

In Joerg Rieger's words, "Theology can no longer be understood without globalization."[31] By this same token, there is an understood relation between Christian theology's role in the process of globalization as well as the now inextricably linked realities of theology and globalization. Globalization cannot be reduced to one or a few simple factors, and likewise, its evaluation must be a broad, complex conversation. Much dialogue is needed regarding the ethical and theological implications of the violence inflicted on all of human life as a result of globalization within the majority world

29. Cavanaugh, Bailey, and Hovey, eds., *An Eerdmans Reader in Contemporary Political Theology*, xxii.

30. Held and McGrew, *Globalization/Anti-Globalization*, 2–3.

31. Rieger, *Globalization and Theology*, 1.

as well as with those on the margins in the minority world. It is common understanding that the negative side of globalization causes drastic effects on human rights, an idea that will be referred to as the commodification of personhood. The role for activists and theologians in faithful Christian witness against globalization begs for greater discussion. This work attempts to enter into that conversation around the globe, criticizing the failure to value holistic community throughout the church.

Too often, as David Fitch reminds us in his challenge of the Evangelical church's response to globalization, our beliefs and practices have become parts of a global system, separated from the ongoing work of God in Christ for the world.[32] There must be a calling toward the undoing of such a dualistic lifestyle between belief and action, where the lives on the margins of the capitalistic system have become by-products of the disconnect between the Christian value of human life and our economic choices. Too many Evangelicals, Justo Gonzalez believes, have become unfaithful to the calling of the Gospel by viewing it as only influencing their personal life and salvation rather than every dimension of society, including the economic and the political.[33] Migrating away from this duplicity looks like participating together with others in the fullness of Christ; even inviting others into God's Kingdom at work in the world, actively working against economic structures that fail to confront sin.

Though there have been strengths of globalization, here we are envisioning the ecclesial communities in regards to these four areas in which globalization has hindered it:

1. The progressive impoverishment and disempowerment of tens of millions of working people and their families, both globally and in the United States

2. The increasing domination by corporate and financial global interest of economic development decisions both worldwide and local

3. The widespread assumption that such globalization is logical, beneficial, and in any case inevitable

4. The systematic promotion of material consumption as a primary goal of life through the expansion of commercial ventures worldwide and their accompanying advertising propaganda.[34]

32. Fitch, *The End of Evangelicalism?*, 128.

33. Benson and Heltzel, eds., *Evangelicals and Empire*, 13.

34. Gillett, *The New Globalization*, 10.

It is impossible to speak of the current ecclesial context without acknowledging how deeply the church is enmeshed in globalization. These four areas in which globalization has hindered the Church have limited the effectiveness of the Kingdom of God by allowing economic and political agendas to take precedence over theological ones. This list is not exhaustive by any means, but it is the four major areas considered here as the challenges to globalization—essentially poverty and marginalization, corporate global interests, the assumption that globalization is a positive good, and the expansion of materialism.

Michael Hardt and Antonio Negri, in their pivotal work, *Empire*, identify globalization as multiple processes not uniform or univocal and that any work against them must redirect such forces to new ends. Two common misconceptions for Hardt and Negri are that "first, the notion that the present order somehow rises up spontaneously out of the interactions of radically heterogeneous global forces . . . and second, the idea that order is dictated by a single power and a single center of rationality transcendent to global forces."[35] Standing with other antiglobalization voices, this work will critique assumptions that globalization was a natural byproduct of capitalism and will present alternatives for how the forces of globalization can be redirected by the Church.

With the tool of Christianity, America utilized a theological dualism that glorified itself as good and "the other" as the one affecting our foreign policy, with rhetoric such as their lives our threatening our freedom and making our nation unsafe.[36] The Church has failed in its prophetic role of critiquing the relationship between global market capitalism and American Christianity. "We need to address the roles and responsibilities of the institutional church in moving globalization processes and strategies towards a justice and life-oriented model of globalization and away from the dominant forms of globalization rooted in individualism and greed."[37] A critique of globalization challenges profits as the guiding norm and requires a fundamental rethinking of the capitalist economic paradigm that currently dominates global economic policy and practice.[38] The role of economic life must be reimagined to transform the values, ideals, and identities of

35. Hardt and Negri, *Empire*, 3.
36. Ibid., 180.
37. Peters, *In Search of the Good Life*, 204.
38. Ibid.,193.

corporations and business communities so that the communities on the margins come to the forefront.

Globalization and the Church

Such a discussion of globalization lays out a clear challenge for the Church. One proposal for countering such widespread abuses is the advocacy of local economies. Voices like that of farmer/economist Wendell Berry argue for a community economy, centered around a local economy, that stands as a critique of globalization because human rights must become the forefront as the ethos of this new economy. This manner of economic structures forces humanity upon globalizing forces, which in itself is a positive force, yet the power of globalization and its industrial complexes often overtakes these glimmers of humanity. This idea is not unlike the critiques of globalization waged by eco-feminist and ecological theologians alike, constantly moving our theological reflections to better represent the entire narrative of Scripture that connects God's story with that of all of creation. Such a critique helps us view the story as one all of humanity participates in and recreates with renewed lifestyle practices, joining in the ongoing work of redemption of all creation. Antiglobalization identifies worldwide responses to globalization by reacting in subversive campaigns and movements to top-down economic and power demonstrations. In his work on the subject, Joerg Rieger speaks to the examples of landless movements in Brazil as well as labor coalitions in the United States as contemporary examples of church partnerships with such antiglobalization movements.[39] He implores this trend to continue when he states, "Many churches are happy to denounce issues like greed and consumerism, but the number of churches that dare to point out that the deeper problem has to do with the structure of free-market capitalism, which fosters the accumulation of wealth in the hands of the few and encourages consumerism in order to be able to keep the lines of production going, is much smaller."[40] Rieger's voice serves as an example of this idea of the church rising as an antiglobalization voice, advocating for local and community economies that connect ecotheology with ecclesiology. Rieger believes this is the role of the Christian Church: to

---

39. Rieger does clarify that these examples are smaller movements subverting the Christian status quo in the West and not typical of the trends overall. Rieger, *Globalization and Theology*, 50.

40. Ibid., 51.

continue the work of supporting movements that subvert globalization as a representation of the Kingdom of God in the world.

The mission must be the definition of the Church. And this is not the traditional definition of mission as conversion-based evangelism, but a renewed understanding as the Church's existence in the world for the sake of working against what Walter Wink describes as the "structures of sin" that keep all of creation enslaved. This missiology must precede ecclesiology and must follow a definition of Christology where Christ's body invites all of creation into the Eucharist for salvation. Our understanding of salvation must demonstrate the impossibility for one to be saved by faith in Christ without also being "in Christ." "We are saved only as we are in Christ, part of an ongoing participation in Christ, as God's mission in the world. We are grafted into a new politic, the people of God, that makes Christ the core from which God is working to make the whole world right."[41] John Howard Yoder casts a similar challenge in which the incarnate Jesus cannot be separated from a concrete, on-the-ground politic in the world. His work, *Body Politics*, references that Christ's reign is present in the church community by the Spirit, birthing a politic in and for the world. In his chapter on the fullness of Christ, Yoder challenges the Church to think of the priesthood of all believers as working against any sort of hierarchy of valuing certain lives over others in the body of Christ. "The people of God are called to be today what the world is called to be ultimately."[42] This entails a shifting of ecclesiology for the Church to serve as an alternative political movement in contrast to the state in its allegiances and treatment of humanity and the environment. In order to do this, Christians must change their posture in the world so that all of their actions identity them with the other, the weakest, and the least.

Alistair McGrath emphasizes the secularization as a natural byproduct of globalization and the need for the Church to inform itself of this reality. Religion may continue to be an aspect of global culture, but he affirms that Christianity must continue to adapt and develop. His prediction is this: "It will revive Christianity's root emphases on healing and prophecy, not least because its adherents will identify themselves with the poor and oppressed who first embraced the redemption healing and blessing that Jesus promised."[43] McGrath does not believe that a secularizing globalized world

41. Fitch, *The End of Evangelicalism?* 137.
42. Yoder, *Body Politics*, 28.
43. McGrath, "The Future Configuration," in O'Mahony and Kirwan, eds., *World*

does not inherently become a problem for Christianity but can, in fact, serve as a motivating force toward a purer ecclesiology. More individuals live in poverty today than in the 1960s at the beginning of the liberation theology movement, and thus the realities of globalization, poverty, secularization and the Church have yet to be fully wrestled with.

Globalization and Colonization

A proper treatment of globalization entails a discussion of colonization and the realities of the postcolonial project. Globalization becomes a form of neocolonialism, as Rebecca Todd Peters propones, and it "reinscribes dependency and control over politically weak and economically impoverished countries."[44] The comparison is often made between the dependency of the colonies and their colonizers to the dependency that exists between contemporary countries and transnational organizations such as the IMF, the World Bank, and other powers. Too often, globalization forces unity and fails to preserve diversity and respect the differences of each particular social location. Each of the women whose theology I am focusing on here— Oduyoye, Kwok, and Aquino—understand themselves as having different unique "colonizers," and yet the reality of globalization levels the playing field as to their collective colonizers. Values such as community, culture, autonomy, and the rights of women are to be fought for when combating the neocolonization of globalization. Peters argues that the social changes that have contributed to a loss of community in the modern era can be traced to the effects of corporate globalization and the byproducts are evidenced on the lives of the people in the Third World.[45] This is not intending to oversimplify or blame all problems related to globalization on the Western nations but only to identify the power realities that have extended beyond cultural exchanges. Postcolonial thought stresses the notion of hybridity, even if those in power have more freedom to escape the powers of Empire than those located on the underside. All three women understand patriarchy and the economic realities of globalization as "colonizers" in their settings. Often, the insistence on male-domination in the institution of religion or "church" serves as a colonizing body.[46] Third World feminist

---

Christianity, 176.

44. Peters, *In Search of the Good Life*, 139.

45. Ibid., 187.

46. This definition of "church," run by patriarchy and preserving its power at the

theologians raise important questions regarding how we understand the Incarnation in overlooked corners of Empire and how the conversations of our globalized world inform a full picture of theology.

As Anselm Min identifies in *The Solidarity of Others in a Divided World*, regional theologies have focused on the concerns and experiences of the liberation of a particularized group. Min understands these as necessary but limiting in our globalized world. The new paradigm he advocates for is for that of the solidarity of others in the body of Christ.[47] Transcending fragmentation allows for interdependent contexts and speaks of the necessity for all to be liberated. One group's liberation cannot happen as another finds itself still enslaved to hegemonic forces. Similarly, concrete subjectivity, Min believes, is intrinsically pluralistic and cannot be reduced to a single category. Black theology can no longer merely focus on race, feminist theology on gender, and so forth. Dynamics find themselves inextricably linked in our modern era. For theological, ethical, economic, and anthropological reasons, theological regionalism must be sublated, Min argues, for a globalized theology to remain relevant today.[48]

One tension theology must continue to straddle is the particular and the universal. "The alternative to the abstract imperialist universalism of Western theology is not the sheer pluralism of theology that absolutizes particularly."[49] Part of the balance in avoiding further colonialism involves an acknowledgement of the "other"—the economically exploited, politically oppressed, socially marginalized—and conceiving and practicing the collective responsibility of solidarity. Solidarity acknowledges interdependence while working to avoid further colonizing by implying complete understanding. It resists individualism and totalitarianism and similarity and is neither universality or complete similarity. Min's emphasis on the interdependent aspect of solidarity lends itself to total liberation rather than isolated, particularized groups seeking an agenda above the salvation of all.

The compelling task of Christian theology, for Min, is particularly for Western Christians to acknowledge the responsibility globalization plays in limiting the liberation possible in Jesus Christ. Future visions of theology must explore the biblical and theological resources that contribute to

---

expense of women, would not be the true Christian Church as any of these women understand it.

47. Min, *The Solidarity of Others in a Divided World*, 135.

48. Ibid.,138.

49. Ibid., 139.

solidarity—solidarity of both humans in community and of all creation in the cosmic universe.[50] Globalization demands with new urgency the progression of theology to respond to violence and alienation and the loss of dignity of so many around the globe. And insofar as theology refuses to address these concerns, it continues the colonization of the least around the world. "Doing justice to this dignity means the praxis of constructing a social system, structure or totality—laws, policies, institutions—that apply to all and actualize and concretize the dignity under particular historical conditions, with all human beings likewise sharing the obligation of this praxis."[51] By humanizing transformation of unjust systems and by now representing others in theology, solidarity and liberation become possible. The positions advocated here, theologically by Min and categorically by Held, would place the Third World feminist theologians in the category of "global transformers," with their focus being on using globalization for equality and justice through greater understanding of theological movements around the globe. This would also entail advocating for a theology that stands in solidarity and responsibility for those on the margins of society.[52] Social justice must extend beyond borders in our globalized context, with peacemaking coming from an expansion of the horizons of one's own framework.

The Context of the Western Christian Church

In this portion of the chapter, the context of Western Christianity will be assessed. This includes an honest look at the statistical realities of the European and American Evangelical movement in contrast with its Third World counterparts. Sociologists predict that by the year 2050, the majority of U.S. residents will be nonwhite, and by 2023, minorities will comprise more than half of all U.S. children.[53] This statistic is significant because even in North America, the majority of Christians will be nonwhite. Currently, African, Asian, and Latin American Christians make up 60 percent of the world's Christians. Similarly, by 2050, African, Asian, and Latin

---

50. Ibid., 229.

51. Ibid., 228.

52. Held and McGrew, *Globalization/Anti-Globalization*, 194–97.

53. "An Older and More Diverse Nation a Half Century from Now," December 12, 2012. https://www.census.gov/newsroom/releases/archives/population/cb12-243.html; as referenced in Rah, *The Next Evangelicalism*, 14.

American Christians will be making up 71 percent of the world's Christian populations.[54] From 1970 to 1985, the church in African grew by six million people whereas during that same time, 4,300 people per day were leaving the church in Europe and North America.[55] The largest Christian church today is the Yoido Full Gospel Church in South Korea, with its 700,000 members. The fastest-growing church on the planet is the Chinese church, comprising over ninety million members.[56] Today the statistical center of Christianity is Timbuktu, Mali. For the first time since the Reformation, the majority of Christians live outside the West. Clearly, global Christianity is and continues to become a nonwhite religion. In The American Church in Crisis, David T. Olson notes that every major Christian denomination has experienced a decline in total attendance between 1990 and 2005.[57] Though the traditional face of American Evangelicalism is changing (with almost 30 percent being Asian, African, Latin American or Pacific Islander in the United States) the leadership continues to appear white and fails to reflect this change in Christian academia or pastoral positions.

Another aspect of the globalization conversation for the West is the economic realities. "In 1960 the 20 percent of the world's people who live in the richest countries had 30 times the income of the poorest 20 percent— by 1995, 82 times as much income. New estimates show that the world's 225 richest people have a combined wealth of over $1 trillion, equal to the annual income of the poorest 47 percent of the world's people (2.5 billion people) . . . The richest three people have assets that exceed the combined GDP of the 48 least developed countries."[58] This says nothing of the reality that health care, food, clean water, and sanitation for the world is $40 billion a year, less than 4 percent of the combined wealth of the richest 225 people in the world.[59] Globalization has life-threatening and staggering economic consequences on the world's most vulnerable. This reality exists while at the same time, the Christian Church is growing in these contexts of economic disparity. No doubt, globalization can bring economic growth and benefits for many, but this small good cannot come at the expense of

54. Ibid.

55. Sanneh, *Whose Religion Is Christianity?*, 15.

56. Barrett, Kurian, and Johnson, eds., *World Christian Encyclopedia*, 191.

57. Olson, *The American Church in Crisis*, 38.

58. The United Nations Development Programme, *Human Development Report 1998*, 29–30, as referenced in Moe-Lobeda, *Healing a Broken World*, 28.

59. Ibid.

widening the gap between the wealthy and the rest of humanity, causing destructive consequences on the earth's resources, and violating cultural integrity and human rights.

The Western church is no doubt its own particularized context, and yet it exists in an ever-increased globalized context. The particular is becoming the universal and vice versa, and theology must continue to work to reflect this reality. The universal emerges out of the particular, which is a positive movement for theology, speaking specifically out of a particularized context and then allowing that specificity to extend to the globalized context. Theology does not have to limit itself to the particular or contextual, but that is the space where theology begins so that it can extend to the global theological dialogue. "We can no longer afford to ignore the theological implications inherent in the demographic reality that Christianity is currently experiencing a precipitous decline in the West and that the vast majority of Christians now live outside the West."[60] Such a reality informs this entire project.

Jenkins's Future of Christianity Trilogy

Three books that will be given assessment here are the sociological and church historical work, *The Next Christendom: The Coming of Global Christianity*; *The New Faces of Christianity: Believing The Bible in the Global South*; and *God's Continent: Christianity, Islam and Europe's Religious Crisis* by Philip Jenkins. The first two books will be given the greatest attention, since their topics apply most to this particular project. These three works are considered his global theology trilogy, works that have greatly influenced the Christian Church's thinking on its current state and future growth. Such thinking also must impact how we do theology, the voices in theological dialogue, and the manner in which we understand our churches (ecclesiology). In short, Jenkins's thesis involves the prediction that the central point in Christendom would soon be the "global south" as he terms it, or the influence of the southern hemisphere. Jenkins even highlights the recent movement of growing churches throughout the world, such as Korea and Nigeria, sending missionaries to the United States and Europe in the hopes of a modern-day reformation to these slowly dwindling areas of former Christendom. Jenkins presents another helpful statistic: "Today half of the inhabitants of this planet are under twenty-four, and of those, almost 90

60. Tennent, *Theology in the Context of World Christianity*, 17.

percent live in the global South." With that, he concludes that if Western
Christianity continues its decline, by 2050 there will be still nearly three
Christians for every two Muslims in the world.[61]

Jenkins's strength as an author is in his background as a historian.
Though the work serves as a brief survey of historical survey of the spread
of global Christianity, his heart is pastoral in guiding the church through
the tool of storytelling. The work serves as a challenge for the Western
church to acknowledge and respond to the movement God's Spirit is doing
around the world. In many ways, Jenkins uses narrative as a celebratory
tool to encourage and also inspire the parts of the world where the Christian influence is dwindling and in fact almost dying. Even the title, *The
Next Christendom*, is a play on the idea of the former Christendom being
an area rarely viewed as a space where the Church has influence anymore
and instead looking at the territory in the Third World as the new area of
church growth.

Jenkins begins by outlining the state of Christianity in the global
world. He projects the number of Christians in the next few years and estimates how the demographic will shift. He also surveys interfaith relations
around the globe, paying special attention to Christian—Muslim relations
and the significance that holds (and will hold) in the near future. From this
point, Jenkins goes on to describe the faith emerging from the rest of the
world as being integrated with a spirituality of culture. Emerging Christendom is not only located in a different geographical part of the world but it
also represents a different type of Christianity, integrating different aspects
of indigenous culture. He speaks of stories throughout the historical development of Christianity around the globe as well as recent movements,
such as the African Independent Churches movement from the past few
decades. Such a survey examines the missionary movement throughout the
past century and discusses the weaknesses and strengths of colonization on
the spread of Christianity. Jenkins examines different sects and branches of
the Church that have taken root. He looks at the future cities that will serve
as thriving urban centers of Christianity as well as the nations he projects
to grow in their percentage of Christian followers.

Jenkins emphasizes contextual theology and uses mestizo theology,
similar to Aquino's, as an example of how the Western Evangelical church
must be open to alternative readings of the Bible if it places such an emphasis on the Word. His project underscores the reality of the lack of growth

61. Jenkins, *The Next Christendom*, 27.

and vitality in the Western church, in particular with his emphasis on Third World nations sending missionaries to the West. Jenkins attempts to hold an honest perspective in regards to colonial and missions projects of the past, unafraid to shy away from their faults yet still hopeful for a changing perspective on Christianity's potential for social change. Confidently, he asserts the potential for Christianity's staying power if it becomes willing as a movement to learn from its growing corners around the world. Jenkins accurately understands that the separation between spiritual and material well-being becomes a luxury for those in the "Global North."

Jenkins's findings demonstrate a Christianity in the Global South focused more on supernatural elements of faith, the authority of Scripture, and the continuing power of prophecy. For example, African believers value the Old Testament as an ongoing, living source of authority in a war that far exceeds the way it is used in the West.[62] In *The New Faces of Global Christianity*, Jenkins identifies how the fastest-growing portions of Christianity, those in the global South, will inevitably shape biblical authority and interpretation. He speaks of the particularized usages of biblical influence as well as the usages of the Old and New Testament in their cultures. In the words of Musimbi Kanyoro, "those cultures which are far removed from biblical culture risk reading the Bible as fiction."[63] The average Christian today is in poverty, and also often a minority in countries dominated by other religions or secular ideologies. Problems such as famine, plague, poverty, exile, clientelism and corruption are the current reality for many around the world that the New Testament scriptures speak to.[64] Issues such as good and evil, the Prosperity Gospel movement of health and wealth, the role of women and men, and so forth are also related to biblical interpretation and greatly influenced by the center of Christian practice: the Global South. And Jenkins is quick to remind us that the fact that these are dead issues for us in the West reminds us of the incredible debt Western Christianity owes to its roots. Jenkins concludes with an emphasis in not dismissing all of Christian tradition because of the movement South, and similarly not taking all interpretation by the global South as accurate. Scriptures ought to be interpreted through culture without distorting the Bible to answer specific questions about modern culture. Compromises with culture lead to distorted theologies in Western churches, with examples from the

62. Ibid., 53.

63. Jenkins, *The New Faces of Christianity*, 68.

64. Ibid.

twentieth century such as eugenics and apartheid doctrines.[65] Acknowledging the development of Christendom in the Global South and the awareness that comes with the Holy Spirit's movement in churches there does not eliminate the need for balanced study and appreciation of history. That said, the historical center of biblical interpretation has been unequally skewed toward those in power and influence in academia and publishing: primarily white men. New voices must be invited to the table, voices from the Global South, without blanket acceptance but with the understanding that the Spirit of God is growing and moving in these corners of the world. Those of us in the West are welcomed to be learners and listeners, eager to understand how new forms of biblical interpretation can guide the church in the twenty-first century.

And lastly, the third book in Jenkins's trilogy, *God's Continent*, engages in the questions of how Christendom's movement south must wrestle with Islam's growing influence.[66] Though not as pertinent for this particular project, Jenkins accurately asserts the pressing challenge for globalized Christianity to wrestle with pluralism and other religious traditions. His discussion of the differences of European and North American Christianity is also significant because the lumped term "West" is not always accurate, yet overall the Western relation with Muslims is a significant opportunity for common ground. Issues such as moral and sexual decadence can be points of agreement, and finding dialogue and commonality will become a key way for Christianity to remain both faithful and self-aware. Both traditions have intolerant moments in their history and intolerant factions still at work today, but both movements also have incredible involvement in public discourse and political movements. For this work, Jenkins significantly highlights the ability of Christianity to sustain amid other religious traditions and growing secularism. "Each issue poses real problems, which demand a rethinking of the nature of church loyalties, the relationship between religion and national identity, and the proper role for the laity."[67] The sense that the faith is decreasing, or even changing, drives reform movements and continues to inspire activists and evangelists worldwide.

---

65. Ibid., 192. Jenkins is correct to remind readers of this balance by highlighting flaws in biblical interpretation in both the West and the Global South. Neither is to be entirely vilified or idealized.

66. Jenkins, *God's Continent*.

67. Ibid., 288.

Conclusion

Evangelicalism's understanding of ecclesiology finds itself undergoing a period of serious transformation. Voices in South America, Africa, and Asia are attempting to hold to the central tenets of Evangelicalism in its churches while detaching it from the cultural captivity of the West. This emerges out of the assumption that the movement is robust enough to respond to contextual issues and that Evangelicalism contains a strong enough identity to form an ecclesiology. Though in transition, the Word-centered movement of Christianity continues to provide a particularized and unique voice in shaping the future of the global Church.

Globalization, colonization, and sociological assessments of the direction of Christianity have been assessed in this chapter. Factors such as transnational associations, interconnectedness, deterritorializations, and social acceleration are just a few of the impacts of globalization on the process of doing theology. Globalization contains the aspects within it of negative consequences—poverty, marginalization, global interests and so forth as discussed previously—yet also can be viewed as a continuation of the unpacking of the Holy Spirit in history, guiding humanity toward the "world historical" movement in the direction of the city in Revelation 22.[68] Powerful Christian themes, such as the Kingdom of God and the universal church provide a tentative "yes" to globalizing realities as expressing to some degree the will of the Creator and Redeemer of all while still understanding the Church's role as critiquing the injustices that come with globalization.[69] The growth of the Christian Church in the third world, as well as the third world's theologians rising as modern teachers serves as an example of that tentative "yes." Globalization often exploits the most vulnerable and ecclesiology is now invited to foster localized communities that liberate and live in an awareness of the diversity of the global Church. The context of the Western Christian church as well as voices such as Anselm Min and Philip Jenkins speak to the reality of the changing landscape of Christendom. Movements such as robust ecclesiology and stances of solidarity lay a foundation for a constructive global ecclesiology.

---

68. This language is borrowed from Hegel, as used in D. A. Fraser, "Globalization," in Dyrness and Kärkkäinen, eds., *Global Dictionary of Theology*, 339.

69. Ibid., 340.

2

Methodology

Political, Feminist, and Quaker Theology

Introduction

THIS CHAPTER WILL ADDRESS the methodology behind this constructive global theology, namely political theology, feminist theology and Quaker theology. There will also be a brief treatment of Trinitarian theology and its influence on ecclesiology as well as discussion on liberation theology and the place of base communities. Critique and engagement of all three positions will be given, but it should be noted that these three methodologies were chosen for their compatibility with this project.

To open, this chapter will give a brief explanation of political theology and why it connects with this project. The Church takes on the character of the Greek term *polis* and structures itself as a decision-making social body with defining membership, set to carry out common tasks. It is with this definition and for this reason the Christian community is a political entity. John Howard Yoder introduces the term nicely: "'Politics' affirms an unblinking recognition that we deal with matters of power, of rank and of money, of costly decisions and dirty hands . . . The difference between church and state is not that one is political and the other not, but that they are political in different ways."[1] Another definition, borrowed from William Cavenaugh's introduction to *The Eerdmans Reader in Contemporary Political Theology*, speaks of the three-part nature of political theology; the vision of God, the people of God, and the reality of perishing. "Vision seems less urgent than food when it comes to what causes people to perish, but the question for political theology in many contexts is, What kind of vision is required to *see* those who die invisibly and quietly, not in spectacular explosions but in silent deprivation of the basic necessities of life? Politics is defined not only by the concerns of those within the Beltway but also by the daily, material concerns that threaten to disintegrate both individual bodies and communal bodies of people."[2] Political theology concerns itself with what *kind* of concrete political practices are being advocated and affirms that the Christian Gospel must resist structural injustice and work to build a more just and humane society.

To address political ecclesiology, particularly how it influenced and shaped the Western Evangelical church movement, our starting place will be the Trinitarian ecclesiology of Jürgen Moltmann, as it gave framework for what became the political theology movement. Later this work will address voices such as William Cavanaugh, John Howard Yoder, and other voices who greatly shaped the movement of political theology. Within liberation theology, a brief discussion of Gustavo Gutierrez and Jon Sobrino will be addressed. Lastly, the movement of feminist theology will be summarized. Both liberation theology and feminist theology serve as precursors for this particular work, and stand as branches from the broader movement of political theology. But any conversations of their contribution within the Evangelical context ought to begin with Jürgen Moltmann's work and how it gave the Church language regarding how it could be a political entity.

The Trinity and Ecclesiology

Much has been said regarding how Jürgen Moltmann's messianic, eschatological theology translates to his ecclesiology. As M. Douglas Meeks said it, "Moltmann's theology is preeminently a Trinitarian theology which provides a consistent Trinitarian view of the Church."[3] The Church now serves as a function of God's Trinitarian history with the suffering world,

1. Yoder, *Body Politics,* ix.
2. Cavenaugh, Bailey, Hovey, eds., *An Eerdmans Reader,* xxiv.
3. Moltmann, ed., *Hope for the Church,* 61.

wherein God is one also suffering, yearning, acting, and working for liberation and reconciliation with all of creation. Looking particularly at his *The Trinity and the Kingdom* and his prior ecclesiological work, *The Church in the Power of the Spirit*, Moltmann originates a communal vision of the triune God in order to best understand the communal nature of the Church. A few secondary works supplementing Moltmann's works, as well as some of his lesser-known writings, such as *Hope for the Church,* will help to locate his ecclesiology as the Church in the world. With his "Kingdom of God" theology, Moltmann affirms a realized eschatology that becomes the foundational nature of the Church, giving the Church the freedom to creatively imagine the Church as a reconciled community in the power of the Resurrection. As the Kingdom of God is present and active in the world today, Moltmann believes that now the Church can focus on innovative solutions to the present sufferings rather than spend time consumed in questions of theological method. For the brevity of this work, Moltmann's focus on the *perichoresis* will be examined as the indwelling foundation for his ecclesiology.

Moltmann's view of the Trinity serves as a strong foundation for an eventual understanding of Christian community. The Trinity is a picture of all members of the Godhead fully flourishing—actively participating in their roles and fully dependent on one another. This is how Moltmann formulates his social Trinity: one with complete freedom and interplay between the persons. His notion of the *perichoresis*, or theological dance between the members, implies that deep freedom is necessary in order that no member of the Trinity is controlling or dominating the others. This is Trinitarian freedom. Borrowed from the Cappadocian Fathers, this *perichoresis* of the Trinity is a revolutionary thought, expanding from classical notions of the Trinity. The social Trinity is now an action shared from one divine essence rather than an individualistic nature of the One Godhead. The three persons are now three hypostases integral in their relation to one another: the Father becomes the Father by virtue of begetting the Son, the Son becomes the Son by being begotten. Moltmann wants to stress the mutuality of love and roles between the Father, Son, and Spirit by all needing one another for different roles. This expands on mystical subjectivity ideas from Nicolas of Cusa and Meister Eckhart rather than the archetypal image of one single God subject perpetuated by Barth, Rahner, and others. To avoid tritheism, Moltmann stresses the shared essence or consciousness as revealed in different persons and roles. Moltmann uniquely extends this idea of the three persons dwelling in one another as essential to human freedom, and as will be discussed here, essential to his ecclesiology.

Moltmann understood one central metaphor for the Church as the space of ultimate freedom. The doctrine of the Trinity is a doctrine of freedom, where the gifts and natures of all three persons work in harmony with one another. As the Church understands itself trinitarily, God's Trinitarian nature breaks into history in the Church. "The triune God, who realizes the kingdom of his glory in a history of creation, liberation, and glorification, wants human freedom, justifies human freedom and unceasingly makes men and women free for freedom."[4] For Moltmann, Trinitarian theology connects explicitly to a doctrine of true Christian freedom, and such a freedom is manifested in the Church in its truest form. It a world so deeply bound, God presents the Church as a community of freedom, drawn together by "the passionate God, the God who suffers by virtue of his passion for people . . . who calls the freedom of men and women to life."[5] In the light of eschatological hope, it is this freedom that now makes the future coming of God. This is the *project*, as Moltmann calls it, of freedom between God and the Church: a creative initiative that transcends the present through the Spirit in the direction of God's future.

From this, Trinitarian freedom models the flourishing of potential within humanity. Now people can understand themselves as beings with possible created futures based on their imagination and creativity—the ways in which they can live in a manner not unlike the Trinitarian *perichoresis*. One aspect of this is the renewed freedom for true friendship. Friendship with God is possible because of the friendship between the three persons of the Trinity. When speaking of the Trinitarian order, Moltmann stresses the differing interplay of the persons based on the particular context. "In the sending, delivering up and resurrection of Christ we find this sequence: Father-Spirit-Son. In the lordship of Christ and the sending of the Spirit the sequence is: Father-Son-Spirit. But when we are considering the eschatological consummation and glorification, the sequence has to be: Spirit-Son-Father."[6] If political freedom focuses on the Godhead and the sovereignty

---

4. Moltmann, *The Trinity and the Kingdom*, 218.

5. Ibid.

6. Ibid., 94.

of God's Kingdom, and communal freedom focuses on the Son and the eschatological vision, then the religious freedom of flourishing focuses on the Spirit forming the Christian community. The indwelling Spirit makes possible the relationship between humans and between humans and God. This serves as a foundation of mutuality, of shared roles and giftings, and a true equality of persons.

The Christ event introduces "godforsakenness" into the nature of the Father and the Son and allows for the classical notion of *kenosis* into these two members of the Trinity. The Spirit now serves as the mysterious life that allows for the life of God to overcome death. God dies for God out of shame and now is raised by God. The divine self-identity now becomes able to embrace the death of God's own self, and this mystery is the eschatological hope for Moltmann. This understanding lays a foundation for Christian community, because it dismantles and unsettles all previous horizons. In the Hebrew Bible, any freedom from captivity or exile now allows for the fulfillment of eschatological promise and true life throughout the experiences of the Israelites. This Emmanuel, ever-present throughout the Scriptures and in particular moments revealed in wisdom and the *shekinah* glory, we see here as a prefiguring of the suffering of God with the people. Through this equality of persons, each necessary in differing forms, God's Trinitarian history now makes possible the *charismata* of the Church. There is a consistent and constant mediation between these three active forces that now interpret each other and become constitutive of one another. Each serves as a precondition of others and makes eschatological hope possible.

Moltmann's Concept of the Kingdom of God

For Moltmann, the Kingdom is always on the horizon, never within our grasp. Hence the social gospel of Rauschenbusch and others is inaccurate to Moltmann, attempting to create a total realization rather than an awareness of the constant critique of our partial, ongoing realization. Likewise for Moltmann, the life of the Kingdom of God is never a constant despair or frustrating infinitely regressing absolute. Instead in his work we grasp a picture of the Kingdom as proclaimed in Jesus, providing critical principles for addressing present inadequacies and recognizing God as the creative vision, and the Spirit as shaping present history. The Kingdom is essentially Trinitarian, requiring all persons of the Trinity to work in interplay in order for the Kingdom to be realized. "The vision of the Kingdom as the source of new possibilities for the future implies a judicious and responsible weighing of alternatives in an effort to find the optimum response at this juncture in time in the light of Jesus's disclosure of the nature of the Father's reign."[7] Such a vision naturally requires the mobilization of the laity, and a removal of hierarchy and polity that limits the work of the Spirit in the people of God.

One could argue that Jürgen Moltmann served as the original practical theologian. His work concerned itself with the dialectic relation between theory and practice and his systematic theology always located itself in specific historical practices of the Church. Similarly, his writings stress the organized nature in which the Church receives theory for its life and practices to most accurately reflect the Gospel. Methodological issues of Eucharistic practices, such as baptism and communion become essential for the Church to accurately reflect the systematic and practical nature of the Kingdom. Each of the Eucharistic practices of the Church, as identified by Moltmann, deserve ample space to be unpacked in relation to the Trinity. However but for the brevity of this work, their significance will only be introduced. Moltmann always squarely placed the future of the Church in the local congregation. The Christian community now becomes this sign of hope, an offering to a hopeless world through such life signs of the Spirit presented in the Eucharistic practices. It is only through this that the Church can understand its true socio-political implications in relation to eschatological hope. "The congregation in which the people are conscious agents of their history with God overcomes the religious passivity which results from political oppression."[8] Complementarian relationships within the Christian community demonstrate true freedom to a dying world, the type of freedom only accurately understood through the perichoretic relationship of the Trinity.

How is such a project of the future intended to look? What are the markings of this free community, representing Trinitarian freedom and demonstrating the charisma of the Spirit? Such a free community is markedly Trinitarian, manifesting the work of the people here in the world insofar as it represents all members of the perichoretic community. "The kingdom of glory must be understood as the consummation of the Father's creation, as the universal establishment of the Son's liberation, and as the

---

7. Moltmann, *Hope for the Church*, 14.

8. Ibid., 41.

fulfillment of the Spirit's indwelling."[9] In this manner, the Kingdom of God is demonstrated through communities that represent this Triune formula. The Kingdom sums up the work of the Trinity and points all members toward freedom and toward God's works and ways in history. Through the Spirit, Godself indwells these manifestations of the Kingdom and this serves as a sign of the eschatological indwelling of God's glory in the world. Now there exists the creation of an open world to the future, an "open system" as Moltmann describes it, in constant creation and open to the true future through the gift of time. This Kingdom of God is not one of power, but of self-emptying and self-limitation of God, one might even say of the "godforsakenness" already witnessed in the crucifixion. Yet in that open future, this Kingdom is also a vision of hope, that in the suffering members of the Trinity now in their self-restricting activity are given space. It is, as Moltmann says, "the great Lord of the universe who preserves the world through his patience that now gives the liberty of created beings space and time, even in the slavery they impose on themselves."[10] As mentioned before, now in this freedom and possibility, the activity of the Kingdom in harmonious community can flourish.

Markings of a Trinitarian Community

In his work, *The Church in the Power of Spirit*, Moltmann himself claims that he has now finally addressed the community after Pentecost.[11] With the sending Spirit, the Church now understands itself not as a pastoral church, with one leader looking after the people, but as a communal church, where the people care for one another in social community.[12] This church, for Moltmann, is an "open" church—open to God, humanity, and the future—as it understands itself primarily existing as the living nature of God, in what he also comes to call a "relational ecclesiology." Moltmann sees relational ecclesiology as the church being defined by its other realtionships: to God's Trinitarian history, to other institutions, and to other doctrines and movements in the world. Because this is not a fixed concept, because this is

9. Moltmann, *The Trinity and the Kingdom*, 212.

10. Ibid., 210.

11. This idea is introduced in Moltmann's preface to *The Church in the Power of the Spirit*, xx. This is of course not to say that other works of his failed to address the Church, which they certainly did.

12. Introduced in Moltmann's preface to *The Church in the Power of the Spirit*, xvi.

a living, "open" relational understanding of the Church modeled after the Trinity, history cannot be fixed to one point and knowledge of God cannot be universally socially located.

> For that reason the church can only understand its own position or abode in participation in the movement of the history of God's dealings with the world, and therefore as one element in this movement. Its attempts to understand itself are attempts at understanding the movement of the Trinitarian history of God's dealings with the world; and its attempts to understand this movement are attempts at understanding itself.[13]

What this now means for Moltmann is that it is only through the experience of the Spirit, in light of the sending history of God and Christ, that the Church can begin this process of self-understanding. The Trinity both opens up history and makes itself open so that all of humanity and creation can understand the sending love of God. The Trinity provides this basis for the eschatological glory and unity of God, opening up the Trinity for the gathering, uniting and glorifying of the world in God and of God in the world. "The relationship of the divine persons to one another is so wide that it has room for the whole world."[14] And this is exactly what is meant for the Church as a redeemed creation, enjoying consummation with the indwelling of God until his full eschatological glory becomes completely unified with the world.

The Gospel now serves as the foundation for the Church, the liberating word that makes such freedom and openness possible. Eschatological hope is found in the Gospel, and centrally locates the Church's charismatic community. Hence for Moltmann, the Gospel is true freedom, the liberating "yes" in the face of resistance. "Every Christian proclamation is an expression in one way or another of 'I absolve thee.'"[15] And likewise, this proclamation always situates itself in a community, with its public activity being the messianic work of the Trinity. This fellowship centers itself on the Gospel of hope, and offers freedom to a world entirely bound. Such a fellowship is a proclamation of the person and work of Christ, made accessible by the power of the Spirit, telling of God's glorified coming. It is

---

13. Ibid., 53.
14. Ibid., 60.
15. Ibid., 223.

through this Gospel that "the Church sees itself in the presence of the Holy Spirit as the messianic people destined for the coming Kingdom."[16]

To become conscious of this freedom, and the task of proclaiming this gospel freedom, the Church must now understand its role in shaping the "open" future through telling and embodying this hope to a bound world. Because of this, another area significantly connecting Moltmann's Trinitarian thinking with the life of the Church is his understanding of the role of preaching. Rather than recent notions of Christian preaching that have come to be characterized as "moralistic, therapeutic deism," Moltmann sees preaching as the vehicle in which the natures of the Trinity are introduced into the Christian community.[17] "For Moltmann, preaching is adequate only as it is consciously Trinitarian: the cross of the Son is the means used by the Father to bring new, reconciled life out of death and create a community that shares the gifts of the Spirit for celebration and service, anticipating the age to come."[18] Preaching must serve a far deeper role, one that creates the space for the *perichoresis* to occur within the midst of the sin-filled state of history and humanity. The Kingdom only has the power to break through insofar as all members of the Trinity are given space to properly represent their personhood. This means that the fullness of the Kingdom of God is limited when our Trinitarian theology limits the relationships of the Father, Son and Spirit. What is essential for Moltmann in the life of the Church is the role of preaching in the formation of the community. "For Moltmann, preaching is '*pro*-clamation' and '*pro*-nouncement,' offering a future which is for human beings because it is an alternative to the forces of death, oppression, and destruction that threaten existence on every hand."[19] God is a being in action, where the creating Father, the reconciling Son, and the sanctifying Sprit are all equally important and necessary aspects of the divine event of God in the world. Preaching now becomes the retelling event, the re-membering of this action in every proclamation where the persons of the Trinity are property acknowledged.

The Church as it serves God's eschatological Word works through the community of persons to bring the ultimate redemption of all things. "Every facet of church practice is meant to call the church and the world into full participation in the mission of God himself as he moves towards

---

16. Ibid, 289.

17. I was first exposed to this term through Horton's *Christless Christianity*.

18. Moltmann, *Hope for the Church*, 11.

19. Ibid, 11.

the ultimate defeat of sin, death and evil."[20] This makes the church what Moltmann calls the "Exodus Church" in *Theology of Hope*. He understands the Church as the pilgrim people of God, without camp as spoken of in Hebrews 13:13. "The Church is then an absolutely non-worldly phenomenon, which in contrast to the planned society of rational ends is described in the categories of 'community."[21] As a community of eschatological salvation, the Church now is one of gathering in and sending out into the horizon of the eschatological expectation. Through this orientation, the Church embodies this proclaimed Word, presenting a gospel of freedom and open possibility. Proclamation exists in this eschatological tension and is true to the extent that it announces the future of truth.[22] As the Word transcends into its future, it is also present in the form of promise and of awakened hope, offering a sign of greater things to come in the eschatological salvation.

In summary, for Jürgen Moltmann, the Church is primarily a Trinitarian community, understanding itself socially through its relations to one another, and dimly attempting to reflect the *perichoresis* of the divine persons. For Moltmann, "it is no longer an eternal cycle of the divine life which repeats itself eternally, but a movement which brings in God's world and draws everything together into the kingdom of glory that is still to come."[23] This foundation serves as Moltmann's renewed vision of Trinitarian thinking, of intending all relationships to be viewed on equal footing. When taken seriously, this naturally has deep implications for the Christian community. "What is 'played out' in God embraces the great 'play' of creation and the 'world theatre' that is so full of suffering."[24] Structures of subordination and power find themselves subverted as authority and obedience are now replaced with dialogue, consensus and harmony in the church. The social Trinity creates in the Kingdom of God a place of freedom, where the "creative passion for the possible" now exists. To conclude, Bauckham's words on Moltmann summarize this idea best: "By enabling the church to recover its bearings within the Trinitarian history of God—its Christological origin, its pneumatological commission and its eschatological goal—ecclesiology should . . . liberate the church to regain the freedom

---

20. Ibid., 67.

21. Moltmann, *Theology of Hope*, 321.

22. Ibid,. 326.

23. Müller-Fahrenholz, *The Kingdom and the Power*, 147.

24. Ibid., 147.

of its messianic vocation and to point to the communal church among the people."[25] To this I believe Moltmann would truly say yes and amen.

John Howard Yoder

John Howard Yoder, the Anabaptist theologian, transformed the Christian church's understanding of the Gospels with his profound work *The Politics of Jesus*. That seminal work deserves the monumental praise it has been given, and in many ways serves as the precursor for his future writings. Because the treatment here centers on ecclesiology, his work *Body Politics* will be the focus of this conversation. Borrowing Paul's metaphor of the Church as Christ's body, Yoder seeks to create a social organism (or *polis*) that makes decision, assigns roles, and distributes powers like a body (in both senses of the term). Yoder outlines five models reflected from the practice of the early church as recorded in the New Testament. Those areas are: binding and loosing, breaking bread together, baptism, the fullness of Christ, and what Yoder calls "the Rule of Paul."

Binding and loosing speaks to the practice of church discipline and practicing forgiveness and reconciliation. This is intended to serve as a model for truth-finding and community-building, which, to Yoder, holds true to the reconciling nature of the Gospel as living in the world. Breaking bread together, or the common meal, is intended to add the account of memory as well as to serve as the space of equality and the formation of a new community. Yoder examines the economic implications of this equal table in meeting needs and uniting in common solidarity. Baptism is to be understood as the process by which God creates a new humanity, and Christians understand themselves as being made into a new and equal society. "Baptism is the formation of a new people whose newness and togetherness explicitly relativize prior stratifications and classifications."[26] Baptism breaks down ethnic walls and inherently creates a multiethnic community of believers. When speaking of the fullness of Christ, Yoder understands Paul's writings describing the breadth of roles and gifts within the Church. This values the priesthood of all believers, including women and laity, and the practice of God's presence as evidenced in all disciplines and vocational spheres. Lastly, the rule of Paul speaks to God's Spirit speaking and acting across faith communities. This idea can be made manifest in

25. Bauckham, *The Theology of Jürgen Moltmann*, 127–28.
26. Yoder, *Body Politics*, 33.

denominations such as the Quakers working to "seek the mind of Christ" in the silent meeting and in ruling their business meetings by listening to the Spirit as made known in consensus. Such an example is one of many intended to stand in the tradition of apostolic practice in seeking God's Spirit for guidance and truth.

Yoder understands these five practices as aspects of the "good news" (*euangelion*) as a true connection between worship and ethics, or a political understanding of an embodied liturgy. His understanding of "evangelical" points to news that aids, helps, and saves by God. Yoder connects the biblical concept of *shalom,* or whole peace, by "telling the world what is the world's own calling and destiny, not by announcing either a Utopian or a realistic goal to be imposed on the whole society, but by pioneering a paradigmatic demonstration of both the power and the practices that define the shape of restored humanity."[27] Each of these processes requires a vulnerability and incarnational existence that creatively provokes a transformation in culture.

William Cavanaugh

William Cavanaugh intends to craft so robust a political ecclesiology that the Christian Church can stand as an alternative to the state. His intention with this is that Christian political relationships can be modeled best within the Christian community, and this provides a different space for these relationships to exist in what he believes are their truest form. Cavanaugh envisions the role of liturgy as a political act in our global, consumeristic age. He understands political theology as an act of the imagination and the Eucharist as the space where Christians re-imagine space and time together in both memory and anticipation together of the work of Christ.[28] Distinctly, he identifies how globalization cannot be confused with Catholicity and participation in the Eucharist unites the particular in the universal. The nature of the Church cannot allow globalization to be seen as synonymous with universal, because an equality of persons must be a marking of the Church, which is not always true within globalization. Working within the realm of political theology, Cavanaugh reminds the reader that the nation—state and civil society only provide alternative myths to the

27. Yoder, "Sacrament as Social Process," in Cavanaugh, Bailey, and Hovey, eds., *An Eerdmans Reader,* 655.

28. Cavanaugh. *Theolpolitical Imagination,* 7.

Eucharistic community centered around Christ as Savior and occupying a public space.

"All political theologies," Cavanaugh declares, "can be read as so many attempts to come to grips with the death of Christendom without simply acquiescing in the privatization of the church."[29] In understanding the church as political, there can be no salvation history apart from political history and similarly, salvation history is indispensible to the church. Cavanaugh understands the political task of the post-Christendom church to be 'to suffer rulers as faithfully as possible, to the point of martyrdom if necessary, to wait upon the Lord and not to presume to rule in his place.'[30] This does not endorse simple quietism, but guides Christians today to as faithfully as possible nonviolently stand against oppressive forces of empire. The church is intended to understand his politics from God's eternal rule and thus to embody a different sort of politics, transforming the world through such a model.

Moltmann, Yoder, and Cavenaugh have been included as representatives of political ecclesiology because of their embodiment of the church as a political alternative to society. Some, such as Yoder, influenced the peace church tradition directly as a Mennonite, but Moltmann and Cavenaugh both indirectly and directly shaped the ecclesiology of many traditions, peace churches being one of the many. Yoder's emphasis reflects the practical aspects of theology and ecclesiology, and Cavenaugh's as well with his analysis of the church in Chile under Pinochet with *Torture and Eucharist,* whereas Moltmann serves the more systematic model with his Trinitarian emphasis. Moltmann wrote the most extensively on the subject, compiling volumes on every member of the Trinity and with extensive writings on ecclesiology, yet it would be remiss not to see each of these three as formative in the understanding of the church as a political entity in the world, following the political model of Jesus.

Liberation Theology

In order to accurately construct aspects of ecclesiology later in this work, the enterprise of Third World Theology must be understood within the broader context of liberation theology. Both liberation theology and feminist theology exist as subsets of political theology, since their understandings

29. Cavanaugh, *Migrations of the Holy,* 123.

30. Ibid., 138. Cavanaugh appears to be echoing a vision shared by Stanley Hauerwas.

of theology from the margins are inherently political. Two voices will be examined here: Gustavo Gutierrez and Jon Sobrino, leading representatives of this movement. Liberation theology began as Latin American Catholicism's reaction to Vatican II Council and the political situation in Latin America. From this context emerged a particularized church that stood for the preferential option for the poor, God as liberator, the poor Jesus as the suffering Christ, and God's liberating reign in the *Eschaton*.[31] Building off Marxist philosophy, liberation theology critiques the structures and institutions that create the poor, including but not limited to modern Christianity as primarily identified with the rich. Theological discourse moves from academic spaces to Christian community, or "nonpersons" as Sobrino calls them, whose basic dignity and rights are being denied. Liberation theology intends to rescue elements of the biblical tradition long neglected by the colonialist church and centers biblical interpretation and theological work amongst the oppressed people, because there you will find God at work. Even the metaphor of "liberation" in exchange for "salvation" or "sanctification" implies the radical nature of soteriology and community transformation. Sin becomes not simply individual moral acts but now unjust structures and systemic inequalities, an aspect that will be discussed at greater length in a future chapter. Much of liberation theology's legacy has been in its methodology: praxis for justice and theology as a reflection on such praxis. It is worth acknowledging that the conditions that set liberation theology have not gone away, but have in fact actually worsened, and issues of the globalized market and postmodernity only necessitate its praxis all the more.

Gutierrez identifies with the poor, a marking of his theology, and understands those in poverty as being irrupted into a historical praxis. He sees this as based on the First World's traits of individualism and rationalism, and valuing those attributes and others at the expense of people on the margins. The poor are exploited in order that industrialization and progress can occur. According to Gutiérrez, this calls for re-interpretation of history based on spirituality and an evangelical life. Gutierrez explores at some length both the universality of God's love and God's preferential option for what he calls "history's last." The heart of Jesus's proclamation of a Kingdom speaks of the love of God for the poor. In his words, "The option for the poor, with all of the pastoral and theological consequences of that option, is one of the most important contributions of the church universal

---

31. Gutierrez, *A Theology of Liberation*.

to have emerged from the theology of liberation and the church on our continent."[32] This idea roots itself in biblical revelation and the history of the church, and for Gutierrez, this idea is the core of what he calls "the new evangelization" that is transforming the Christian faith today.

For Sobrino, the Reign of God stands as the central aspect of liberation theology. This situates itself as a historical theology, a prophetic theology and a praxis-based theology. Sobrino emphasizes Jesus's teachings and ministry as presenting a vision of what the Reign of God is to be like. Liberation theology emphasizes *life* as the historical context of the Reign of God because, as Sobrino points out, "In the Third World, poverty means proximity to death and the poor are those who die before their time."[33] This idea of the Reign of God is both an event and a movement in history. Sobrino expands the thinking of Gutierrez and other liberationist voices by emphasizing the ecclesial implications of its movement. Rather than form an ecclesiology, Sobrino discusses basic problems faced by the Church in *The True Church and The Poor* and contrasts European and Latin American ways of doing theology. "The poor are therefore structural channels for finding the truth of the Church and the direction and content of its mission."[34] He understands the true church to be formed on the basis of the poor and with the poor as the center of the whole, which is not for him another Church alongside the Catholic or Protestant church, but instead he believes that "the Church of the poor is in its structure the true way of being a Church in Jesus; that it provides the structural means of approximating ever more closely to the Church of faith; and that it is more perfectly the historical sacrament of liberation."[35] Sobrino speaks of evangelization as the mission of the Church and highlights celibacy, poverty, and obedience as markers of following Jesus in the Third World. He believes these churches bear witness to life and understand the realities of persecution and martyrdom. This vision continues from New Testament ecclesiology and allows for the Church to expand its own work toward liberation through God in Christ. Sobrino's understanding of ecclesiology, as with other liberationists, still serves as a bold proposal that many would take issue with, yet their

32. Gutierrez. "Option for the Poor" in Cavanaugh, Bailey, and Hovey, *An Eerdmans Reader,* 193.

33. Sobrino. "The Central Position of the Reign of God in Liberation Theology" in Cavenaugh, Bailey, and Hovey, eds., *An Eerdmans Reader,* 211.

34. Sobrino, *The True Church and the Poor,* 95.

35. Ibid., 123.

challenge to classic ecclesiology encourages believers to embody communities of justice centered around Jesus.

Feminist Theology

The final subset explored within political theology for the sake of this project is that of feminist theology. This explores the unique voice of women in systematic assessments of theology as a reaction to patriarchal, inadequate representations of theology. These women integrate women's experience and context into Christian discourse and emphasize the restoration of women into full personhood in church communities and leadership. Rather than finding itself limited to a systematic enterprise, feminist liberation theology is an advocacy theology, one that looks to do more than just speak from a specific position but also to overturn male-dominated systems. Feminist theology encourages its readers to understand how diversity as represented in gender forces the Christian Church to wrestle with embodiment and the whole body of Christ cannot ignore human bodies, both female and male, if it wants to be true to Christ incarnate. One of the points the feminist theologians advocates for the church continue to be a proactive body, aware of the sociocultural context it is currently in and continually speaking for those society is oppressing. Feminist theology understands itself within the liberation theologies, advocating that a definition of sin should broaden to include alienation from one's true sense of identity and liberation from the structural sin of sexism. Metaphors for God and human relationships, such as the earth as the Body of God as articulated by Sallie McFague, are stressed by feminist theology, with their limitations emphasized. Feminist theologians see church history as an empowering agent for women within church, reclaiming early Christian history as a period where women disciples, missionaries, prophetesses and ministers exercised spiritual power and promoted societal changes.

The feminist theological project is particularly political in ecclesial settings. The church must be a liberating community, engaging in the struggles of all peoples on the margins, but especially women. "The working assumption of this feminist theology has been the dynamic unity of creation and redemption."[36] Feminist theology advocates that the justice of the Kingdom of God can be achieved in communities of faith today, rather

36. Ruether, "The New Earth: Socioeconomic Redemption from Sexism," in Cavenaugh, Bailey, and Hovey, eds., *An Eerdmans Reader,* 378.

than being limited to the *eschaton*. A comprehensive vision of feminist theology can only exist within the Church as embodying the theological alternative society within the world. Feminist theologians would say that one of the roles of theology is to speak of the need for societal justice as advocated by the Church, justice in this case for females. Experience is one of the factors that impacts theology just as much as sex, gender, bodies, and all that those differences entail.[37] This becomes complicated when Christianity and the Christian churches are at once locations of women's oppression and marginalization yet at the exact same time the space where such discourse and liberation is possible.[38] Letty Russell also speaks of this vision in her work, *Church in the Round*, and describes a feminist church setting as one with a roundtable, as opposed to pews, in an attempt to reconcile her love/hate relationship with a broken church that she struggles to abandon.[39] The metaphor of a circular church around a common table speaks to the vision of Christian community that practices hospitality and serves as a household of freedom and equality for those on the margins on church and society. Feminist ecclesiology emphasizes sisterhood and connected relationships, the communal struggle for justice, and the Word preached and celebrated in service to the poor. She emphasizes a spiral method of action and reflection that "makes connections between context and tradition as a means of theological table talk."[40] Women believe their understanding of God is at work in their lives must be evident through language, thought, and action within the church, particularly as those oppressed themselves and understanding the realities of the "oppressed of the oppressed" in speaking for injustice.

Redemption in Christ contains a social dimension that cannot individualize or spiritualize salvation and sin. The manner in which this is avoided is by creating communities of Christian faith that affirm the equality of women in the image of God and restore them to their full personhood in Christ. The three women examined in this work (Mercy Oduyoye, Kwok Pui-Lan, and Maria Pilar Aquino) all stand firmly within this tradition and the liberationist theological tradition as well, merging the two into their own contextual political, liberationist, and feminist theology. The liberationist model has re-examined itself in society today, with a broader scope

37. Watson, *Introducing Feminist Ecclesiology*, 25.
38. Ibid., 42.
39. Russell, *Church in the Round*.
40. Ibid., 30.

than merely the revolutions in Latin America. Liberation Theology now voices the methodology for theological reflection in every corner of the world where injustice exists, and provided the lens for these women to theologically reflect from their corner of the world. Though waning in its influence today, Liberation Theology may find itself at a point in history to speak most directly to orthodox Christianity, as the Christian church becomes more and more aware of the injustices within its midst and perpetuated by its narrow theologies.

Quaker Ecclesial Tradition

This portion of the chapter seeks to identify and unpack the Quaker ecclesial tradition as a methodological framework. The author was raised in this tradition and continues to identify with the Anabaptist, low, free church tradition. The Quakers served as a community that viewed Jesus Christ as the center and necessary element to the flourishing of human beings created in God's image. As a peculiar people, the Friends movement saw their communal ethos and faithful witness in the public square as an apologetic tool. In the context of Christian history, the Quakers often have had a quiet voice, yet nevertheless they provide a unique contribution into alternative approaches to church identity and growth. Quakers looked to identify the "light of Christ" living in all people, as George Fox so aptly identified in his conversion, and use this as an impetus for missions work worldwide. Human flourishing, for Quakers, involves all peoples understanding the light within them as God working. Salvation for this people of God centers on the understanding of the centrality of Christ in the glorious, Spirit-filled community and all habits of life must stem from this core. After a brief history of the Quaker Evangelical movement, two examples will be given of how social justice was deeply connected to Quaker ecclesiology. American Indian rights and the abolitionist movement served as two areas where the Quakers could flesh out their embodied ecclesiology. Viewing all peoples as equal was a core conviction, or "testimony," and this distinctive found significance in lived communities. This chapter will end with the manner in which the Friends still believe in Jesus's living presence today as the key to true conversion of both the individual and the entire faithful community. Two Quaker women—Margaret Fell and Lucretia Mott—will be examined in further depth in the chapter on constructive peacemaking, since their legacy centers on embodying the Quaker distinctive of equality of persons and extending that to the feminist and peace concerns.

"The Lord showed me, so that I did see clearly, that he did not dwell in these temples which men had commanded and set up, but in people's hearts . . . his people were his temple, and he dwelt in them." The words of George Fox echo throughout the ages and serve as the framework for the entire Society of Friends. This famous experience of encountering God atop Pendle Hill instigated a movement and ushered a missionary work that extended throughout the continents and the centuries. Fox believed that there was only one, Jesus Christ, who could speak to the condition of humanity, and when he heard this voice, his heart did leap for joy. In his frustration with the condition of the church in England in the fifteenth century, he lamented the sense that none of the religious leaders could speak to his condition but only through the one who enlightens could Fox find the grace, faith and power to do the work. He speaks of this as his "opening," wherein the Spirit of God revealed a new and truer understanding of Christian belief so that rituals need not be the only basis for spiritual experiences. Now the Holy Spirit was to be the only bestower of gifts, not just to those who have practiced religious study but also in the hearts of obedient people outside church buildings. God's presence now had the potential to be experienced anywhere. Fox went on to be known for public preaching in various unorthodox places and gathered other preachers to roam the English countryside and teach the Scriptures. This led to suffering and persecution and, for many, imprisonment in the early movement, yet this only encouraged its growth and expansion to the Americas and West Indies. With the emphasis on the personal and corporate guidance of the Holy Spirit, Quaker spirituality began to form, and with it concerns for specific testimonies such as simplicity and integrity that served as signposts to continue to guide the movement. When all around them the Quakers observed complex ecclesial structures, the Friends arose as gatherings marked by plainness and quietude.

The Society of Friends or Quaker movement grew as a Spirit-led movement in the pathway of emanating Christ towards the cross. For the followers of George Fox, their understanding of the true heart of Scripture moved them towards the development of "testimonies," such as the equality of all peoples. Social justice became a hallmark of Quakerism. Amongst Christendom, the Society of Friends found significance in world history for becoming the first religious group to publicly denounce slavery and require its members to free blacks held in bondage.[41] Examples such as this are reasons why the Quakers can prophetically speak to the sinful human condition by addressing the issues of social justice from the foundation of its movement until modern day. Though brief, this survey of the social justice will highlight two areas of the work of the Quakers—Indian and slave rights—and intends to give a glimpse of the depth and breadth of such convictions as a cornerstone to their unique voice in Evangelicalism.

Early Roots and Testimonies

From its genesis in the mid-seventeenth century in England and Wales, Quakers reacted to British religious life through an infusion of direct experience with the living Savior. From the thinking voices as early as George Fox and Robert Barclay, the Friends viewed the mark of a Christian as a transformed life, one that changes in all patterns and habits to reflect God's Sovereignty and Christ's active presence. Consequentially, a transformed life implied a transformed view of humanity—with all peoples created in the image of God, reflecting the light of Christ in all and believing that "there is one, even Christ Jesus, that can speak to thy condition."[42] Fox believed that God's light was in the heart of all men, and human sinfulness can impede our ability to fully reflect God's image in us. From this theological understanding, the Quaker imperative of evangelism was understood. "Quaker evangelism united the political and the spiritual in the same manner in which the Old Testament prophets denounced their kings for 'grinding the faces of the poor.'"[43] Quakerism grew as a reaction to religious oppression, both spiritual and social. A concern for equality of all persons and social justice were cornerstones of their evangelism in so far as these principles grew out of early Quakers' religious beliefs. From its beginnings, the Quaker movement always married evangelism and social justice.

Another unique aspect of Quaker theology was the development of convictions or testimonies. Friends' testimonies came to be represented in four major areas: truthfulness, simplicity, equality, and peace as leadings from the Inner Light, or Spirit of God. Equality came to embody refusing titles, an equal humility toward everyone, and the belief in God's ability to speak through any receptive person—rich, poor, young, old, educated,

41. Barbour and Frost, *The Quakers*, 119.

42. Fox, *The Journal of George Fox*, 82.

43. Spencer. *Holiness*, 22.

uneducated, women, and men. This was emphasized in women's role in teaching and worship and also God's ability to speak in non-Christian cultures. "Friends assumed that God's Spirit worked through Turks, Chinese, or American Indians, as well as through the Englishmen who knew that the Spirit's proper name was Christ."[44] It was from this testimony that the Quakers found a grounding point for their work in social reform as characteristic of their movement. The Friends testimony of equality of peoples compelled them to respect and care for Native Americans and hold significant leadership role as abolitionists, two areas this paper will explore further.

Such an opening serves as simply a brief sketch of the origins of the Quaker movement. As the denomination grew, many splits and branches emerged, and I am speaking from the Evangelical Friends International strand, looking in particular at its global focus of its tradition and how it cannot be separated from its theology of the community. As stressed by Fox, the Quakers would entirely support this theological notion, though rarely are they known for their systematized theology as much as their embodied practices. With their extreme and almost excessive posture of reaction, as accompanied other Reformation sects, the Quakers believed in the core position of all peoples as equal before the Lord. Stemming from 1 Peter 2:5—9, the Quakers affirmed the posture of the priesthood of all believers, taking this so literally as to do such things like record giftings of preaching and teaching rather than ordaining, treating women as equals of men, calling for the abolition of slavery, advocating for the native populations, working with those in prison and in mental institutions, and treating the government officials as equals rather than those in a higher posture. Each new convert, as they joined what the early Quakers referred to as "the Lamb's War," undertook roles in the movement and in the responsibility of starting fires in other human hearts. In the words of Quaker scholar Hugh Barbour, unlike other movements at the time, "Each Friend themselves came to know the same direct power which George Fox had announced. Several hundred Friends shared fully in Fox's own roles as preacher, tract-writer and gatherer of Quaker Meetings. Above all, Friends shared Fox's experience of the total world."[45] This same adherence led to the significance of abstaining from war and taking a posture of peacemaking with all peoples, one of the famous tenets of Quakerism. The aim from very early on was

44. Barbour and Frost, *The Quakers*, 43.
45. Barbour, *The Quakers in Puritan England*, 1.

never to establish a new church or denomination but merely to transform the whole nation and likewise the world as they boldly saw a vision of the great work of God in the earth. No account represents this better than that of the description of early Friend Edward Burrough:

> We obeyed the Light of Christ in us, and took up the Cross to all earthly glories, crowns and ways, and denied ourselves, our relations, and all that stood in the way betwixt us and the Lord. And while waiting upon the Lord in silence, as often we did for many hours together, we received often the pouring down of the Spirit upon us and our hearts were made glad, and our tongues loosed, and our mouths opened . . . and the glory of the Father was revealed; and then began we to sing praises to the Lord God Almighty and to the Lamb forever, who has redeemed us to God and brought us out of the captivity and bondage of the world, and out an end to sin and death.[46]

God, as they viewed it, had made his dwelling with the people and had this glory poured over them, giving them a unity of spirit and of peace. Only through the Spirit's awakening would any even be so bold as to speak in Quaker meetings. Practices such as this were intended to safeguard from the self-centered or fleshly thoughts and instead only true words from the Lord spoke into their midst. Yet even in this practice, all could share and speak rather than just the minister, again stressing the equality of all believers as a part of the Body of Christ. This created a living fellowship, with a vivid life of the movement even apart from its leaders like Fox. For the early Quakers, they truly did share one another's burdens and support the family members of those in their community who were taken to prison. At times, the children in their midst kept meetings going after all adults had been thrown in prison, and this was not viewed as uncommon but rather as part of the Quaker way of mutuality and equality.

Little framework was given to this movement over the years by means of polity such as creeds or church government. The Quaker way of life was not seen in an affirmation of words but in the actual life of its people. Apologetics was inextricably linked with the early Quaker movement and continues to be a beacon of the Friends today. Whether it's the social justice work of the liberal Friends or the conversion missions movement of the Evangelical Quakers, each movement has chosen to highlight different sides of the same coin. Both streams took seriously the Quaker value of the light

---

46. Trueblood, *The People Called Quakers*, 11–12.

of God alive in all people. Unlike other missions movements, the aim was never one of bringing God to the unsaved heathens but rather to awaken all of sleeping humanity to the work of God already present within them. The earliest Quakers needed not assemble a missions board or committee because the entire movement was a missionary movement. There was no option for the early Quaker, as they understood the Christian Scriptures, to keep the Gospel at bay in their own heart. Public proclamation and sharing appeared to them as the only recourse after being awakened to the truth of God within them. The focus was on both word and deed, with the lifestyles of the early Friends being just as significant as the actual proclamation of the Gospel.

American Indian Rights

Over the centuries, the Quakers became known as a people devoted to the equal treatment of all peoples, and this included the American Indians. Before the 1750s, the Quakers had been a people of simple, quiet testimonies with little emphasis on voluntary associations. Both the Friends in America and in England shifted to the creation of voluntary associations to address the rights of Indians. In America, this became known as the Friendly Association, a gathering created to regain the confidence of the Delaware Indians through gifts and representation.[47] This decision came as a result of the injustice created in the (non-Quaker) business decision called the Walking Purchase of 1737.[48] This move took the Indian's lands from them after the Quaker William Penn had worked at great length to make a genuine treaty with the Indian chiefs for their land. The Quakers did these ventures at the risk of their lives from the frontiersmen, yet knowing that this conviction represented their conviction of the Inner Light of Christ in all of humanity.

The proper treatment of indigenous peoples applied to any venture of the Quakers. "It is a striking fact that, when John Woolman, in the eighteenth century, went as a missionary to the American Indians, he told them that he had done so in order to learn something from them."[49] Woolman's missional work with American Indians as well as slaves represented his detailed understanding of the relationship between conversion and transformation within the Quaker way of life. Woolman's *Journal* is filled

47. Barbour and Frost, *The Quakers*, 126.
48. Trueblood, *The People Called Quakers*, 151.
49. Ibid, 78.

with writings questioning and imploring fair treatment to those whom the settlers had displaced. Woolman worked to establish a "Meeting for Sufferings" to aid the American Indians "in their distressed state on the frontier settlements" as a byproduct of the French and Indian War.[50] Woolman's theology reflected an understanding that the Christian life implied the impossibility of being separated from the sufferings and deaths of others.

George Fox's words and life established the precedence of such care and equality with all people of the world. This can be best represented in his missionary work in Barbados. His famous *Letter to the Governor of Barbados* was a reflection on his two years there in which he opposed accusations that Quakers were stirring up the slaves to revolt and tried to affirm the true nature of Quaker beliefs in valuing the indigenous Indians. In his own words: "Now, negroes, tawnies, Indians, make up a very great part of the families in this island; for whom an account will be required by him who comes to judge both quick and dead at the great day of judgment, when every one shall be 'rewarded according to the deeds done in the body, whether they be good, or whether they be evil'; at that day, we say, of the resurrection both of the good and of the bad, and of the just and of the unjust, when . . . he shall come to be glorified in his saints, and admired in all them that believe in that day."[51] This passage represents the tensions the early Friends lived in as they balanced the demonstration of the orthodoxy of their beliefs with their testimony of the God in all people.

This view continued on years later, as even into the 1800s the Friends were known for their defense of the American Indians. Elizabeth L. Comstock became known as one voice of many who advocated for the equal pay and working conditions of all people, especially minorities.[52] She was quoted as saying that American Indians deserved to "go where they like, do what they like, and earn good wages anywhere."[53] Her attitude, as well as that of her contemporaries like Rufus M. Jones, expressed the Quaker value of the treatment of peoples and the role of advocacy within Christianity even when solutions had not been reached. During this era, Friends such as William Tuke and Elizabeth Fry advocated for the establishment of asylums for the mentally ill and humane treatment of prisoners, both of

50. Ibid, 149.

51. Evangelical Friends Church Southwest, *Faith and Practice*, 2001, 30. Taken from Fox's *Letter to the Governor of Barbados*, 1671.

52. Hamm, *The Transformation of American Quakerism*, 158.

53. Ibid.

which are extensions of the value of equality amongst people that was given precedence with the American Indians.[54]

Slave Rights

The Quaker Holiness Movement of the 1650s expressed concern for a strong agenda of social reform—in particular, abolition, temperance, antiwealth and materialism, concern for the poor, educational reform, pacifism, and equality. As characterized by historian Carole Dale Spencer, "Social outreach had an importance place, but its immediate challenge, eliminating slavery from within its own ranks, became paramount in its desire to be a holy community."[55] These values carried as the abolitionist movement gained steam throughout the early 1700s. In 1713, John Hepburn of New Jersey and William Southeby of Pennsylvania spent time in the New England countryside preaching against slaving and eventually publishing the what would come to be known as one of the most sophisticatedly argued tracts of the era. This led to the first official Friends statement against slavery being issued in 1729 by the Philadelphia Yearly Meeting.[56] Anthony Benezet, a contemporary of the better-known John Woolman, was a valuable example of a Quaker who championed the rights of slaves and Native Americans. He wrote many tracts on the slave trade, one of which was later borrowed and used by John Wesley in his own tract on slavery. Benezet first saw the connection between the Christian perfection movement and social reform that was also voiced by Woolman. John Woolman's treatise on slavery that was printed in 1746 came to be one of the most forceful tracts in the movement.[57]

One of the most famous British abolitionists was William Wilberforce. His movement throughout England was surrounded with other lesser known but equally vibrant antislavery champions. Sir Thomas Fowell Buxton was the leading abolitionist that led to the vote in Parliament in 1833 that ended slavery in the British colonies. From England, Parliamentarian John Bright worked for the end of slavery in American even at the expense of mills and workers such as his own family in Lancashire.[58] The

54. Ibid., 156.
55. Spencer, *Holiness*, 93.
56. Barbour and Frost, *The Quakers*, 121.
57. Ibid., 123.
58. Ibid, 296.

victory came after William Wilberforce's ten years of efforts to sway British public opinion and after the publication of "Appeal on Behalf of the Slaves" in 1823.[59] The ultimate victory of the Slavery Abolition Act represented multiple voices campaigning through a variety of means to achieve equality, especially the Quaker activists.

The Friends in America played a strong role in the antislavery movement. As a general rule, Friends freed their slaves long before the Civil War, and some served as the chief conductors of the Underground Railroad.[60] Thomas Garret held an Underground Railroad stop at his house and Richard Dillingham housed runaway slaves, both of these actions ending with imprisonment for the two men. Levi and Catherine Coffin were known to have helped thousands of runaway slaves passing through Indiana gain freedom.[61]

Later in 1833 John Greenleaf Whittier sacrificed his chances of a career in politics by publishing a tract advocating for the immediate and unconditional emancipation of slaves and continued a work for the next twelve years in the abolitionist movement. He wrote poems and essays and arranged speaking engagements where he could continue to abolitionist agenda. Such a work eventually compelled Whittier to found the Liberty Party as a political vehicle for the antislavery movement that helped to elect multiple abolitionist senators.[62] Overall, the American Quakers utilized the Republican Party as a means for advancing their testimonies, especially that of abolition. During the 1850s and 1860s, the Friends were not all convicted to be involved in politics, but the ones that were became known as those who would never vote for a "proslavery" candidate.[63] One sect of the Quakers, the Gurneyites viewed themselves as renewal Friends who saw their commitment to the testimonies as a continued conviction despite earlier schisms over the abolition. The Gurneyite gathering of the Anti-Slavery Friends that formed in the 1840s eventually dissolved because of how fervently the various sects of Friends united together to continue the Evangelical emphasis on fighting to end slavery in America, making such a small yearly meeting unnecessary.[64] Even in recent times, Friends from a

---

59. Ibid, 180.

60. Fox, *Faith and Practice*, 6.

61. Barbour and Frost, *The Quakers*, 306.

62. Ibid., 375–76.

63. Hamm, *The Transformation of American Quakerism*, 61.

64. Ibid., 62.

variety of yearly meetings still find themselves united over the testimony of opposing modern-day slavery and human trafficking all over the globe.

Modern Developments

In recent years, Evangelicalism saw the emergence of liberalism and its effect on the fervency of social movements. Yet under this wave, the Quakers saw continued energy for its causes such as caring for the oppressed and underrepresented. In many ways, the Friends work of bringing the Kingdom of God to earth through social action took a variety of new forms throughout the 1900s.

One major development in the modern era was the creation of the American Friends Service Committee (AFSC). In 1917, the Quakers created an independent organization whose services were similar to the Friends Ambulance Unit in England as well as the War Victims Relief Committee formed a few years previously.[65] The AFSC demonstrated the love of country and Christ by serving its people and all of humanity most in need as a result of poverty, war, famine, violence, and so forth. Through following Christ, the Friends have sought to reconstruct nations and people groups equally as a nonpartisan organization, making it notable for its work in Israel—Palestine in what some consider to be its anti-Jewish bias.[66] Alongside the British Friends Service Council, the AFSC was the recipient of the Nobel Peace Prize in 1947 and received much recognition for its constructive alternatives for conscientious objectors to military service. Other goals of the AFSC are public works such as domestic programs aimed at urban poor and minorities as well as pacifist causes like nuclear proliferation. Overall, the AFSC continues to work as a voice that represents Friends views through policies, works, actions, and legislation with the intent of relief and social reconstruction.

The changing face of America since the 1950s also presented the Quaker movement with creative options for engaging society with a cry for reform as an aspect of Christianity. "In 1960s when racial crises and the Vietnam War had prepared many liberals to call for the total reorganization of society, Hugh Barbour and T. Canby Jones revived for young Friends James Nayler's symbol of 'the Lamb's War,' calling humans to enroll in God's

65. Barbour and Frost, *The Quakers*, 252.
66. Ibid., 254.

struggle against evil simultaneously in their own hearts and in society."[67] The Lamb's War had become an image for the Quakers from its early roots, harkening back to King Philip's War in New England when the Friends were known for their service as mediators.[68] Now in the 1960s and 1970s, the Friends saw fringe movements aligning with Marxist voices and others who argued for a total restructuring of society toward greater equality. Another example of this was the creation of the Brandywine Alternative Fund that made it possible for Friends to avoid paying war taxes and instead giving to a peace tax fund.[69]

Others took more moderate approaches, with similar evocations to the Friends social roots. Many Yearly Meetings participated in "sit-ins" and became active voices in the civil rights movement.[70] The Quakers looked to become a more integrated group by listening to black voices through tools such as the Philadelphia Yearly Meeting's creation of the Economic Development Fund to underwrite black and other minority business ventures.[71] In similar moderate approaches, other Quakers balanced their convictions with civil engagement by working to mobilize the poor and embracing simpler lifestyles of voluntary poverty. Quaker groups in New York and Pennsylvania worked to mediate and restrain police brutality as well as work on alternative ways of housing and supervising delinquents as a part of reforming the entire prison system.[72] Similarly, in the 1960s, Quaker activist Eric Baker worked to establish Amnesty International as a tool for giving equal treatment to all people accused of crimes or imprisoned.[73]

Different than other Evangelical missions movements, the Quakers say from their foundation that their mission work was influenced by beliefs about the Holy Spirit, interpersonal relationships of peace, convictions that the human condition involves both physical and spiritual needs, and the belief that a passionately holy life full of integrity was what the Lord God was requiring of them as missionaries.[74] The truth is that the Living Christ has, all along, been reaching out to all humanity wherever their position

67. Ibid,. 267.

68. Ibid,. 247.

69. Ibid., 267.

70. Ibid., 266.

71. Ibid., 267.

72. Ibid., 268.

73. Ibid.

74. Stansell, *Missions by the Spirit*, 2.

on the globe. Quakers have from their early missionary work been ever so careful as to not seem presumptuous or imperialistic, with the focus being on the mutual receiving and sharing of God's Spirit. For the Friend, no one is ever so rich in spiritual resources that they can afford to neglect whatever can be learned from any teacher. There are anticipations of the Gospel in every world religion and this for the Quaker does not minimize the missionary movement but encourages it. The assistance of one another as brother or sister in the family of God helps the spiritual truths within each of us come to actuality. "If Christ is already speaking to everyone, we need to have the help of one another to learn more fully what it is that He is saying."[75] Because of these roots, Quaker missionary work often connected the inner religious life with the improvement of the total economy. The quiet center of the believer became deeply tied with social concern and outward expression in the quality of life. The Church, as understood by the Quakers, is not on mission but *is* mission and must therefore hold to the spiritual and social in one context. In the presentation of the Nobel Prize for Peace jointly awarded to the Friends Service Council and American Friends Service Committee in 1947, it was noted how in the Quakers the world has seen it possible to carry out a desire to aid others without eliminating dignity and with no regard to race or nationality.[76]

This transitions well into another Friends distinction: namely, the removal of the separation between the sacred and the secular. As observed in the discussion on mission work, evangelism and social justice were intertwined for the Friends from its genesis. In regards to spiritual practices, the Quakers take a similar posture of immersion. "What is done in the legislature or the factory or the household must be as much under Christ's immediate leadership as what is done in the prayer meeting."[77] To the Quakers, the world is a sacramental universe, which often is the distinguishing feature of it today in comparison with other traditions. Communion and Baptism no longer served as necessary marks of the Church but the condition of the heart is the Quaker's primary concern. Both are acts of the Spirit, in which some may find the participation in the sacrament helpful. But for the Friends, the physical ceremony is neither necessary nor sufficient, and is merely an outward expression of the inward reality. Rather than banning sacraments, the Quakers view themselves as truly enlarging

75. Trueblood, *The People Called Quakers*, 255.

76. Ibid., 257.

77. Ibid., 262.

and expanding the Christian vision of idea. Everything does not become a spiritual practice, but everything does have the *potential* of becoming a spiritual practice not merely certain spiritual ceremonies of initiation. Because of a strong affirmation of the church practices, the Quakers took such a posture as to never let anything devolve into ritual without deep spiritual meaning behind it. Christ's presence may be as vivid in the consumption of basic food in a humble house where the husband and wife toil away to feed their children as it is at any alter consecrated by a priest. As one Quaker author describes it, "The ideal which seems a high, but may not be too high, is that every home should become a Christian society and every common meal a sacramental experience."[78]

Another example of such an idea of human flourishing is the Adult School Movement, which started not exclusively, but largely as a Quaker idea to address the illiteracy of the English working class in the middle of the nineteenth century. Sunday served as the only free day so thus the schools met then and taught on religious and secular subjects as a model of outreach to the neighboring communities. The Quaker hope with the creation of these "schools" was to create spaces of divine confrontation, where insights into God can be recognized and developed in the beloved community. The movement has always been a missionary movement with all vocations and various forms. Adult Sunday School was simply one way in which the Quakers, to paraphrase John Woolman, worked to "turn all the treasures they possessed into channels of love as the business of their lives." May that same sense of the Spirit being active in its missionary ventures to meet contemporary injustices carry it forth.

At this point, I want to be sure and explicitly touch on the idea of ecclesiology for the Quakers. Though already implied here, the Quakers have little actual writing on the subject, yet as a contemporary Quaker, I see the concept as central to the nature of the Friends movement. Never was this movement systematized or presented as a formal theology, yet the Quakers serve as a fantastic example of an embodied theology, less written and more told through its lived history. Its action is never divorced from its convictions, and the community of believers becomes the space where such convictions are lived out. The closest examples of a written ecclesiology are the Quaker writings on the spiritual disciplines and how these are lived within both the individual and community of faith. One Quaker, Hannah Whitehall Smith, wrote specifically on this topic in her famous work, *The*

78. Ibid., 146.

Christian's Secret of a Happy Life. Though this title appears trite, her work intended to identify how the Quaker Christian sees action as connected to belief. This classic came out of her sincere plea to God to show her the secret of how to find joy in a life with Christ. She affirms that all of God's children feel instinctively, in moments illuminated by the Spirit, a duality of inward rest and outward victory. For her, a total abandonment of self to God results in an absolute faith. From this faith, the believer can now move past emotions and understand the sheer joy and happiness that comes in entire surrender and absolute trust. Believers now can *be* rather than just *feel* as a part of our union with Christ. As we continually put self to death in all the details of daily life and let Christ instead work and live in us, such a constant repetition cannot help but transform the attitude of our whole being. Other significant Quaker voices, such as Thomas Kelly and Richard Foster, similarly write about such spiritual transformations. In the Quakers there has been little organized theology or philosophical foundations, but deep mystical writings on the process a self-centered individual undergoes as the Living Christ consumes them. As Thomas Kelly says, "The Inner Light of Christ is the truest guide of life, showing us new and unsuspected defects in ourselves and our fellows, showing us new and unsuspected possibilities in the power and life of good-will among men."[79] This inner center of life, for the believer, is the true space where Christ dwells and the truest spot of joy and amazing life in all of the world. This is the spirituality that the Quakers bring to the discussion of human flourishing.

It is true, no doubt, that there is a vast disparity between the Quaker numbers and the Quaker influence. Though the Friends movement has never been the largest or even one of the larger movements in Christendom, their voice is a particular and necessary one in the dialogue. Their number may hardly exceed 300,000 today, yet their influence has been significant based on their way of life as what D. Elton Trueblood calls a "holy worldliness." Quakers sought to embody the idea of each person as a life fully alive to God, basking in God's good glory and pleasure, and living out Christ's words of being salt and light in the world. In the words of famous Quaker William Penn, "True Christians carry Christ about with them, who exempt not themselves from the conversation of the world, though they keep themselves from the evil of the world . . . but it enables them to live better in it and excited their endeavors to mend it."[80] I reference the foundations of the

79. Kelly, *A Testament of Devotion*, 6.
80. Trueblood, *The People Called Quakers*, 19.

Quaker movement not to idolize or idealize that era in its history but to remind myself and its other contemporary followers that the movement is one of the Holy Spirit, ever changing with the contemporary context and always looking to reinterpret how to be a "peculiar people" who are fully alive to Christ today.

There can continue to be a faithfulness to the Spirit with an extremely different version of Quakerism being present in our modern era. As each experience in our contemporary world is filtered through the light of Christ alive in the community, then the Quakers can best discern today how to be faithful and intelligent, and that need not be dressing in "Quaker greys" anymore or buying up all of the town liquor licenses. The manner in which the early Friends resisted unjust laws and stood for the equality of all is to me a great inspiration as to how the missions movement and social justice convictions can still provoke a small denomination to have a strong voice in Christianity today. "The time has come again when, as in primitive Quakerism, every Christian can be and ought to be a missionary. If she is not, she has not rightly understood her vocation."[81]

Conclusion

In many senses, the Quakers appear to be an ecclesial movement, similar to other peace and free church movements, inclined towards a constructive global ecclesiology. Quaker ecclesiology entails a form of revolutionary subordination, as introduced by Anabaptist voices such as John Howard Yoder elsewhere in this work. "The Christian community is not responsible to 'redeem' society but simply to live in it but not of it, to witness to it, knowing we cannot essentially change its dynamic and direction."[82] With a belief in the doctrine of the priesthood of all believers and a distinctive of equality of persons, the Quakers position themselves easiest to listen to the teachings of their sisters and brothers around the world and in the overlooked corners of Empire. By focusing less on academic spheres and pontificated theology, it becomes easier to bridge the gap between theology and embodied praxis. Each community of faith must wrestle with the idea of constructing theology from entirely different spaces and in entirely different ways in our globalized world today, but for the Quakers, there is room within their tradition and practice to continue their small yet unique

81. Ibid., 256.
82. Dyrness and Kärkkäinen, eds., *Global Dictionary of Theology*, 343.

and particularized voice in the broader theological dialogue. I believe the value in beginning to create a formal Quaker ecclesiology is to continue to expand the growth and influence of the Quaker movement. Though not necessary for the Quakers, or for that matter any denomination living its ecclesiology rather than writing it, the significance in using it as a lens and model can continue to develop ecclesiological reflection.

As demonstrated here through the works and brief treatment of Moltmann, Yoder, Cavanaugh, Gutierrez, Sobrino, Ruether, and Russell, the discussion of political theology centers itself on the Church as an alternative politic in society. These perspectives—political liberation, feminist and Quaker theology—all synthesize together to form a framework for building a constrictive global ecclesiology. Each movement critiques the normative center of theology and deconstructs ecclesiology in a manner that allows for a rebuilding from theologians on the margins. Theologically, this grounds itself in an adequate treatment of the perichoretic nature of the Trinity and the nature with which the Church embodies the eschatological vision. This foundation paved the way for liberationist and feminist theologies, both seeking to extend the Church's vision to the margins of society and the overlooked voices of the poor and women by adequately addressing the systemic nature of sin and the liberatory nature of salvation.

3

___

Third World Feminist Ecclesiology

Mercy Amba Oduyoye, Kwok Pui-Lan,
and Maria Pilar Aquino

Introduction

In speaking of Third World feminist theology, this project centered around three women who focused their writings on ecclesiology. One woman from each of the continents from the Global South was selected as a representative for African, Asian, and Latin American women's theology, respectively. From Africa: Ghanaian Mercy Amba Oduyoye; from Asia: Hong Kongese Kwok Pui-Lan; and from the Americas: Mexican Maria Pilar Aquino will serve as the theological guides in identifying the Christian Church as they see it. Though each of these women come from unique denominational backgrounds—Methodist, Catholic and Episcopal—this work is examining how their ecclesiology can still influence the Evangelical tradition. Each woman takes the role of Scripture seriously as a starting point for theological reflection, making each of their ecclesiologies still relevant.

Utilizing a thorough summary of their works and theologies, each of their unique perspectives on Third World feminist theology will help to form constructive global theology—a theology including voices from the entire globe for the entire globe. From their points of similarity, intercultural dialogue and discussion becomes possible. Despite particularized geographic experiences, Oduyoye, Kwok, and Aquino can together begin to form an ecclesiology that speaks to the Church worldwide. Though now educated and published, each of these women writes with a deep awareness of the underrepresented communities they speak on behalf of. Greater than their distinctions or separations is their shared sisterhood and positioning of liberative theology from the margins. Similarly, each of these women understands the power contained within the unity of Third World theology for the formation and direction of the Church. This theology stands as a representation that both reflects their experiences as marginalized women as well as their interpretations of Scripture. Here, these three voices will harmonize together for a picture of experience, methodology, and feminist theology from each of their continents.

Mercy Amba Oduyoye

Background

Mercy Oduyoye's experience as a Ghanaian woman provides a unique perspective on the Third World feminist movement. She is Akan, Asante, and Brong in background and a part of the Methodist church as a fifth generation in Ghana. Oduyoye grew up in a large family that shared a compound together. "I saw births, sickness, cooperative economic activities, death . . . I did not have to imagine community, I *had* community."[1] She believes that African Christianity emphasizes sharing struggles and triumphs as a community to encounter the presence of God among us. Her grandfather was a cocoa farmer, and so she does her theology always asking, "What difference does it make?"[2] It is significant to her that the vision of the Christian life she describes in her writings always considers those on the margins and brings the good news of the Gospel into their experience.

Since she was raised in a matriarchal culture, Oduyoye first encountered patriarchy when she left Africa for higher education in the West. But through her education and also her awareness of the realities of other women in different parts of Africa, Oduyoye began to articulate her own African feminist theology. She believes that women in Africa have a unique voice to contribute regarding the role of the Church. Her writings have led her to positions such as the Deputy General Secretary of the World Council

1. Oduyoye, "Re-imaging The World," 83.
2. Oduyoye, "Be a Woman, and African Will Be Strong," 35.

of Churches, and ecumenical dialogue is an area of great significance in her work. Oduyoye, as both a Ghanaian and a Methodist theologian writing specifically from the context of African women, believes that Christian tradition and African tradition need to find a harmonious place together.

Oduyoye also understood her context through the remnants of colonialism. European missionaries came to Ghana in the early nineteenth century and sought to undermine the coherence of the communities there. She believes that though missionaries attempted to convert belief systems as well as cultures, the Ghanaian people could not be completely taken over. "The result of this interaction [between Christianity and African spirituality] is a distinctive African Christianity with its own spirituality, partly creative, partly imitative, and in large measure a mixture that is identifiable as Christian and African."[3] In this setting, she understood the embodiment of Trinitarian theology, lived in communities that reflect the perichoretic nature of the Father, Son and Spirit. Through her Akan community, postcolonial as it was, she witnessed the care, love, and mutuality of the community of three persons. In her words, "If a company of three can be manifested as one, then I could live with the blundering attempts of the Akan community."[4]

Gatherings such as the Ecumenical Association of Third World theologians (EATWOT) have been helpful in extending the growth of liberation theologies from the Third World. However for Oduyoye, she understands a gender divide even among Third World Theologians, with a lacking in cross-gender dialogue and the difficulty for women and men to talk together about the women's issues in theology, the church, and the world.[5] Patriarchy, she believes, still continues to reign even among Third World theologians. In spaces where there is a consciousness that women have been discriminated against in both church and society, if nothing is done to rectify this with action, then such oppression continues. In her words, "The dividing line of gender is most dangerous where it is masked by 'friendship,' polite conversation and avoidance of conflict."[6] The problem, even within spaces like EATWOT, Oduyoye believes, is that women's conversations can become their own space within the space (or "subjectness" as she sees it), rather than a consciousness that shapes the entire conversation.

3. Oduyoye, "Re-imagining the World," 86.

4. Ibid., 87.

5. Oduyoye, "The Impact of Women's Theology," 90.

6. Ibid., 95.

Her desire is that the direction of Third World theology continues to stress cross-gender dialogue and addresses the sexism within its midst. Her hope remains that liberative nature of theology can free both women and men from "dominant structures that stifle the process of transformation . . .[and minimize] the fullness of life."[7] Oduyoye understands an aspect of her background as being associated with Third World theologians, yet believes that one of her tasks is to help articulate the feminist consciousness and increase women's participation in theological discourse.

African Spirituality

In speaking of spirituality of resistance and reconstruction, she declares, "It is this violence against women that generates a spirituality of resistance to dehumanization."[8] She believes that the violence that Africa suffers stems from the racism and exploitation built into her relations with the Euro-American world. African women cultivate a spirituality of resistance that avoids hiding the violence against women. "In African Christianity, spirituality can and is understood as what propels us to resist death and to foster and create life."[9] Her emphasis on this truth of African spirituality is what compels Oduyoye and others to working with men for women's discourse, creating one earth community with mutuality for all.

African religious beliefs must find their place within African Christianity. There are a host of areas that must be addressed in order for Christianity to truly represent Africa rather than colonialist representations of Christianity. Oduyoye believes that the overlap is greater than often recognized. Christianity shares African belief in the divine origin of the universe and that humanity is intended to be a steward of this universe.[10] Recognition is needed of one God from whom all movements of the spirit take their origin. God is the Originator of all humanity, and all humanity is one family. The value of ancestors is a strong emphasis in African belief and

7. Ibid., 109.

8. Oduyoye, "Spirituality of Resistance and Reconstruction," 161.

9. Ibid. 170.

10. This understanding of the "Divine" (God) would be critiqued by orthodox Evangelical theology, but for the sake of representing her theology best I am including it here. For Evangelicals, God would be Creator that is separated from the created universe and thus separated from humanity as well, but this African notion of divinity understands a greater interplay than such a harsh separation.

must find its place in Christianity as well. Past, present, and future generations are one community. Ancestors enable us to remember our source and history. Christianity will have to take seriously the African belief that God delegates authority to intermediary beings, or the "divine rights of kings." This comes as interconnected with the very realistic attitude of the power of evil in Africa. Another area, covenant making, is a central characteristic of African life. Likewise, reconciliation has a central role in African religion and practice because the value of one's word and one's community takes centrality.

When viewing the person, African religious belief asserts that selves must be viewed as one whole without separation between body and soul. All lives are intended to be viewed in a unified fashion and also as a part of one unified whole. "Spirituality is a holistic and continuous process of becoming. It enables me to look at others with mutual respect. Spirituality is always coupled with justice."[11] Women are integral parts of humanity and not just integral parts of the male. One other major area of African religious belief as translated through the context of Christianity is Christian liturgical traditions. Most rites of passage performed by Christians in African have been enriched by African culture. Drumming, dancing, extemporaneous prayer, dramatic methods of conveying the word of God, robes, exorcisms, healings, and so forth are all Christian concepts that have found richer meaning and practice in the African context.

Methodology

A major component in her methodology for theology is the role of story. Story now serves as a source for theology, valuing a perspectival approach and affirming ancestors and familial lines as teachers and leaders. This she believes will create spaces for all types of prayers and spiritual expressions, not merely Western liturgy or Scripture. A storytelling approach becomes a source for this theology so as to give women the opportunity to tell their own story especially in a context where those stories have remained unwritten for so long. This lends itself to a narrative view of Scripture based on the strong role of oral tradition in African lifestyle. Rather than using analysis or critique, African women engage in what she terms a "perspectival approach" stemming from a dialogue that questions the traditional

11. Ibid.

views while also contributing the creation of new theologies that integrate in women's spiritualties.[12]

Women as living stones is one framework coming out of the African context. This idea emerged from Cameroon, where living stones are known for being movable, portable, and usable. This cultural tool, the living stones, is now given a spiritual metaphor when compared with women. Living stones are used for cooking and have a vital purpose in the life of the community. They are used in the wedding ceremony and signify the bride and groom building their house together as one family. Because marriage and sexual relationships are such a significant part of stepping into adulthood, these roles become an inevitable and inescapable context for theology and are themselves theological issues. Peter uses the image of living stones to signify the Church as a community of believers that serve and witness to the world. Grace Eneme speaks of how women, a majority of the church members in Africa, make up a small minority of the leaders and decision-makers.[13] Odudoye appreciates this example and references Eneme's metaphor as the power of scriptural concepts in the African context. The status of African women in the church serves as microcosm for their status in broader African society. This metaphor of living stones serves as an example of the power of imagery and story as theological norms for women understanding their role in transforming society. For Oduyoye, the human being is still an integrated person in Africa; the private and the political cannot be separated.[14]

Scripture

Oppression, war, famine, and poverty are sadly far too commonplace realities in Africa. This setting compels Oduyoye to practice a lived reality of the Deuteronomic principle.[15] This affirms obedience to God's principles as outlined in the Torah, whereas disobedience brings destruction and curse. As theology develops in Africa and contains a liberatory element, it must continue to emphasize both literal and psychological liberation. The internal transformation brought through salvation in Christ must counter the fear of change with the redemption God can bring. Christian bodies

12. Oduyoye, *Introducing African Women's Theology*, 11.

13. Ibid., 76.

14. Oduyoye, *Hearing and Knowing*, 101.

15. Oduyoye, "Liberation and the Development of Theology in Africa."

are intended to be temples of the Holy Spirit, spaces where the Living God works within humanity in each particular space and culture.

In speaking of the liberative power of African women, Oduyoye takes John 4:42 as key, advocating that now they have heard for themselves and speak that Christ is indeed the savior of the world. In creating a new Christology for Africa, Jesus takes on new models as personal friend and savior, as embodiment of the Spirit, and as prophet. "For Christ to become meaningful in the context of African women's search for emancipation, he would need to be a concrete and personal figure who engenders hope in the oppressed by taking their (women's) side, to give them confidence and courage to persevere."[16] When Christ stands on the side of the powerless, he enables them to speak for themselves. This Christ is actively concerned with the victims of social injustice and dismantling those structures that keep society unjust. Such progress would be a movement away from colonial models of Christ as an imperial, conquering warrior King and toward a vision of Christ apart from the oppressive ways the colonialist church has presented him.

African Liberation Theology

A key aspect of liberation theology in the African church context is the role of psychological transformation and internal liberation as a part of salvation. Too often, women and the poor understand their humanity as of less worth, and liberation must not only create new spaces for them to thrive and lead but also must affirm their worth in God's Kingdom. She calls for the need for "liberation from the mentality that keeps women coping with marginalization and repression rather than resisting it."[17] The church in many ways has served as a structure of sin in Africa by keeping women in lesser positions. Women often serve the church diligently with their time and service, yet rarely is their voice elevated to positions on boards or as ministers. "The church has never tried to build a dynamic community of women and men. I never cease to be astonished at how little we have actually accomplished in community-building."[18] Her impression is that too often the feelings of women in the church are ridiculed, and this attitude works against any formation of spirit-led community. All people find their

16. King, *Feminist Theologies from the Third World,* 267.

17. Ibid.

18. Oduyoye, *Hearing and Knowing,* 125.

needs met, their lives valued, and their stories affirmed in the true Church. God becomes an active, power-giving spirit that empowers the people of God to combat the powers that threaten humanity through prayers, prophesies, and songs that speak a new world into existence.

Part of the work of the church in African women's liberation theology is to stand and cry that enculturation is not sufficient. Enculturation is only worthy if the culture being reclaimed promotes justice and supports the life and dignity of African women.[19] African culture must first be redeemed toward women and their full personhood in order that any steps toward incorporating culture into the church represent the vision of God's community. The church must become a body of enculturation and reconstruction, one that is both personal and ecclesial. As a body, it must reconstruct its dealings with management structures, financial policies, pastoral care, human resource development, research, family education, service, and witness. All of these are areas in which women are easily exploited and underrepresented within a patriarchal culture. She believes in a postcolonial trajectory for a future history of Christian theology that is dialogical, uses narrative genres, respects all cultures, and addresses gender dynamics in complex ways.[20]

Too often in Third World theology, women are viewed as "slaves of slaves" in Oduyoye's perspective. "Rituals that use sexuality to divest women of power and enthrone men for the same reason are found in African religion as in Christianity, making the African Christian women a creature that has little hope of being defined by anything but gender."[21] Women experience entirely different socioeconomic realities than even men in the Third World. Areas in which Oduyoye views this slavery are in many of the women's reproductive rights: marriage, procreation, ability to reproduce, genital mutilation, and so forth. In the African context, women view mother-centered communities as the norm and see this as a source of strength. This strength is co-opted when patriarchy takes over and forces purity and control. In Oduyoye's own words, "Men make God and women worship them."[22] Women carry life-giving burdens and need to name themselves and participate in a Christianity that gives them the opportunity to do that.

19. Kwok ed., *Hope Abundant*, 26.

20. Kwok, "Mercy Amba Oduyoye," in Kwok and Rieger, eds., *Empire and the Christian Tradition*, 485.

21. Oduyoye, "Christian Feminism and African Culture," 447.

22. Oduyoye, "Feminist Theology in an African Perspective," 166.

"Feminist theologians remind the 'male' processions that the majority of the people they pass by are women and that ministry should be service in the name of Christ to and by all these baptized people."[23] The feminine aspects of God must also be better represented in African Christianity, for as Oduyoye points out, most African languages contain God in the female as the "source-Being."

Ecclesiology

Oduyoye begins by longing for the church to recognize its role as a structure of sin, keeping both women and culture subjugated in order to perpetuate its hierarchies. Likewise she believes that salvation in African Christian theology must include questions of racism and liberation from material need. She calls for a reconstruction of all church hierarchies that will provide channels of accountability. She longs for a model that is more than just an enculturation or an integration of partial African experiences as long as the church leadership approves of them. "An African who is a Christian and who feels herself part of the global sisterhood has to cope not only with all that Western Christian women have to contend with, but in addition there are elements of African culture even more deeply rooted than Christianity that militate against her image in of herself as a genuine and full member of those who see themselves as created in the image of God."[24] Instead she boldly propones that all churches in Africa need to become African Initiated Churches (or AICs), where African religions can be seen as equal, and all experiences can be viewed as valid in theological conversation.

Her seminal work, *Beads and Strands*, intends to call the Church to account. Western churches implanted in Africa so as a result, too often African women mirror their Euro-American predecessors. Her belief is that now African churches must work toward redeeming Christianity from its image as a force that coerces women into accepting roles that hamper the free and full expression of their humanity. She propones that the place of women in the church is perhaps the most crucial issues in our century for the total work of evangelization. Biblical interpretation and Christian theology in Africa have previously had the effect of affecting secular culture in a negative fashion and forced the marginalization of women's experience, even in traditional African religions. The African church needs women to

23. Ibid, 170.
24. Oduyoye, "Christian Feminist and African Culture," 441.

form its theology and make decisions that affect the entire church. Historically, the church in Africa tends to be a "reaction" church, rarely visible on the front lines and often delayed in arriving on the scene. Instead, Oduyoye affirms that African Christians who form the visible church must boldly identify as sin the suppression of the full humanity of persons.

If the church is to understand itself as perpetuating sin, then the African church must take on the role of exorcising demons. These demons may need to be exorcised in objects, structures, and people. This is an example of African tradition finding its place in the Church as it calls out the sin that suppressed life and practices any and all rituals to eliminate it. The African concept of the spirit world is on the side of protecting life, and this must be nurtured and valued, with its opposing forces exorcised and called out.

And finally, Oduyoye speaks of the church with the language of *harambee*. This African concept tells of cooperation and sharing that characterize self-help groups of urban or rural women in Africa. Normally used as a local community term, she believes that this metaphor extends to the Church and speaks to the ways in which salvation provides a fullness of life now. When the church is reconstructed in its hierarchies, with African religions leading and all experiences valid, then the church can move beyond its role as a structure of sin and become a life-giving resource for the community.

Speaking of rural faith communities in Africa, a larger picture of the definition of church must surface. Some move as far as to say that African religions must be understood as equivalent to African Christianity. Voicing this opinion in regards to the ways in which the institutional church of Africa has limited the role of women, Denise M. Ackerman responds: "We are the church. When they locked our churches, we held church under the trees and we baptized our children in the river. When the commissar *(commissioner)* tried to stop this, we took them to the sea at night. We just kept on being church. Tell them, we are the church."[25] This speaks to the idea that for women in the church in Africa, the Nicene creedal statement, "I believe in one, holy, catholic and apostolic church" becomes a contradiction. Mercy Oduyoye believes that they are many churches, divided and "being church" in a number of ways all throughout Africa. One unified Church can only emerge if greater expressions of church are validated in their representation of African Christianity based out of African culture. Each of these spirit-led

---

25. Ackermann, *After The Locusts*, 46.

representations of God must be acknowledged and vindicated in order to bring women into full personhood.

The *Oikonomia* of God

Throughout her theology, Oduyoye appreciates the metaphor of the *Oiko-nomia* (household) of God as significant for African women because of the cultural emphasis of homemaking. She extends the African metaphor further with the idea of "hearth-holds," or an extension beyond one house dwelling to the community with women as the central points/mothers/ethical leaders. Hearth-holds is the Nigerian concept of all who are nourished from the same fore-place and for African women, this extends to all the lives that an individual woman is responsible for. "It has, therefore, become important for women theologians that they see the Church as the hearth-hold of Christian within the household of God."[26] This furthers the biblical metaphor of the household of God and, in Oduyoye's estimation, moves the concept closer to the New Testament idea of the metaphor. The reason for this is two-fold: women-headed households in biblical times and household divisions within the people of God extend beyond biological lines to the new family of God.[27] This community participates in healing actions, as Oduyoye calls them, and carries on that ministry as a part of its mission.

The *koinonia,* or the sharing of a common life in the Church, implies working together, and sharing equally in all that God has given to creation. *Koinonia* centers on a community of equal persons, functioning in a communion that because of its mere existence stands against injustice. Biblical passages such as Ephesians 5:28–31 identify the Church growing into a space of mutual sharing and participation. One instrument that advocates for the true house-hearth or *koinonia* of God is that of true theological education. This is not limited to academic spheres, but exists anywhere where justice and participation are better understood after a deep reflection on the Scriptures. Another example is the sacrament of baptism. Actions such as participation in the baptismal community of faith invite new believers into the nonhierarchical *koinonia* of God. "Baptism," Oduyoye writes, "is the rite that confers 'citizenship' in God's Commonwealth."[28] Oduyoye un-

26. Oduyoye, *Introducing African Women's Theology,* 79.

27. Biblical examples of women heads-of-households are that of Hagar, Lydia, and Martha/Mary.

28. Oduyoye, *Introducing African Women's Theology,* 87.

derstands the experiences of women as working to promote the equality of all persons, and sacramental actions such as baptism, with many deep theological implications, also signifies equality to the outside world.

In speaking of women's experience, Oduyoye believes that women in Christianity are working to build a church that is inclusive to all despite all the temptations of compromise. "Re-imagining community is women living *beyond* patriarchy in the midst of patriarchy."[29] Similar to baptism, the Eucharist is related to the experience of community as well as the continuing equal community of persons being maintained in the Church. The Eucharist is not to be reduced to merely the equality of the human community, but Oduyoye understands that the Eucharaist does contain this capacity. Women's imagery of church provides a vision of a Church in the Round, a sense of connectedness and solidarity, and many other visions and metaphors extended from the Lord's Table. Often the experience of women in the church is a lack of hospitality, and Oduyoye believes that an entirely new vision of community must be crafted in order to be faithful to the liberative nature of the Gospel. In her words:

> The eucharistic community that our churches pretend to represent only approximates what it is called to be if it is a home where looking different is accepted and appreciated, a home where one's gender and the tone of one's skin make no difference to one's participation or partnership. If we have ringing in our ears words like racist, apartheid, ethnic cleansing, and low-caste exclusion, then we are not re-imagining community and the church is failing in its duty to mirror the community of the Trinity.[30]

Oduyoye understands women theologians in the Church are needed to offer themselves up as resources and to commit to continue the development of building Trinitarian communities that participate faithfully in the sacraments. She continues to create spaces for African women theologians to do just that, and her vision of representation continues in her teaching post in Ghana.

29. Oduyoye, "Re-imagining the World," 87.
30. Ibid., 88.

Kwok Pui-Lan

Background

Kwok Pui-Lan, as a Chinese woman who grew up in Hong Kong, understands the role of the church for marginalized people. Her observation is that the missionary movement in China, even with all its colonialist faults, brought tremendous good for women in China by working to end the footbinding movement, creating temperance unions, providing education, fostering literacy campaigns, and securing more healthcare. Those are just a few examples of how she came to understand that the Church can serve as a liberating agent for those caught in oppression. "Christianity offered women new symbolic resources with which to look at the world and themselves, helping them to affirm their sense of worth and dignity."[31] Kwok's ecclesiology stands on the foundation that Church must be an alternative vision of society and human relationships. This background propelled her scholarship into the area of postcolonial feminism.

Her emphasis on China's history comes out of her awareness of the potential the Church can have for either good or evil in each context. Chinese women found themselves drawn to join the Christian community in search of an alternative vision of society and human relationships. "Although the majority of Chinese female Christians were little educated and believed in an individualistic evangelical faith, the more articulate leaders had begun to relate their faith to the needs of China at the time."[32] She sees herself as in part a church historian as well as a prophetic theologian, called to continue to expand the understanding and reach of Asian feminist theology. There were some clear, tangible benefits from early missions movement to China, such as meals, security, famine relief, protection, and escape from abusive marriages. Out of this foundation of the strength of the Church to provide salvation and community, Kwok speaks for the reality of Asian women and the injustices still faced today. "Christian women believed that Christianity enabled them to struggle against all forms of discrimination against women, since Christian doctrines stressed the equality of all human beings before the almighty God."[33] This vision is what motivates her to speak out of the liberationist framework, and her desire is not to present a

---

31. Kwok, "Chinese Women and Protestant Christianity at the Turn of the Twentieth Century," in Bays, ed., *Christianity in China*, 200.

32. Ibid., 208.

33. Ibid., 207.

new vision of Christianity in China as much as to expand on the historical framework and now have Asian women provide for their own resources.

Postcolonial Theology

One aspect of Kwok's theology to be addressed is her work at moving beyond liberation theology into the space of postcolonial theology.[34] She attempts to take seriously the fact that Christianity can never be assimilated with empire and colonialism and must seek to provide alternatives to the status quo. Theology, for Kwok, never emerges in a vacuum but is always in an ongoing process of negotiation with power structures—economic, political, ecclesial, and the like. Her emphasis on globalization includes the hybridity of theology and politics and the need for shifting bases of authority. The conceptions of God and the problems of history cannot be divorced from one another. Particularly, she articulates that liberation theology contains the blind spots of its Eurocentric bias in interpreting modernity and secularity, assuming Christianity is the global dominant religion, and demonstrating a lack of sensitivity to issues pertaining to race, gender, and sexuality.[35] Liberation theology, she attests, struggles with truly representing the poor because of the class and educational privileges of its authors. The caution is that theologians from these communities "can easily be co-opted into the multicultural theological marketplace or the carnival of postmodern difference."[36] Theology must be self-critical of its own position and continue to work to be representative of its communities of accountability, and this challenge is heavily present in Kwok's work. The question that drives her postcolonial theological project centers on how globalization can exist "from below": "What can Christian theologians contribute

---

34. The difference between liberation and postcolonial theology is a minor one, and deserves deeper discussion. My reason for the distinction comes from Joerg Rieger's Introduction to the "Postcolonial Challenges" portion of *An Eerdmans Reader in Political Theology.* He includes Kwok in the postcolonial category rather than the liberationist category, as do the volume editors. Rieger, "Introduction to Postcolonial Challenges," in Cavanaugh, Bailey, and Hovey, eds., *An Eerdmans Reader,* 476.

35. Kwok, "Theology and Social Theory," in Cavanaugh, Bailey, and Hovey, eds., *An Eerdmans Reader,* 604. I find myself unsure if this bold claim can be fully supported with the breadth of voices included under the heading of liberation theology, and Mercy Oduyoye's work in particular appears to be a strong counterexample to this idea.

36. Ibid., 609.

to a social imaginary that will benefit the oppressed and marginalized?"[37] Ultimately for Kwok, issues of race, class, gender, sexuality and colonialism are not added on or second to theology, but instead must become the spaces where this work is done. Doctrines of God, Christology, ecclesiology, and so forth must integrate embodiment and human relations into its conversations.

One area in which liberation theology needs to expand is to that of gender, sexuality, and women's reproductive issues in order to "demythologize and demystify theology."[38] By focusing primarily on class, male liberation theologians failed to integrate deep liberatory issues, such as gender and sexuality, into their project. Alongside this, Third World and indigenous women's theologians must deeply engage in cultural criticism, particularly in regards to the effects of colonialism and the role of religion in shaping gender identity. Kwok herself has written that she prefers the use of the term "Third World" as mentioned in the introduction because it connotes the power imbalance and keeps that imbalance in the forefront of changing the theological conversation.

Intercultural and Minjung Theology

A more appropriate term that Kwok Pui-Lan creates to describe the hybridity of her particular theology is that of "intercultural theology." She works with a host of other Third World feminist theologians to further support her foundation of intercultural theology as not a new concept but the true intent of theological discourse. Intercultural theology works to deconstruct homogenous agendas and identify the struggles of all peoples on the ground. Within globalization, there must be an acknowledgement of the diversity within each cultural context for dialogue and continued theological development. Kwok Pui-Lan works to employ transnationalism as the ability to understand the globalization of changing religious identity in Asia. Women become both "subjects" and "objects" in these exchanges of capital and labor, and Kwok believes that feminist theological writings must reflect this more and work to disrupt imperialist agendas. God, she believes, is located in the "interstices," the spaces between social systems where divine power energizes and "readjusts and shifts to find new strength, and discover hope

37. Ibid., 610.

38. Kwok, *Hope Abundant*, 6.

in the densely woven web of life that sustains us all."[39] This intercultural theological framework informs her value on churches serving as spaces that reflect people of diverse ethnic backgrounds within their midst.

Similar to intercultural theology, Kwok sees the values of *minjung* theology and the theological concept of *han* as helpful in creating a multicultural feminist ecclesiology. These two notions, borrowed from other Asian liberation theologies, value the role of individual suffering as well as the role of suffering in the community, since it follows after the suffering contained in the nature of God. *Minjung* theology values the suffering community and the gathering of the marginalized. Asian churches remind us of the value suffering has in our understanding of God, and that theological conversations and communities cannot exist when suffering is minimized. Pain finds a place in the heart of God that broke and suffered in the crucifixion, and that continues to break over the realities of sin in our world. This must be integrated into our ecclesial communities as they continue to also reflect multicultural and feminist voices. Kwok does emphasize that even in the *minjung* church context, women, who are the *minjung* among the *minjung*, often play a lesser role in shaping the church.

Christianity in Asian Women

Kwok Pui-Lan advocates for the process of re-rooting Christianity into Asian soil. Part of her story as a theologian and biblical scholar involves coming to terms between the two identities she felt caught between: being Chinese and being Christian. Her mother was a folk Buddhist but she herself became acquainted with the local Anglican Church. She began to see strong similarities between Jesus and Buddha, with both emphasizing forgiveness, sacrifice, and love. She connected the capacity of attaining Buddhahood in all beings to the concept of the living Christ as Redeemer. In her article "Chinese Non-Christian Perceptions of Christ," Kwok emphasizes that Christ can fit in the Chinese framework as a reassessment of Western Christianity.[40] The challenge for Christianity is that it must now think of how it is understood by outsiders, recognizing that some of those "outsiders" are its faithful adherents who fail to fit within its kyriarchial norms.

---

39. Kwok, et al., eds., *Off the Menu*, 19.

40. Kwok, "Chinese Non-Christian Perceptions of Christ," 24.

As Kwok Pui-Lan experienced more of the Christian Church in Hong Kong, she found herself mixed about its role in salvation and liberation. On the one hand, Christianity stimulated social change, including the emancipation of women. "Chinese Christian women were not just onlookers in the unfolding drama of the missionary movement in China. They were integral members of the Church, participating in worship and organizing their own Bible study groups and prayer meetings . . . writing religious confessions, testimonies and short theological articles, giving us information about their journeys of faith and understanding of Christianity."[41]

On the other hand, Kwok Pui-Lan contrasts the history of Christian women in China with the realities they are experiencing today. That history was summarized earlier and gives the foundation for her passion over liberation. "The same Christian community, which was prophetic in terms of women's emancipation in the nineteenth century, seemed to be caught up by traditional patriarchal ecclesiologies, failing to catch up with the changing circumstances of the time."[42] More and more, the Christian women she came to know and wrote on behalf of began recognizing that the Church teachings inherited from the missionary movement no longer fit both from the point of women and from the point of Asian people's struggle for liberation.

Scripture

Kwok Pui-Lan affirms that Scripture needs to be reconceptualized based on experiences in the non-Western world. Eurocentric reading method of Scripture has become the accepted norm for interpretation. First of all, Scripture needs to be broader than the Bible because the reality has been that women's voices have, for the most part, been left out of the canon. The experience of women has been that the Bible became used as a tool to justify slavery, hegemony, patriarchy, and so forth. Kwok's proposal is that a postcolonial reading of Scripture needs to propel biblical studies forward. One example she gives of this is the story of Hagar as one living under colonial powers.[43] Examples like this are one of many that will continue

41. Kwok, "Chinese Women and Protestant Christianity at the Turn of the Century," 195.

42. Kwok. "The Emergence of Asian Feminist Consciousness of Culture and Theology," 92.

43. Kwok,. "Racism and Ethnocentrism in Feminist Biblical Interpretation," 101.

to expand the possibility of postcolonial biblical readings. Kwok builds off the vision of Elizabeth Shussler Fiorenza by affirming that the written text often fails to represent the actual experiences of women. To continue this process, such interpretation must include nonwritten forms, performed exegesis, and other interpretations that defend the reality of Scripture as a living, continuous process. She affirms that Scripture cannot be fixed and bound as the sole point of God's revelation.

She postulates that so few minorities and women are in the field of biblical studies for a host of reasons: institutional barriers, financial burden, and the general alienation of racial and ethnic students in biblical studies. Racism, classism and sexism are interlocking forces of oppression working against minorities and women in biblical studies. She values the approach of each interpreter entering the text from a particular vantage point to further the idea of postcolonial biblical studies. In reaction to prior scholarship, she desires to reclaim the term "native," one categorized as negative by the biblical scholar Albert Schweitzer, and view Jesus as the native rather than the noble savage. Constructions of Jesus of Nazareth as developed in the modern biblical studies enterprise are influenced and limited by its Eurocentric bias. Another example she gives is that of the Quest for the historical Jesus, which she believed was a Western obsession and addressed the anxiety of the construction of modern society.[44] She does believe that the good that came from the emphasis on the historical Jesus was that it created a figure to serve as the perfect human being, demonstrating the highest potential of humankind. Overall, she sees the modern study of the Bible as emerging simultaneously with bourgeois culture and was highly influenced by the expansion of Europe. This framework must change in biblical Interpretation, implores Kwok Pui-Lan, in order to create a new framework for ecclesiology.

Even in the project of feminist biblical interpretation, Kwok understands that racism and ethnocentrism still exist in its biases. In recalling her heritage, she writes, "I grew up in the nonbiblical culture of Asia, and I do not believe that we can abstractly speak about the divine elements or the central message of the Bible without historical specificity . . . and the concept of the 'authority of the Bible' does not have any meaning or might even sound offensive to the majority of Asians who are non-Christian."[45] Kwok's value would be on discovering cross-cultural interactions in Scripture, and

44. Kwok, "Jesus the Native," 70.
45. Kwok, "Racism and Ethnocentrism," 102.

using cultural comparisons with the Confucian classics, the Bhagavad Gita, and so forth. She believes that interpretation comes in the community of women and men who read the Bible and, through their dialogical imagination, appropriate it for their own liberation.

Asian Theology

One example of Asian Theology that Kwok emphasizes is the spiritual and practical concept of recycling within ecology. Recycling is a theological theme in the East, like a circle, and it functions as equivalent to a crucifix. Asian Christian women at times model this principle by binding themselves to one another in a circle. This relates to the significance of the interconnectedness in the circle of life and how it affects the weakest in the chain—women and children in particular. This ecological model moves away from hierarchy and moves away from human being centered to bio-centrism. In this ecological theology, spiritual becomes holistic and expands from simply ecclesial solidarity to now including an ecological solidarity as well.

As stated before, Kwok longs to demythologize and demystify theology. These are concepts she stresses repeatedly throughout her work, especially in regards to the role of the Church. Theology needs to become an enterprise inclusive of gender and sexuality and it also must take into account people's stories and cultural experiences as well as Scripture. "A postcolonialist theological interpretation does not name all men as the enemy in an essentialist manner, but acknowledges that some men and women have more power than others."[46] Her example in broadening the field of theology beyond the traditional voices extends to some women who have more power than necessary. She stresses that we cannot let white women, such as her example Mary Daly, speak to the experiences of non-Western women. She begins to call this an "inclusive theology," not to be confused with the inclusivist position regarding salvation but instead inclusive of a variety of norms for doing theology. Her attributes of an inclusive theology are as follows:

1. Move from the Bible as the only normative source for theology to the value of people's stories for theology

2. Move from a passive reception of the traditions to an active construction of Asian women's own theology

46. Kwok, "Unbinding Our Feet," 78.

3. Move away from a unified theological discourse to a plurality of voices and a genuine catholicity.[47]

Ecclesial communities need to become spaces for theological praxis, and particularly this needs to occur with multicultural feminist voices. "Women in Third World churches . . . bear witness to a faith that empowers people to break through silence and move to action."[48] The Church must continue to integrate cultural learning and criticism into its theology to remain relevant in our world today and also faithful to the Gospel message.

Ecclesiology

Here a more robust treatment of her ecclesiology will be presented. In its past, Kwok laments the manner in which the Church has contained a hegemonic role on doctrinal teaching and biblical interpretation as opposed to intervening for justice for its most vulnerable. This she believes came at the expense of cultural insights and movements of God outside of the Christian tradition. She affirms that Christian identity must include cultural experiences with cultural metaphors and so forth. Experience bears on the interpretation of the Christian faith and dares to challenge the established teaching of the Church. From this framework, she herself even began to question the Catholic idea, as one in the high church tradition herself, that outside the church there is no salvation. This questioning stemmed from her dual identity of being both Christian and Chinese and finding herself feeling conflicted between those two worlds. Her charge is for the church to move from a monolithic theological discourse to a plurality of voices. Projects of hers such as her recent editing of the work *Empire and the Christian Tradition* are beginning stabs at re-interpreting Christian history and significant texts from non-Western modes of criticism. The problem has become that, with the focus on Europe in Christian history and tradition, modernity and secularity become the assumed centers and other significant world religions and types of spirituality become minimalized in comparison to Christianity. Too often, the European Church and its interpretations have served as the sole explications of significant Christian resources as well as the funnel through which significant texts have been

47. Kwok, "Mothers and Daughters, Writers and Fighters," 151.
48. Ibid., 24.

persevered and neglected. Because of this, one of Kwok's major theses is the value of Christianity as indigenized into the Chinese culture.

The Church contains a host of 'symbolic resources,' as Kwok observed for the women in the early missionary movement in China, and she believes that these resources need to be continually used by the Church for the poor and oppressed. Literal and symbolic resources contained within the Church as an institution must work toward the dignity and worth of all. This must involve the Church moving away from viewing anyone as missiological objects or theological subjects. This limits personhood and perpetuates the Church as a means of exploitation. Likewise, ecclesiology must integrate cultural traditions into theology and move from theological discourse to a plurality of voices in order to experience true catholicity. Kwok advocates for a missionary ministry of the Church, not in the sense of the colonialist missiological enterprise but instead in the notion of the good news being delivered to the poor. This is less of a hierarchal—clerical ministry and more of a vision of co-laborers in the vision of Paul. Co-laborers partner women and men together in ministry, often working outside of the church context, and engaging the social spheres to work against injustice as a part of fulfilling the Gospel.

In regards to developing a global ecclesiology, Kwok affirms that women are the majority of members in churches around the world, but often marginalized to the minority in church leadership and development. Her vision affirms the church as a partnership of equals: a power-with-others rather than a power-over-others in terms of gender, sexuality, race, socioeconomic status, and all other means of oppression. This extends beyond her Asian context, but she does believe these inequalities are ever-present in Asian ecclesiology. "The subordination of women in the church is due not only to misogyny within the Christian tradition but also to understandings of purity and taboo in respect to women in Asian religious traditions."[49] The model Kwok gives for egalitarian church leadership is that of a 'partnership of equals.' She delineates authority from power, believing that authority comes from the Spirit of God and rightly belongs to those with the appropriate giftings. Power, however, often becomes much more complex and contains other dimensions of injustice within it.

Lastly, Kwok Pui-Lan describes five areas that must mark the Asian church in order for it to be the true Church:

---

49. Kwok, *Introducing Asian Feminist Theology*, 99.

1. Free of sexism
2. A true community of women and men
3. A grassroots movement of the poor
4. Engaged in the prophetic ministry of Jesus, working against injustice
5. A peace church.[50]

What Kwok intends with these descriptors is to give a clear list of the distinctives that must be present for the community of faith to accurately represent the Gospel of Jesus. Too often, in the Asian context, faith communities emerged that claimed the Christian Gospel and perpetuated the marginalization of women and the poor.

Maria Pilar Aquino

Background

Maria Pilar Aquino grew up as the daughter of a migrant farmworker from Nayarit, Mexico. She traveled with her family to San Luis, Arizona where her father worked with Cesar Chavez being active in the farm workers movement. Her family worked during the U.S. 'Bracero program,' and this background and struggle for justice continues to frame her theology as rooted in liberation. She found herself drawn to the theology and continues to work within the Catholic Church by teaching Catholic theology in the university setting. She understands theology as seeking to "accompany the spiritual experience of the grassroots Latina feminist women and men who struggle for authentic liberation in view of new civilization based on justice, equality, and integrity for all."[51]

Based on her experience growing up in Mexico, Aquino observed firsthand what is needed for the Latina church. Her life experiences and insights convinced her that the fate of the church in Latin America is tied to both women and the poor. From this treatise she began to understand the communal praxis of the struggle for liberation. As she began to identify with the liberation theology movement, she also found her voice in the feminist movement and saw the development of both as tied to ecclesiology. Her desire is to rethink theology and spirituality in terms of the

50. Ibid., 112.
51. Aquino, *Our Cry for Life*, 139.

feminist language and landscape, while also being faithful to the realities and struggles of the Latino people.

Methodology

Theology, for Aquino, is intended to be a shared perspective. For Latino/a theology, the difficulty in doing theology comes in dismantling the Western theological tradition and the need to historicize the fact of theological diversity. Aquino intends for the project of Latino/a theology to critique dominant intellectual traditions and redefine and broaden the terms of theological discourse. No doubt, this is done on the back of Latin American liberation theology, but she believes the expansion of Latino/a theology must take in intercultural theological dialogue, not remain stuck in the "university world," include the feminist Latina perspective, and denounce the problematic nature of dominant ideologies.[52] Epistemologically, the foundations for this are connected to Catholicism, immersed in an adverse social context, struggling for self-determination and demonstrating resistance to defend the Christian and ethical dignity of the human person. Theology, for Aquino, needs to become more particular so that it can become more universal and truly be a culturally plural Christianity.

Latina feminist theology seeks to join efforts to eliminate the systemic kyriarchal forces that daily erode the dignity of women and those around them. One major difference in this theology is in its normative sources, which for Aquino is using divine revelation as a fundamental principle of knowledge. This integrates experience into theological discourse and forces an interdisciplinary ecclesiological conversation with expanded sources of data and methods. This is the manner is which Latina Feminist Theology can adequately address a globalized kyriarchal paradigm marked by unceasing growth of poverty, inequality, social exclusion and social insecurity. Experience must be a valid source and God's revelation must exist in the midst of and as a critique of Christian theological tradition so that globalization can properly be dismantled.

Aquino views daily life, or *lo cotidiano*, as a category for theological analysis. Women doing the work of theology must be free to speak their own word, must speak in solidarity with others not in a position to speak, and must radically broaden the sources that serve as truths. Theology exists in ordinary spaces where asymmetrical relations are produced against

52. Aquino, "Theological Method in U.S. Latino/a Theology," 41.

women and where women believe they must contribute to the perpetuation of these spaces. "Women's contributions are a commitment because they know that the fate of the church in Latin America is closely linked to what becomes of the poor masses."[53] Truth becomes culturally plural and must now become receptive of this new reality. "This theology must show that the grace of God and the strength of the Spirit are causing the transformational practices of these women."[54] Daily life, therefore, must and should be liberating. Everyday gender and socioeconomic encounters hold great potential for dismantling systems and liberating women by the anticipatory dimension of justice made possible in the Gospel.

Latin American feminist theology synthesizes knowledge and practice in what Aquino refers to as *cariño*. This affection speaks to the constant interplay of reason and emotion in feminist theology. Intellectual perception and theological doctrines must not be divorced from compassion, human realities, and lived spiritualities. Aquino believes that this *cariño* supports an ecumenism from below, where women's full participation in theological discourse and church practice becomes possible. The experience of Latin American women is one of hope despite their realities within the Church. Such an understanding leads to the task of asserting the authority given by God in theological discussion, yet continuing to do so with *cariño* and considering the neglected voices from below in crafting a new ecumenism.

Feminist Latina spiritualties are "creatively demonstrating the possibilities of the present historical situation to engender a new world."[55] The value in this methodology is the ability to stand up to the homogenizing avalanche of kyriarchal spiritualties but strengthening the voice of women from the margins. This involves dismantling the spiritual mechanisms that support false determinism of kyriarchal systems and strengthens a feminist vision of transforming society. This also understands how globalization is inevitably wrapped up in kyriarchy and must support and motivate feminist endeavors throughout the world. Aquino sees feminist perspectives represented in the Spirit, the Divine Wisdom, which gives a vision to a new world with justice and dignity, different than the present realities. She believes that many priests or leaders see this as dangerous because this moves God's Spirit from controlled places of power to the

53. Aquino, *Our Cry for Life*, 161.

54. Aquino, "Perspectives on a Latina's Feminist Liberation Theology," 25.

55. Aquino, "Towards a New World in the Power of Wisdom," 130.

reality of where it truly is: present and at work in all, especially those working for the Kingdom of God.

Lastly, as a methodology, Aquino speaks of feminist hermeneutics as the intentional placement of theology done amongst the world's poor and oppressed women. Christian tradition, biblical texts, and spiritual experiences are mediated through women's social locations. "Feminist theologians understand the lived experience of women struggling against patriarchal power relationships in the present context of the world market economy as the primary criterion for interpreting with legitimacy and authority our own experience of faith."[56] Feminist theology works with a methodology that understands the core of theology as a life-giving alternative to the "divisions, antagonisms, and death for most of the world's population."[57] The justice of church in society is to be measured by the liberation of people from 'hierarchical socioecclesial relationships' within feminist theology. Feminist theological language intends to reveal liberation, to subvert forces of oppression and to bring to light the violence done to women within church and society.

Latin American Feminist Theology

At the center of Maria Pilar Aquino's ecclesiology is her Latin American feminist Theology. She believes that the liberation theology movement and the women's movements converge in Christianity over "relational, inclusive and realistic understandings of the Gospel message and the faith experience."[58] The concern for eliminating the oppression of women begins with the radical transformation for the causes of their suffering. She identifies these as polemical interlocutors, or structures that prevent the emergence of women. This is for Aquino a 'struggle for life,' a concept that becomes central to her theology. Women's struggles are against the various forces, systems, and relationships that keep women oppressed. Feminism is not a foreign concept or experience for Latinas.

She extends the vision of the abundant life in John 10:10 to the concrete necessities of daily life by distancing itself from cultural frameworks that support hierarchical social relations. In the context of Latin America, both church and society are identified as containing deep inequalities in

56. Aquino, "Latin American Feminist Theology," 105.

57. Ibid.

58. Ibid., 90.

terms of human rights and resources. The social reality, originating from European colonization and the growth of structures of oppression keeps Latin American women in "asymmetrical and antagonistic relationships of power."[59] The theological task becomes envisioning alternative forms of living and working together with other women who share a similar vision of justice.

Aquino believes that Latin American feminist theology is more particular than Western feminist theology. She gives the analogy of womanist theology, emerging in a specific context and tradition despite its shared geographic spaces. Feminist theology done in the Americas contains a variety of particularized perspectives, and Latin American women have created a space of self-affirmation within the feminist tradition. She believes they need not shed the term 'feminist' for the creation of a new word, but instead can create a particularized version of feminism for Latin American women. "Latin American feminist theology proposes a respectful dialogue among the diverse feminist perspectives that respond to concrete sociocultural realities and a move away from unnecessary antagonisms that only weaken our common task."[60] The framework of liberation theology began to emerge in Latin America, helping shape this movement, but it was not until the feminist theology movement emerged that Latin American women could find a particular home for themselves. Voices like Rosemary Radford Ruether and Elisabeth Shussler Fiorenza began using the term 'feminist theology' in the US in the 1970s, but for Aquino, this term was not being used in Latin America until the late 1980s.[61] As it became a source of identification for Latin American women, there now was a language for the reality already being created in their spaces.

Latin American feminist theology works to create a universal solidarity. This expands on critical feminist theory to create new intellectual frameworks. It is important for Aquino to note that their theological reflection cannot be reduced to merely the faith experiences but must also press into theological questions that address the sexism in society, church, and theology. This is not a universal starting point for theological work, as it must specifically begin with the excluded groups on the underside of society to be able to relate to all. Yet in crafting a new intellectual framework, feminist theology contains the capacity to transcend current realities and

59. Ibid., 91.
60. Ibid., 95.
61. Ibid., 102.

begin the task of telling a new story, one already embodied in Latin American women's everyday lives.

Theologically, the elimination of this becomes possible with the faithfulness to the liberative nature of the Christian Gospel. "The people of God are the true church, whose mission—consistent with the gospel of liberation—is to eliminate the sins of oppression, exploitation, violence, and dehumanization."[62] Her conviction is that feminist emphasis of sense and communal development as opposed to intelligence alone stresses theological realism. This emphasizes transformation over continuity with the establish order. Spiritually, Aquino believes that this theology must be willing to exorcise demons rather than be afraid to name them. Women's experience cannot be relegated to a single category or an abstraction, and instead there must be ongoing naming of the particularities of each woman's encounter with God. There is an interconnectedness of women's shared concerns for justice and vulnerable social groups despite various geographic factors that diversify their experience. Feminist theology sees the embodied experience as the central starting point of theology, as opposed to Christian tradition that conceptualizes space outside the body as the area for theological reflection. Feminist theology can now react against its androcentric tradition and discern the implications of violence against women.

Ecclesiology

Aquino begins to form what she calls "mestizo intercultural communities."[63] Her use of the term *mestizo*, or *mestizaje*, refers originally to the mixed people from both Spain and Mexico. She begins to co-opt the term as a theological concept, referring to the hybridity of theology in churches, blending cultural norms and traditional Christianity, and blending multiple cultures into one community of faith. Her value on the term 'intercultural' comes from the strong affirmation that churches are not intended to comprise of one particular culture, but should instead reflect the diversity of cultures evidenced in the Kingdom of God. *Mestizaje* becomes a category of theological method, a manner in which all can do theology by understanding the mixed perspective one brings to the table of discourse in the globalized era. Her emphasis is not on particularized, limited communities holding

62. Aquino, "Latina Feminist Theology: Central Features," in Aquino, Machado, and Jeanette Rodriguez, eds., *A Reader in Latina Feminist Theology*, 137.

63. Aquino, *Feminist Intercultural Theology*.

to theological discussions and norms but instead all cultures sharing their theological insights with one another.

Aquino values Leonardo Boff's term of 'ecclesiogenesis' and desires to reclaim the concept in feminist terms as well. Boff believes that ecclesiology needs to be reborn, or needs a 're-genesis' of entirely new base communities, better reflecting equality and the removal of hierarchies.[64] For Aquino, for this 'ecclesiogenesis' to be truly effective, women must have a key role in the leadership of the re-genesis of the church. She appreciates the ecclesial model other liberation theologians in Latin America have proposed: that of base communities. Base communities start at the ground floor level, removing the role the institutional church has in the oppression and continual subjugation of women and the poor. With the elimination of hierarchies, base communities study Scripture together, live life in community together, provide for one another's needs, and model an egalitarian, shared structure in church leadership. Aquino affirms that the church's structure, organization, and mission must exist with the poor or else she believes that, as an institution, it is continuing to keep the poor in places of poverty, whether directly or indirectly.

In order to react to kyriarchy, or the term she borrows from Elizabeth Shussler Fiorenza regarding the multiple levels of oppression (sexism, racism, ageism, ableism, etc.), Aquino believes that ecumenism must start at the base and reflect an equality of all persons in leadership of the church.[65] If the Spirit of God truly works between all persons of all genders, then that must be reflected in its positions and social location as a group of believers. She begins to use the language of the church as a baptismal community in the discipleship of equals. This works to overcome ecclesiocentrism with an ecclesiology of dialogue and ministry. Baptism is intended to end hierarchical relationships and cultivate the idea of the Church as communion-*koinonia*. The focus now is on the gifts received and the ministries exercised. Under the Sacraments, all people find equality as they move toward the model of Christ together.

In rethinking ecclesiology as a dimension of the entire theological enterprise, Aquino affirms that the church must form a theology critical of capitalist globalization. Too often, she writes, the church in its existence as an institution has remained silent on or even supported globalization. The problem with this is that for the Latino church, liberation as key to

64. Boff, *Ecclesiogenesis.*
65. Schüssler Fiorenza, *But She Said.*

salvation must be articulated in its Gospel message. Liberation involves reacting against all forms of oppression and structures of sin, and capitalist globalization has affected those on the margins primarily. Globalization is no longer an abstract concept but instead a reality in their everyday life. In her ecclesiology, Aquino values socio—ecclesial practices and believes that theology should be characterized as an intercultural activity.

Lastly, Aquino speaks in her ecclesiology about women as actors and subjects in the church. Women cannot function in a 'token' role, occasionally elevated above men, or treated as the 'weaker' subject in need of saving because of their lesser position. Instead, she believes that women are to be both actors and subjects in the drama of the Gospel message proclaimed in community. Women need to take on all roles in the continuation of these new mestizo intercultural communities. Aquino observes four marks of the church, in her work, *Our Cry for Life*:

1. Proclamation

2. Witness

3. Celebration

4. Unity.[66]

If these four marks of the church are visible, then Aquino believes that the church truly has been reborn, as the vision of ecclesiogenesis implies. This church sees its true proclamation of Gospel and witness in the world as a stance of solidarity with women and the poor, calling out the injustice of capitalist globalization and other forces that threaten true freedom and equality. Aquino believes that older theological metaphors can find new meaning for the church today, especially when women now have a role in the re-genesis of the Church. One metaphor that Aquino desires to revive is that of the Church as mystery, stemming from the analogy between love and divine mystery. Just as God is a mother who feels for the child in her womb, the Church needs to continue to cultivate both activism and compassion as a part of connecting with the mystery of the Divine.

For Aquino, the Church of the poor is a sacrament of liberation for the oppressed masses. This church must be structured on the basis of equal participation of all members. The experience of women in Latin America affirmed the reality of a patriarchal Christianity characterized by conquest and racism against indigenous people. Women found themselves violated,

---

66. Aquino, *Our Cry for Life*, 170.

raped, and viewed as war booty. The transformation beyond this previous colonialized reality involves women interpreting their own worlds to re-define Christian identity. The truths of salvation as embodied in ecclesiology combine suffering and hope and blend the best elements of one's own ancestral cultural symbolic world with the Gospel message. Now in these ecclesial base communities, women reclaim their right to be the Church and regarded as creative participants in it. This calls for a re-ordering of the Church's structure, organization, and mission to exist within the poor and marginalized.

There are a few clear areas that Aquino identifies that must be re-assessed with this renewed vision of the Church. A new Bible reading is required, one with a critical spirit, denunciations and re-interpretations of biblical claims and rights. Pastors must play a true diaconal role of service, animation, and defense for all peoples in their congregation. Theology must be connected to pastoral action on behalf of the poor. Existing on the side of the poor and oppressed involves a reformulating of our own Christian history and identity. This will look like an ecumenicism from the base that creates a spirituality of hope in the struggle.

Conclusion

Mercy Amba Oduyoye, Kwok Pui-Lan and Maria Pilar Aquino describe a Church that liberates those most on the margins of society. These women are not complete representatives and cannot speak from every African Christian, Asian Christian, or Latin American Christian, but their theological reflection can serve to teach and to guide. These women are also sensitive to including as many voices in their writings as possible and their words come with an awareness of the voices they write on behalf of, the women whose names will never be known but who faithfully live out their Christian faith in contexts of persecution. Christian spirituality must continue to incorporate these voices into theological discourse. One of the many complications of presenting a robust, global theology is the lack of access to theological works produced by feminist theologians around the globe. These three served as the strongest examples with the most writing on ecclesiology, yet the lack of others speaks to poor material and financial resources to facilitate theological work. Each of these women crafts theology from their particular context, yet attempts to articulate and converse with other women on their continent where their voices can be represented.

And it also should be noted that the Third World church is not a perfect one to be esteemed without critique. Injustice and oppression occurs throughout, and often women theologians such as these write critiquing their own church as much as the Western one. Yet their voices have helped inform the Third World Christianity, and will continue to faithfully call to truer representations of the Gospel. Third World feminist theology continues to expand through their developments and now serves as a framework for building a constructive global theology.

4

Constructive Global Ecclesiology

Salvation and Sin

Introduction

THESE THREE WOMEN, SERVING as sample Third World feminists from Latin America, Asia and Africa, find multiple points of commonality in their renewed ecclesiology. A few will be highlighted here. First, since all three are operating out of the liberationist framework, each of them values salvation as liberation, particularly from kyriarchal oppression and the structures of sin. Too often, the Western church understands salvation in a limited manner, focusing primarily on individual, internal salvation instead of salvation as a tool for countering structures of sin and forces of injustice. Naturally, this implies an understanding of sin as both individual and structural. Rarely is sin communicated in this broad manner in the Western church. Implied with this line of thinking, these women believe that the Church must take a stance against globalization, particularly the injustices caused by economic and militaristic realities, and confess the Western church's role in supporting such forces. Whether this occurred directly or indirectly, the Western church rarely acknowledges its role in valuing large businesses and corrupt governments, partially creating the realities of income disparity and power structures in the world today.

Related to this, the use of critique and how one type of theology can serve as a signpost for another allows for the continual growth of the

Christian Church. Critiques are never intended to vilify one tradition at the expense of another, but they can serve as a means to identify where the Holy Spirit is working in a particular era. This convergence of location—the Third World—and church growth moves beyond sociological reality and cultural observation into theological reflection here. Critiques are intended to strengthen, and these theological themes are intended to better refine Godtalk in the West and worldwide.

From this point forward, there will now be a discussion of various themes of constructive global theology.[1] Constructive theology seeks to re-define what has been historically known as systematic theology. This attempts to not force particular conversations or themes but rather present openness to the themes or dialogues as is pertinent. Feminist theologians, such as Catherine Keller, Serene Jones, and Sallie McFague, believe that systematic theology builds itself upon overall systems that are patriarchal and Western in nature, and this term is no longer accurate for the room that theology needs to re-form in a manner that reflects all vantage points.[2] Each of these voices understands constructive theology as the future enterprise of theology and sees this as a particularized or contextual manner in which theology should be done. Constructive theology, a lens that existed before the horizon of feminist theology, does become the most appropriate label for this project given the feminist methodology as well as the nontraditional approach to the practice of doing theology. Similarly, 'constructive' implies that a new horizon of theology is being envisioned together, as a variety of voices and perspectives build anew from the ground up. No longer must these women fit their theology into male-created systems, but now women from the margins are constructing the new landscape of theological inquiry.

Global theology intends to use each of these three voices as representative and form their perspectives into one unifying non-Western voice. The hope with using the term 'global' is to imagine such robust themes that can stand regardless of geographic location. Global also speaks to our

---

1. Lamin Sanneh draws a helpful and important distinction between "global" and "world" Christianity, with "global" Christianity as an imported term to Africa and Asia and "world" Christianity rooted more in the lives of Third World inhabitants. With respect to this thinking, I stand with Philip Jenkins in believing the distinction is difficult to implement. I will continue to use global Christianity in this work as I begin to form a constructive global Christianity, in Jenkins's words, "in a broad and nonjudgmental sense." Jenkins, *The Next Christendom*, xiii.

2. For more on this, see Jones and Lakeland, eds., *Constructive Theology*.

globalized world, and the reality of theology being done as a transnational project. The constructive ecclesiology created here will be my attempt at appropriating the methodology and theological foundations of Third World feminist theology to begin articulating a theology that critiques and dismantles particular norms within Western theology. Particular themes have emerged as points of commonality between these three voices. For the sake of brevity, we will focus on the following ecclesial themes: salvation, sin within this chapter, and in the following chapter peacemaking, women in leadership, and multi-ethnic churches. The process of narrowing was a difficult one, since each of the women represented in this work values a host of particularized marks of the Church. Each voice contains their own sets of cultural experiences, and yet their combination attempts to be a movement toward universal, essential aspects of the Evangelical Christian Church.

These women are not identical carbon copies of each other's theology, yet in Kwok, Oduyoye and Aquino I found points of commonality to serve as a methodology for my construction of aspects of ecclesiology. The political ecclesiology discussed in chapter 2 in particular serves as lens to move theology beyond the individual or limited context and into a broader, more global discussion. Areas such as sin and salvation have implicit overlap with political, economic and social realities in our globalized context. The interface of politics and theology is unavoidable in the modern world, and the political vantage point from which these Third World theologians write from implies that the Church cannot be faithful to the Gospel if it is not understanding itself as political. Engagement in injustices, extending our definitions of aspects of theology, and requiring that our ecclesial spaces reflect the values of the Kingdom of God are political endeavors, working to create the justice and righteousness of God here on earth.

Salvation

For global theology, salvation is to be understood through its nature of being both/and. Soteriology is both individual and social, both present and future, both local and cosmic, both spiritual and material. Traditionally, much of Western Evangelical theology tends to only highlight one side of each of those coins, to which now Third World feminist voices will attempt to broaden the conversation. Because this paper is working from an Evangelical context in dialogue with Third World feminist theologians, the uniqueness and particularity of salvation as only possible through Jesus

Christ must be stressed. The Jesus of Nazareth and the Christ of Faith serves as the only means by which salvation is made freely available to all. The Evangelical emphasis speaks to the biblical language and narratives that give framework to what is occurring in salvation. The Third World feminist theologians introduce experience and liberation for those on the margins as key aspects of the Gospel. These two ideas of salvation as individual and communal need not be in opposition but rather inform each other in a constructive fashion. Feminist theologians have also helpfully articulated the interconnected, interrelated nature of salvation, whereas humans are inextricably linked to their neighbors, creation, and the entire worldwide community. Primarily here the focus of salvation will be on its movement to be saved into the family of God, where whole communities and households receive salvation, and this salvation provides literal life-saving material resources for the Body of believers.[3] After framing and defining the conversation of salvation, the primarily example this chapter will use for global soteriology is that of Mozambique's *Transforming Arms into Tools (TAE)* program. This Christian aid initiative serves as the embodiment of salvation as community transformation, extending beyond the individual and providing transformation to an entire people.

Framework of Salvation

To address salvation from a global perspective, a few major questions will serve as a framework.

1. Who saves?

2. Saved from what?

3. How is salvation accomplished?

4. Personal or corporate salvation?

5. When is salvation?[4]

---

3. The contextualization of aspects such as atonement, significant as that theological conversation is within the realm of salvation, will be acknowledged but not included in this work. Just as the definition of salvation must be broadened and contextualized, so much the work of Christ on the Cross. Future writings in global theology can expand on Christ as, for example, the Great Liberator of established evil structures, as is one atonement metaphor in the African context.

4. I am borrowing the very helpful framework for a global soteriology from Baker and Le Bruyns, "Salvation," in Dyrness and Kärkkäinen, eds., *Global Dictionary of*

God in Jesus Christ, providing healing and liberation to creation in bondage to sin initiates salvation. God's saving activity is directed against everything—be it slavery, injustice, death, oppression, illness, displacement, and so on—that threatens life in all of its fullness. Passages such as Romans 8:21 extend salvation beyond humans to all of creation, and present a vision of future freedom from a reality even greater than sin. Alienation and broken relationships between God and creation, humans and creation, and humans with each other extend to the biblical vision of salvation. Salvation in Jesus Christ offers forgiveness from sin and victory over death, making reconciliation possible for all—both between God and creation and humans with each other.

In speaking of a broader or corporate understanding of salvation, Scripture gives examples of God liberating Israel from oppression in Egypt. Exodus 2:23—25 tells of this:

> The Israelites groaned under their slavery, and cried out. Out of the slavery their cry for help rose up to God. God heard their groaning, and God remembered God's covenant with Abraham, Isaac and Jacob. God looked upon the Israelites, and God took notice of them.

As the Exodus story progresses, the author tells of how God liberates the children of Israel from bondage and culminates in the words of Exodus 15: "The LORD has triumphed gloriously."[5] From this biblical story, salvation is understood as liberation from brokenness, restoration of harmony with God, and the ability for reconciled relationships with all of creation. Salvation offers wholeness for this entire community, offering reconciliation as fellowship into the community of God's people. God is a God who liberates the oppressed, and salvation comes as initiated by God, leading to a rejection of powers of empire. This corporate vision of salvation also tells of God's committed, ongoing healing process with creation that overturns the structures of power in this world. God's salvation for the Israelite people also included the provision of the establishment of an an entirely new way of living. God's salvation included the gift of place, an alternative social and economic system, and an entirely new identity and vision of self-worth. This all-encompassing salvation for the entire community becomes the vision extended by Jesus in providing life to the fullest in John 10:10.

Theology, 778.

5. Exodus 15:1. The entire Song of the Sea in Exodus 15 recounts the saving work of God through extended metaphor of song.

Salvation affects individual change (anthropological), broader change for the common good (social), change in identity and belonging (cultural), change in human understanding and vision (ontological), and change in providing life-giving power in all spheres of creation (vitalistic).[6] The social and structural nature of sin, which will be addressed later in this chapter, mandates a broader understanding of salvation extending beyond individual extension into eternal life. Sin serves as the great disorder that has disrupted the work of God, and thus salvation is the overcoming of this disruption. Such an overcoming need not be relegated to a future reality, but as a reality that has begun in the crucifixion and resurrection. Voices such as biblical theologian N. T. Wright have been helpful in extending Protestant understandings of salvation to beginning in present-day, emphasizing an inaugurated eschatology that God has already begun to initiate through Jesus Christ.[7] Yet a global soteriology extends beyond salvation, affecting modern-day realities as well as a future redeemed vision of creation. Salvation takes on an interrelated nature, moving beyond the Western, individualistic notion of being mere recipients of salvation. Participating in God's saving activity invites Christians to contribute to the salvation of others and of creation by working toward justice and equality in all areas of life. The Body of Christ is invited through salvation to partner with God in the expansion of God's Kingdom of healing and liberation.

Salvation takes on a metaphysical dimension in that it extends across time. The Cross initiated salvation two thousand years ago, salvation points to a moment of conversion, and salvation speaks to an ongoing reality where each person and community of faith is continually being saved. There also extends a future vision of complete salvation, speaking to the new heavens and a new earth, reordering life completely, which 2 Peter describes as a "total salvation." Similarly, the vision of Revelation 21—22 tells of an end of death and pain accompanying eternity with God as the final completion of salvation. In this sense salvation is past, present, and future all at once. Salvation can never be limited to a particular moment in time, for this minimizes the multifaceted dimension of salvation's extension beyond human concepts of time.

Metaphor is the means by which salvation is understood, giving room for various biblical authors to employ the metaphor most helpful for their audience. The author of Hebrews emphasizes the priesthood and sacrificial metaphor, whereas the author of Colossians leans on cosmic language for

6. Ibid., 779.

7. For more on this, see Wright, *Surprised by Hope.*

God's saving work. Feminist theologians, in this same vein, speak to the value of metaphors for giving the female experience language in salvation. One helpful example is that of Sallie McFague, whose works center heavily on metaphor and language. Her text, *The Body of God*, gives a metaphor of the world as God's body and sees this language as helpful in redefining salvation. "Christianity, and especially Protestant Christianity, has been concerned almost exclusively with the salvation of individual human beings (primarily their 'souls'), rather than with the liberation and well-being of the oppressed, including not only oppressed human beings, body and social (or better, spirit), but also the oppressed earth and all its life-forms."[8]

It is important here to note that McFague's vision of salvation cannot devolve into pantheism or panentheism. God's salvation occurs within the world, but the world cannot save itself without the work of Christ in the world. Christ is the particularity that keeps this salvation from pantheism and is the only means by which salvation occurs. Metaphor, she believes, is only language's attempt at articulating the mystery of God saving the world. McFague builds upon the language of the Patristics and Teilhard de Chardin in speaking of the "economy of salvation," with the ability to provide different currency in different situations and working within the natural order to transform in multiple modes at the same time. Teilhard de Chardin's language frames the idea that salvation through Christ works throughout the world and through time to meet exactly what is needed in every aspect of sinful existence. If salvation is to extend a vision of another possible world, then it must meet the basic, physical needs of each creature on the earth, whatever those needs be and only be possible through the cross of Christ.

Third World Feminist Soteriology

Aquino defines salvation as liberation from all oppression. The struggle for this liberation is a communal praxis, gathering together the hopes and expectations of the people of God to work for justice and peace. She describes her vision of salvation here:

> The core content and ultimate finality of God's revelation is resumed in the term *salvation*. As the most precious gift of God to humans and to the world around us, salvation is understood by Latina feminist theology as liberation from every oppression. Thus the historical process of liberation from poverty, social injustice,

8. McFague, *The Body of God*, 31.

and exclusion becomes the most effective and credible manifesta-
tion of God's salvation.[9]

This vision of salvation is grounded in the lived experience of this world,
rather than focusing on the eternal, otherworldly aspects of salvation. A
renewal of earth qualitatively alters the lived experience of humans today,
freeing them from kyriarchal exploitation and dehumanization.

Aquino stresses Jesus's salvific identity as connected with his *mestizo*
and border identity. This is a salvation that stands in solidarity with the
marginalized, provides liberation for the poor, and demands that his saved
people now function critically within society of dominant spaces of power
that continue the oppression of others. Jesus is a *mestizo*-Galilean, a Gali-
lean Jew who occupied the marginal, border reality of his time. This vision
implores the Christian community to turn to the borders, the spaces where
their Jesus occupied, in order to understand the true gift of salvation. What
humans have rejected, God chooses as his own. "God chooses an oppressed
people, not to bring them comfort in their oppression, but to enable them
to comfort, transcend, and transform whatever in the oppressor society
diminishes and destroys the fundamental nature of human dignity."[10] This
vision of salvation is offered by a Jesus who accompanies, who calls for solidarity as an expression of salvation. "To walk with Jesus is thus to walk with
the wrong persons in the wrong places."[11] The historical work of salvation
must continue to be an ongoing reality in the present, guiding the saved
people into the corners of oppression in the world today so that they too
may be a people who accompany others.

Kwok describes the saving work of God as emphasizing the freedom
and liberation available now through Christ. "The message of salvation, if
concerned primarily with redeeming individual souls and life after death,
has little relevance in an Asia plagued by issues of survival under foreign
domination."[12] She stresses the Western influence that held salvation captive
as simply an individualistic enterprise. Even the concept of Jesus as 'Lord'
contained domineering, subjugating overtones for Asian peoples. Salvation
must address those who are not just sinners but also sinned against, viewed

9. Aquino, "Latina Feminist Theology: Central Features," in Aquino, Machado, and
Jeanette Rodriguez, eds., *A Reader in Latina Feminist Theology*, 151.

10. Referencing Aquino's vision of salvation. Gonzalez, "Jesus," in Aponte, De La
Torre, eds., *Handbook of Latina/o Theologies*, 21.

11. Ibid., 23.

12. Kwok, *Introducing Asian Feminist Theology*, 79.

as the outcasts of their society, as many Asian women are. Salvation becomes not only a personal and spiritual relationship with God but also liberation from bondage, the opportunity to develop one's potential, community and family well being, freedom from violence, hope and security for the future, and the availability of a life-sustaining ecosystem.[13] This for Kwok echoes the biblical vision of *shalom* as total liberation that connects ecological language into the wholistic vision of redemption. Jesus as Savior is not one of the oppressors, but one of the *minjung*, or masses. This salvation is solidarity, a God who suffers with and provides redemption from systems of oppression.

Oduyoye speaks of salvation in its multifaceted nature, but one example she gives from the African context is that of freedom from shame. "Jesus's delivering people from shame is particularly meaningful in societies where new sources of stigma such as HIV/AIDS have emerged with full negative force in compromising the experience of life in all its fullness for HIV-positive persons."[14] HIV/AIDS serves as one example of shame, but others identified in the African context are that of societal shame due to age, disability, employment, poverty, or racial and/or nationalistic identity. Salvation now offers human dignity and inclusion in an entirely new family. Jesus becomes the one who removes all stigma, being identified as the "friend of sinners" in Luke 7:34, and cultivating relationships with those stigmatized by society. God in Christ removes the stigma and hostility that keeps humanity separated from God and one another. The remedy for shame in salvation is removed disgrace, offering a new identity and overcoming exclusion by restoring honor and reincorporating those individuals into community.

Oduyoye also understands salvation as both communal and individual, with her discussion of the devastating impact colonialism and hegemonic missionary movements had on African Christianity in emphasizing the individual over the communal. "The missionary told the Africans what they needed to be saved from, but when Africans needed power to deal with the spiritual realms that were real to them and their community, the missionary was baffled."[15] The transformation of entire communities was ignored in the language of salvation, with emphasis being on the Ten Commandments and a Christianity of "thou shalt nots," or individualistic legalism, emerged. Instead, she writes of African-Initiated theology of salvation,

13. Ibid., 81.

14. Baker and Le Bruyns, "Salvation," in Dyrness and Kärkkäinen, eds., *Global Dictionary of Theology*, 783.

15. Oduyoye, *Hearing and Knowing*, 41.

where God is Guarantor (*Okyirtaafo*) who transforms their experiences of "hell" on earth into a "heaven" that can be experienced in present-day liberation from oppression.[16] This does not negate the internal transformation Christ brings in salvation but rather extends it to the overcoming of external physical enemies. This rings of Isaiah's vision that Yahweh will contend with those who contend with his people.[17]

God answers the cries of all who need salvation and the language of liberation broadens salvation beyond mere economic, marketplace terminology. In Oduyoye's words, "God snatches us away, separates us from the oppressive environment, breaks off unjust relationships, and tears down dehumanizing structures."[18] God here is concerned with the wholeness of human beings and for the relationships implied with this wholeness—both between the individual and God and between the individual and other human beings. This liberation comes with an intention in the Kingdom of God: to make us truly human. "In Jesus, God brings to us a style of life that puts others first, that saves others, leaving God to bring about the resurrection that will transform one's own wretchedness."[19] Salvation and liberation provides the examples for turning the other cheek, for praying for our enemies, and for refusing to stand by while others are being exploited. Good news for Africa is a willingness to die to all that dehumanizes, both personally and corporately. Whatever the culture, Oduyoye believes that Christ offers a particularized experience of liberation.

A theology of solidarity understands individual salvation as connected with the salvation of others. Rebecca Todd Peters believes that the term *metanoia* is more helpful when speaking of the salvation of the whole person. Practices of sustainability and social justice encourage the New Testament concept of *metanoia*, or transformation of the body mind and soul. This extends deeper than just repentance in salvation and instead invites the type of transformation that makes an entirely new person. Behavior and lifestyle must be connected to an entire move of salvation. "It is this kind of transformation of one's understanding of the world that is required in order for people to generate the political will to work together towards a different vision for the world. For those first-world Christians who are shaped and formed by dominant cultural attitudes and expectations about

16. Ibid., 100.
17. Isa 49:25.
18. Pss 35:17; 136:24; Deut 6:27–28. Oduyoye, *Hearing and Knowing*, 104.
19. Ibid., 106.

economics, development, consumerism . . . *metanoia* is a prerequisite."[20] This eliminates the idea of solidarity-as-charity or any engagement that does not address the global ramifications of injustice. Salvation here must be liberatory moves away from injustice rather than simply charitable actions. Rieger echoes this same liberatory nature of salvation when he speaks of the difficulty for the oppressed in understanding salvation the same as their oppressors. "The images of God that had endorsed the top-down globalization processes of Europe and the United States were called into question in this context . . . The God of the masters and the God of the people could no longer be considered to be one and the same."[21] Christianity must now rethink the imagery of this God of salvation so that true transformation can occur in the lives of all peoples worldwide.

Global Soteriology

Evangelical pneumatology integrates speaking of the Holy Spirit with Scripture as its basis when speaking of the true extent of salvation. Emerging from both the Evangelical and Pentacostal traditions, global theologian Amos Young describes in his marks of the Church a robust vision of salvation. "Full salvation, involving abundant life according to the gospel promise (John 10:10), cannot but also address, encourage and empower these material domains of life."[22] Young believes that if salvation is not extended to embodied word and deed in communities, it fails to live out the Spirit-led vision of the community at Pentecost. Young utilizes the example of Zacchaeus to serve as the archetype for the multidimensionality of salvation.[23] Salvation takes on a five-fold Gospel nature:

1. sanctification
2. healing
3. forgiveness of sins (justification)
4. adoption (into a new community)
5. new life (regeneration).[24]

20. Peters, *Solidarity Ethics,* 60.
21. Rieger, *Globalization and Theology,* 47.
22. Young, *Renewing Christian Theology,* 188.
23. Luke 19.
24. Young, *Renewing Christian Theology,* 230.

Salvation, he further declares, must be a Spirit-empowering process that extends into eschatological implications. Young attempts to balance the classical, individual terminology of salvation with the expanding, broader understanding of all of salvation's implications. He describes this tension here:

> Assuredly, any contemporary Christian theology of salvation must explicate what happens in individual hearts and lives. At the same time, the renewal experience of divine salvation is increasingly being understood in broader terms. God saves people in families and communities, even while people are saved not only as souls but as embodied, as material, economic, social and political creatures, and as environmentally and ecologically situated—hence the "full gospel."[25]

This vision of salvation implies God's works as making a difference in the concrete realities of human lives, including, but not limited to, reconciling individuals, families, racial differences, and entire communities.

Global soteriology also emphasizes salvation as the means possible for stopping the cycle of violence. The Cross breaks the ongoing nature of violence by absorbing it into God's self and through Jesus's response of forgiveness and love. Jesus's life and death on the Cross broke the cycle and extended the liberating love of God to heal our violent, broken world. Any transformation, newness of life and renewal of creation is only possible because of God's love. Sin no longer becomes the most powerful force and now by the Spirit of Jesus, Christians can utilize the resource of God's love to break the cycles of violence in this world. Evil powers, in all forms that oppose life to its fullest, no longer have the final word. The Cross is the resource that overcomes economically oppressive and culturally repressive principals because in God, Jesus has overcome these principalities. Such forces are now exposed for what they are: failures and liars. "The cross opens up the possibility that one does not have to obey the powers. The resurrection was not only a defeat of the powers in the sense that Jesus came back to life, but also a validation for Jesus's way of living."[26] Salvation reveals other powers, forces, and principalities to be pseudo-powers, lacking in the ultimate say. The Cross both judges and reveals, vindicating those on the margins that society has overlooked and also holding accountable

25. Ibid.
26. Baker and Le Bruyns, "Salvation," in Dyrness and Kärkkäinen, eds., *Global Dictionary of Theology*, 785.

those committing injustices. Cultural practices, economic structures, unjust governments, and other structures of sin will now be revealed as forces in opposition to the Kingdom of God, unable to ultimately reign victorious. God in Jesus not only reveals the ideal way for humanity to embody the way of salvation but also the power to overcome these forces at work in the world.

Salvation is a particular work, with contextual uniqueness to it based on the differing sins overcome in each location. Salvation can mean healing against environmental degradation, empowerment for women in patriarchal communities, empowerment of Christian discipleship in spaces of pluralistic religiosity, and humanizing lives caught in fatalistic Caste systems. Salvation identifies, names, and challenges existing systems of injustice. "In this case, salvation transforms human beings into human doers, persons who interface with others."[27] Christian salvation implies a particularity in each context, and with this contextual salvation comes a response by the saved person. For example, African terms for salvation intimately connect the concept with the physical welfare of life. God is identified as the Protector of the poor (*Tutungaboro*, as the Barundi call God) and the Deliver of those in trouble (*Luvhunabaumba*, as the Ila of Zambia call God).[28] This idea of salvation speaks to the exact needs of those tribes and the manner in which God provides for them.

The cruciform community is to be a liberative people in the world, extending justice to others on political, economic, and other levels as an expression of salvation. The parable of the sheep and the goats (Matt 25:31—46) presents a vision of salvation (for sheep) coming as a result of ethical practices of feeding the hungry, showing hospitality to strangers, clothing the naked, and caring for the sick. Such a parable opens up the possibility of the unsaved meeting the mystical body of Christ in and through the least in the world.[29] This echoes Jon Sobrino's vision of no salvation outside the poor, that Jesus lived among the poor and called them blessed, and this space among the poor Sobrino believes is where the True Church dwells.[30] He understands this vision of salvation as biblical and serves as a wake-up

27. Young, *Renewing Christian Theology*, 251.

28. Mbiti, "God, Sin and Salvation in African Religion," in Barr, ed., *Constructive Christian Theology in the Worldwide Church*, 167.

29. Young identifies this interpretation as the minority amongst biblical scholars, but the importance of acknowledging such a possibility is relevant here for our broadening description of salvation. *Renewing Christian Theology*, 317.

30. Sobrino, *No Salvation Outside the Poor*.

call to take seriously the helplessness of our world and how glimmers of salvation are found with those on the underside of history.

In a multidimensional sense, salvation also extends to relationality. Relationality speaks to salvation as understood through human relationships, particularly in familial and household units. Global salvation also emphasizes salvation as spoken of in Scripture through household units as well as through the metaphor of adoption. Returning again to the example of Zacchaeus, Luke's Gospel proclaims "Today salvation has come to this house, because he too is a son of Abraham."[31] The good news extended beyond Zacchaeus to both his household and the entire community witnessing Jesus's actions. "The prejudices of the people are thereby exposed and to the degree that they believed in and accepted his proclamation, they also would have embraced Zacchaeus and thereby experienced their own salvation from conventional stereotypes and discriminatory behaviors."[32] Zacchaeus's reconciliation to God also included reconciliation to others, including, assumingly, his enemies. His story embodies how the relational aspects of salvation also include social, political, and economic aspects of salvation as well.

Constructive Soteriology

In contrast with systematic theology, constructive restructuring of the language of salvation introduces new starting points for theological reflection. With globalization comes increased plurality, both within the Christian tradition and as Christianity exists alongside other faith traditions. Understanding diverse opinions within Christianity regarding positions of salvation becomes part of the reconstruction of soteriology.[33] In the process of re-constructing theology, a new construction of salvation must be a starting point. Romans 14:7–9 extends a vision of entrusting ourselves to God in death as in life. It declares:

> We do not live to ourselves, and we do not die to ourselves. If we live, we live to the Lord, and if we die, we die to the Lord; so then, whether we live or whether we die, we are the Lord's.

31. Luke 19:9.

32. Young, *Renewing Christian Theology*, 226.

33. Salvation can be understood through theological categories such as exclusivist, inclusivist and pluralist, but that conversation is best had elsewhere than this particular work.

This echoes the philosophizing contained in Ecclesiastes 3. As with dust, human lives as with all lives in creation are given finality apart from salvation, and thus the need for God's salvation is clear. The only New Testament reference to *apocatastasis*, or universal restoration or salvation, comes in Peter's sermon in the temple to the Jews in Acts.

> Repent therefore, and turn to God so that your sins may be wiped out, so that times of refreshing may come from the presence of the Lord, and that he may send the Messiah appointed for you, that is, Jesus, who must remain in heaven until the time of universal restoration [*apokatasastis*] that God announced long ago through his holy prophets.[34]

This usage of Peter echoes the Old Testament understand of *apocatastasis* as the restoration of God's people as done by God. God's eschatological kingdom is understood as universal in scope, with all nations coming to God through the people of Israel. Christianity uniquely partners human freedom and accountability before God with the sovereign and universal saving act of God in Christ, and these two aspects of salvation are often difficult to reconcile into a coherent soteriology. Salvation's ethical imperative becomes humanity truly living out the hope they confess. "Hope for the salvation of all requires that radical love and solidarity in our relations with others which Christians recognize on the cross."[35] This hope in salvation demonstrates a faith that works for the justice and love of God here in the world today.

In speaking of the current impacts of salvation, theologian Joerg Rieger wonders if salvation can be reconstituted without being centered in the capitalistic economy. He thinks of how economic language of salvation has become so distorted through Western economic principles:

> Notions like Christ's love and charity are conceived in terms of the economic principles of compassionate conservatism, Christ's justice in terms of . . . the expansion of free-market economics, Christ's redemption in terms of the freedom of the market from

---

34. Acts 3:19–21. Other New Testament passages, such as 1 Tim 4:10 and Titus 2:11 speak to the universal scope of God's salvation in Christ, but the Acts passage is the only explicit use of *apocatastasis*.

35. Sachs, "Universal Salvation and the Problem of Hell," in Barr, ed., *Constructive Christian Theology*, 536.

challenges like the starvation of millions of children each year, and salvation through Christ in terms of success.[36]

Rieger wants to dismantle Christ as Savior from an image that creates a Christ today who functions as a CEO, lifestyle coach, or "friend in high places" that relate the work of salvation to economic transactions. Instead, a truer understanding of salvation is that the Kingdom of God challenges the status quo and subverts the powers that be. The wisdom of the Cross, as Paul speaks of in Corinthians, provides a salvation that baffles those in power.[37] Salvation's wisdom comes not in a simple solution to suffering but in presenting the power contained within it to access the life with God. Mark's parable of the Wicked Tenants speaks to how the tensions and sufferings in the present age are produced by the powers that be, and Christ's salvation exposes that and "lays open the ways in which we are all part of the system, encouraging repentance and a new start."[38]

Transforming Arms into Tools

The primary example utilized here to embody a global soteriology is that of the Christian Aid and the Mozambican Christian Council's program called *Transforming Arms into Tools* (TAE).[39] Shortly after its independence from Portugal, Mozambique devolved into civil war. The civil war in Mozambique claimed almost 1 million lives and displaced over 5 million people between the years of 1977 and 1992. After Mozambique's civil war ended in 1992, there were believed to be roughly seven million guns buried all over the countryside. The intent was for United Nations troops to disarm both sides, yet many of the weapons remained hidden. Beginning in 1995, one year after the country's first free elections, the Christian Council of Mozambique (CCM) began a work of helping individuals exchange tools of war for tools of living through the TAE program. Common tools for living were construction materials, sewing machines, roofing materials, tractors, hoes, and bicycles. A group of Mozambican artists then took the tools of war, cut them up, and rebuilt the pieces into sculptures.

36. Rieger, "Christ's Offices Reconsidered," in Jones and Lakeland, eds., *Constructive Theology*, 191.

37. 1 Cor 1:22-25.

38. Mark 12:1–12. Joerg Rieger, "Christ's Offices Reconsidered," in Jones and Lakeland, eds., *Constructive Theology*, 195.

39. Diocese of London, "Transforming Arms into Tools."

This project found support in the Mozambican government and committed not to prosecute former rebels for surrendering weapons in an effort to build peace. Much of this peace negotiation was the work of Anglican Bishop Dinis Sengulane. He understood this project as a literal outworking of the vision of Isaiah of swords being beat into plowshares and spears into pruning hooks.[40] As a result, over 600,000 weapons have been exchanged for tools over a nine-year period. Art professor Jonathan A. Anderson speaks to the salvific implications of this work:

> These sculptures and the TAE initiative behind it give powerful form and testimony not only to the terrible groaning of creation under the weight of evil but also to the orientation of Christian hope, which proclaims that the wondrous works of God in the world are organized around the redemption of all that is presently broken and dysfunctional in God's good creation.[41]

Reconfiguring these instruments of violence into symbols of life evokes the redeeming work of salvation. This process of rebuilding and transformation takes time and recalls the eschatological hope that Christian salvation points creation toward. God in Christ is reconciling all things to himself, whether in heaven or on earth, as the language of the hymn in Colossians envisions.[42]

The British Museum displayed one of these sculptures, entitled "The Throne of Weapons," in its series in partnership with the British Broadcasting Corporation called "The History of the World in 100 Objects."[43] This sculpture is the work of Mozambican artist Cristovao Canhavato Kester in 2001. Kester himself describes one of the visions in the sculpture in this way: "At the top you can see a smiling face, and there is another smiling face . . . and they are smiling at each other as if to say 'now we are free.'"[44] The British Museum's curator, Chris Spring, says this about the sculpture: "The Throne is also a contemporary work of art with a global significance, linking . . . Mozambique with the global arms trade. None of the guns in the Throne were made in Mozambique, none in Africa, thus it becomes

---

40. Isa 2:4.

41. Anderson's commentary in Young, *Renewing Christian Theology*, 232.

42. Col 1:20.

43. BBC, "A History of the World: The Throne of Weapons." http://www.bbc.co.uk/ahistoryoftheworld/objects/97OnxVXaQkehlbliKKDB6A.

44. Ibid.

a sculpture in which we are all, one way or another, complicit."[45] In many ways, The Throne and the sculptures like it serve as a type of war memorial that remembers those lives lost. At the same time, these sculptures also celebrate the victory of the lasting peace and the ongoing heritage of a rebuilt nation. The *Transforming Arms into Tools* initiative truly is an example of salvation in Mozambique.

Structures of Sin

This chapter, with its focus on salvation and the structural nature of sin, continues to expand the project of Constructive global ecclesiology. Hamartiology, or the theology of sin, often finds itself limited to the individualistic aspects in the Western context. As addressed here, liberation theology helps broaden the doctrine of sin to include systemic structures that perpetuate injustices. To form a global ecclesiology, the primary example given in this chapter will be the treatment of women in the DR Congo. As a body of work, the writings of liberation theology deeply move this author, a privileged white Western woman, to learn from and stand in solidarity with the plight of women everywhere. These are my sisters in Christ and sins committed against them, particularly as a result of globalization and their bodies as spaces of victimization in the globalized economy, are sins committed against me in the Body of Christ. Their suffering is interwoven into my reality here. The broader postcolonial project of liberation theology begs for each community to speak with their own voice but also challenges the global Church to unify in crying against institutional-based suffering and injustice wherever it is located.

In the past few years, I have been fortunate to spend a few months in Rwanda and Uganda working with the Quaker efforts toward peacemaking and the rebuilding of these formerly war-torn nations. The treatment of women, especially in the Congo has come to light in recent years, particularly where rape is used as a tool of war. The use of women as a tool of war in the Great Lakes region of Africa sickens me, and my faith compels me to respond. That being said, this brief work serves as a small step toward a theology of liberation for Congolese women. This particular work will only briefly discuss the topics of sin and the Church based out of their unique experience of suffering. Little has been written about this atrocity in the past few years from the perspective of a liberation theology. As a

45. Ibid.

foundation, this will build off of the works of Mercy Oduyoye and Kwok Pui-Lan primarily, as well as the thoughts of a few others to create a theology of suffering with recent African and indigenous women's liberation theologies. My hope is that other Congolese women are writing their own liberation theology and that this work can just serve alongside theirs, crying out for justice for the oppressed.

As discussed, though my focus is on the example of the treatment of women in the Congo as a structure of sin, the intent will be to use this example to understand the systemic, structural nature of sin when discussing global ecclesiology. Visions of church in the Western context cannot understand a holistic definition of sin without seeing their lives here on earth as interconnected to the sins of others. As Rebecca Todd Peters understands it:

> From the Christian perspective, behavior that does not seek to democratize power, care for the earth, and promote social well-being of people must be decried as sin. This includes an unexamined consumer behavior that complicity contributes to the degradation of the earth as well as the impoverishment of the Third World and the poverty of the marginalized in our hometowns. Recognizing our behavior as sin is essential to the transformation process because it is a critical first step towards taking responsibility for our actions and changing our lifestyle.[46]

Sin is multifaceted, complex, and clearly extends beyond individual choices. But to accurately represent a global ecclesiology, sin must involve my ignorance and indifference to the injustice in both my community and around the world. Now for a brief discussion of the condition of women in the Congo.

The Condition of the Women in the Congo

The Democratic Republic of the Congo has been struggling to recover from what has been called Africa's "world war" in which approximately three million died between the years of 1998 and 2003. Government forces, supported by Angola, Namibia, and Zimbabwe, fought against rebel troops encouraged by Uganda and Rwanda. Though a peace deal was reached with the formation of a transitional government in 2003, the nation has since remained in conflict from militia groups and its own army. Starting in 2008,

46. Peters, *In Search of the Good Life*, 186.

various coup attempts and Rwandan Hutu militia clashes with government forces constantly displaced thousands as a byproduct. Peace deals have been signed on numerous dates, but currently the eastern areas remain entrenched in violence. Though ongoing violence primarily remains in the northern providence of Kivu, much of the country still remains unstable, with the ever-present reality of threats of clashes from the militia or the government.[47]

With the start of the conflict came reports of the extreme treatment of women as tools of the warfare. Women were used as human shields in Ituri province from as early as 1999.[48] But this was just the beginning of the injustices done to women. Increased reports emerged of the sexual violence inflicted on women, including incidents of gang rape and mass exploitation. The United Nations eventually came to understand the incredible effects the treatment of women was having on the conflict in Congo, and in 2008 its Security Council voted unanimously in favor of a resolution classifying rape as a weapon of war. Rape had become a tactic in warfare and a threat to national security when used to "humiliate, dominate, instill fear in, disperse, and/or forcibly relocate civilian members of a community or ethnic group."[49] As modern warfare shifted, the United Nations came to recognize that violence done to women can significantly exacerbate situations of armed conflict and greatly hinder the restoration of peace, economic security and social stability of nations.

This acknowledgement on the part of the United Nations came as merely the tip of the iceberg in the broader global community becoming aware of the sexual abuse inflicted in the Congo. Reports emerged in August 2010 of rebels occupying neighborhoods and gang raping as many as 200 women and baby boys before leaving.[50] The Democratic Republic of the Congo developed the reputation as "the rape capital of the world" with an estimated 8,000 women raped as a result of civil conflict in 2009 alone, 60 percent of those instances being gang-rapes and over half occurring in the victims' homes. In a study done by the *American Journal of Public Health* in May of this year found that forty-eight rapes occur every hour in

47. This rough sketch of the history of recent conflict in Congo comes partly from my own memory and partly from the BBC News Country Profile on the Democratic Republic of the Congo. For a more in-depth account, visit http://www.bbc.co.uk/news/world-africa-13283212.

48. BBC News, "UN Classifies Rape a 'War Tactic.'"

49. Ibid.

50. BBC News, "UN Was not Told about 'Mass Rapes.'"

the Democratic Republic of the Congo.[51] Rapes in the past year increased dramatically, with over 400,000 females reporting as victims in the last twelve months. Many believe that the figures reflect better reporting rather than more instances occurring, but "even these new, much higher figures still represent a conservative estimate of the true prevalence of sexual violence because of chronic underreporting due to stigma, shame, perceived impunity, and exclusion of younger and older age groups as well as men."[52] Because sexual violence has been used so prevalently in warfare in Congo, the study found that the practice has spread into civilian society and areas apart from warzones. The shift in perpetrators has moved from soldiers as the norm to relatives or neighbors. Yet incidents of mass rape by soldiers do continue to be reported. One of the scientists voiced the sentiment that "rape in the DRC . . . has emerged as one of the great human crises of our time."[53]

This is not to say that nothing has been said or done by women in the Congo to stand against such deep injustice. Just last year women in Congo held their first march against sexual violence, led by first lady Olive Lembe Kabila.[54] In response to recent reports of government and rebels engaging in mass rapes, thousands of women walked through the streets of Bukavu, the capital of the South Kivu province. Nene Rukunghu, a doctor in a hospital in Bukavu, declared of the march: "We must fight against impunity, so that the perpetrators of violence are punished, to allow women to regain their dignity. Despite what they endure, Congolese women are strong and able to stand up again."[55] In the midst of injustice, hope remains. The continual challenge in the face of such suffering is to weave together the liberating perspective with this specific context.

Liberation Theology in Africa

Part of translating liberation theology for the Democratic Republic of the Congo begins with understanding the African backdrop of liberation theology. According to Emmanuel Martey, liberation became seen as a protest word or a violent word in many African contexts, "upsetting existing

51. BBC News, "DR Congo: 48 Rapes Every Hour, US Study Finds."

52. Ibid.

53. Ibid.

54. BBC News, "DR Congo women march against sexual violence."

55. Ibid.

political order which brings with it chaos and insecurity."[56] For many years, liberation theology was understood as a political movement limited to Latin America and connected to the Marxist overthrow of governments. This broad generalization of the genesis of the liberation movement created a situation where any new representations of its theology must recontextualize and become relevant when oppression takes different forms. So to begin, liberation theology must be separated from other contexts (Latin America and black, for example) and envisioned uniquely in Africa, where the hope is to re-frame the current societal structure in order to better represent God's justice for women. This begins with building off of previously written works of African women's liberation theology.

The fact is that sexism is part of the intricate web of oppression in which most women live, and having become accustomed to it does not make it any less a factor of oppression. This must come to the forefront of any conversations about African society as the context of African women's theology. "To understand that while you are preoccupied with, say, equality or abortion rights, your sister is anxiously awaiting her husband's release from South African police detention is consciously to accept responsibility for her freedom in her terms. What is important for you may be merely incidental for her by comparison with the suffering she experiences because of the color of her skin . . . I am not saying that the issues which affect middle-class women are unimportant, but I am saying that, if some of us have platforms, we must speak on behalf of others who have no platform."[57] True equality for African women must emerge on every level of the feminist agenda, yet the core of their liberation begins with freedom from violence and military threats. With regards to national policy and broader legislation to advocate change, part of liberation theology in the African context argues for women not only being granted rights in the home sphere but also serving as those who shape the legislation and policy in broader society. "Justice for women would involve a just definition of development which implies that women participate in defining national development."[58]

Kwok Pui-Lan's recent collaborative effort, *Hope Abundant*, is a smattering of Third World and indigenous women's theology. One area in which liberation theology needs to expand is to that of gender, sexuality, and women's reproductive issues in order to "demythologize and demystify

56. Althaus-Reid, Petrella, and Susin, *Another Possible World*, 80.

57. Ibid., 28.

58. Chetti and Joseph, *Ethical Issues in the Struggles for Justice*, 157.

theology."[59] By focusing primarily on class, male liberation theologians failed to integrate deep liberatory issues, such as gender and sexuality, into their project. Sins such as pride, egotism, and sexual aggression are more likely to be displayed in a male-dominated society, and Kwok stresses the sins of women that often get overlooked. "The sins of women are more likely to be passivity, the lack of strong ego, acquiescence, sloth, and accepting fate as their lot."[60] Women in Third World contexts have often been the victims of the sins of those in power in their society, but this does not minimize their complicity in these structures of sin as well.

Alongside this, Third World and indigenous women's theologians must deeply engage in cultural criticism, particularly in regards to the effects of colonialism and the role of religion in shaping gender identity. The Kenyan theologian Musimbi Kanyoro introduced the term "engendering cultural hermeneutics" to describe the analysis of cultural ideologies in regards to gender roles, violence against women, power dynamics, and women as both victims and perpetrators.[61] Hers is one example of an African theologian taking concepts like feminist theory and postcolonial theory, and revealing it through her African context to bring a gender and feminist perspective to inculturation.

Though Native American and not African, Laura E. Donaldson speaks of the value of indigenous theology for women to address the sexual violence against women as a continual strategy of conquest.[62] The spiritual world behind sexuality is one of deep significance in many indigenous cultures and its exploitation becomes a grave misappropriation of traditional identity. Within many spirit-based cultures, such as the African one, sexuality serves as more than an expression of physical existence. The rights of passage at different stages of life are mere examples of the harmonizing nature between physical existence and supernatural forces. Ceremonies and divination rites are parts of African traditional religions and any action that limits the impact of these expressions is another form of colonization and conquest. Though African society is often very hospitable to life and especially to new life, the physical bodies of women have become sources often avoided in theology. African women must continue to provide a postcolonialist theology of women's agency because of the life-giving power of

59. Kwok, *Hope Abundant*, 6.
60. Kwok, *Introducing Asian Feminist Theology*, 80–81.
61. Ibid., 7.
62. Ibid., 8.

their bodies came become a source for spiritual growth. Bodies become expressions of spirituality and spaces for worship, opportunities for women to shape the future of norms for indigenous theology.

Sin

Sin takes on a broader nature in the African context than the orthodox Western church often defines it. Multiple norms are used in the African contexts beyond the biblical text. The African worldview and human condition become strongly valued sources as well, speaking into a situation entrenched in structures of sin such as slavery, colonialism, and racism. For Africans, liberations became the theological choice for "anthropological dignity over against anthropological poverty."[63] For women in the African context, issues that confront the androcentric bias blatant in Africa must be addressed in order for it to heal the brokenness and transform the society. Because African life takes on a political nature based on its context, a greater unity between all aspects of personhood must be considered within the realm of sin. Much of society creates a dichotomy between the elements of human well being, especially in regards to the spiritual and physical when speaking of sin. The human being is still an integrated person in Africa; the private and the political cannot be separated.[64]

Sin becomes issues like fear of sexuality (which works against matriarchy), violence against women, ritualistic processes, and other practices that are oppressive to women. Within the context of African women's sexuality, issues uniquely arise such as widowhood rites, polygyny, barrenness, secret societies, clitoridectomy, bride-wealth/price, *purdah* (the practice of concealing women from men, such as through wearing the *burqa* or *niqab*), and child marriage.[65] Likewise, Oduyoye speaks of many of the cultic African practices that view women and girls as not fully human because of their ritual impurity of menstruation. This has been the position of African women, serving as custodians of cultural practices with strict observance. Despite serving at times custodians, a role that gives agency, women are often themselves the object of these practices and diminished by them. Even if such practices are harmful, they are not to be discussed. Alongside that, many of the sexual sins listed rob women of the agency they possess and

63. Althaus-Reid, Petrella and L Susin, *Another Possible World,* 81.

64. Oduyoye, *Hearing and Knowing,* 101.

65. Althaus-Reid, Petrella and L. Susin, *Another Possible World,* 84.

any pleasure or ownership of their own sexuality. The ways in which single women, barren women, and widows are stigmatized is one area in which African women need liberation.

Oduyoye speaks of salvation as saving African women for psychological liberation and internal transformation. She calls for the need for "liberation from the mentality that keeps women coping with marginalization and repression rather than resisting it."[66] The church in many ways has served as a structure of sin in Africa by keeping women in lesser positions. Women often serve the church diligently with their time and service, yet rarely is their voice elevated to positions on boards or as ministers. "The church has never tried to build a dynamic community of women and men. I never cease to be astonished at how little we have actually accomplished in community-building."[67] Her impression is that too often the feelings of women in the church are ridiculed, and this attitude works against any formation of spirit-led community. Ridicule is different than being ignored or repressed because both of the latter attitudes admit that women have valuable contributions, but men choose to discredit them, whereas ridicule dismisses the possibility that women strengthen the community, as though the idea is some type of joke. Musimbi R. A. Kanyoro believes that one way such liberation can happen is through women pastors being able to talk about the reality of women's experiences in their sermons, and therefore being able to make connections between church, home, and society.[68] If the everyday experiences of women, be it struggles or celebrations, are introduced into church conversation, deeper theological expression and spirituality will emerge.

Part of sin for Oduyoye is the process of saying "No" to where God is working in and amongst Africans, furthering chaos. An active effort against structures of sin involves fighting against cynicism and distrusting in the power of God in the midst of the women in Congo. "All that prevents us from living a life of absolute trust in God, living out the values of God's kingdom, is sin."[69] In African traditions and culture, the spirit-filled nature of everyday life allows for the demonic to emerge. "Demonic" becomes defined as any area where the spirits contained in objects, structures, and people are held captive to evil forces. In the African context, sin involves

66. Ibid.

67. Oduyoye. *Hearing and Knowing*, 125.

68. Kwok, *Hope Abundant*, 21.

69. Oduyoye, *Hearing and Knowing*, 103.

acknowledging the demonic in structures and the potential for things to become demonic when distorted by patriarchy. "We seek empowerment from the gospel to dismantle what is demonic in society and to exorcise the demons that turn persons into oppressors."[70]

One specific area of sin relevant to the context of the Congolese women is that of a deeper suffering. Any theological study in Africa takes place situated amongst a context where both women and men have suffered greatly. As if illness and diseases were not enough, warfare is a constant reality and repressive regimes rule all over the continent. In speaking of the suffering of African women, Musimbi R. A. Kanyoro speaks of times when people are unable to cry and tears are preserved only for mourning the dead or else women would be crying all the time.[71] This connects with the work of Rebecca Chopp on suffering as a theological praxis for women. She believes that suffering and its quest for freedom is the fundamental reality of human experience as well as the location of the church in history. This could not be more accurate for the situation of Congolese women today. Liberation theology today, Chopp believes, must relate the Christian narrative as the focal center of God's liberating activity in the midst of suffering.[72] This Christianity radically engages with the world to represent human freedom and demonstrate God's action with and for those who are oppressed.

Liberation theology becomes a reorientation toward transformation rather than merely reconciling one's existence and reality because suffering demands transformation. A concrete, lived theology of Congolese women must integrate how their experiences of oppression speak of a God who enters their existence and suffers with them. "For liberation theology risks a wager that only by standing with those who suffer—the poor and the oppressed, the living and the dead—shall we see the reality of human existence through their eyes and experience in their suffering a God of grace, of hope, of love."[73] Giving African words to this idea, Mercy Oduyoye writes this poem:

> Suffering grows a spirituality of persistence
> aided by faith in God who enables them to make
> a way where there is no way . . .

70. Ibid., 148.
71. Kwok, *Hope Abundant,* 25.
72. Chopp, *The Praxis of Suffering,* 4.
73. Ibid., 151.

suffering sprouts a spirituality of resistance,
Refusing to be blamed for the hurts one endures;
Refusing to be shamed by the violence on one's self;
Telling when the telling itself is taboo,
Speaking it out is half the resistance, for,
It reveals that one is alive to one's full humanity.[74]

Too often suffering is connected with sin, be it sin in another life or lack of obedience to God. For African women, suffering needs to be reclaimed as a part of what it means to be human and retold as a testimony of how God enables them to "make a way where there is no way." This process of reclamation reveals a feminist spirituality that strengthens the Church through its own agency and an instance of humanity stepping into the heart of a suffering God. Sin has been inflicted on African women through structures of oppression, but the way in which African women redeem this suffering becomes a part of their humanity. This is worship, and this must become central to the spirituality of the African church, as we will proceed to discuss.

Sin in the Democratic Republic of the Congo

Any adequate Congolese women's liberation theology must address the unsafe structures and conditions that have allowed rape to become so commonplace in the nation. Part of that is due to the inadequate view of women around the world and the androcentric bias of society, particularly in African society. Structural sins of slavery, colonialism, and racism for the Congolese women are similar to the experience of their other African sisters. Likewise, any colonialist imprints of church in the African context become a structure of sin, keeping Congolese women in lesser positions and therefore limiting their full humanity. All of these understandings hinder a true woman's spirituality, one based out of God's presence amongst Africans in their traditions and religious understandings of the world. By keeping Congolese women from seeing their traditions and religious understandings of the world as true Christianity, the colonialist church has inflicted sin upon them. Sin becomes anything that keeps the African church from seeing the Holy Spirit and the potential for the demonic behind everything.

74. Oduyoye, *Introducing African Women's Theology*, 75.

138

The most significant perspective Congolese women could bring to the movement of liberation theology in the area of sin speaks to the sexual suffering inflicted on women. This attitude undercuts their full personhood and separates women from their full agency through their sexuality and sexual pleasure. Specific areas of this fear that Congolese women must reclaim for their own personhood are all aspects of sexual culture that lead to violence against women and ritualistic processes such as clitoridectomies that oppress women. Women must address sexual-related issues that keep women in a lower place in society, such as the bride price, childhood marriage, widowhood rites, and polygyny, so that their nature is not understood as inherently sinful.

The Church in Africa

Women in African churches often view their role as spirit-directed. They take serious the charge in Acts 2:17 that daughters shall take a role as diviners, prophesying in the context of worship and relying on the Spirit of God as they have understood it through some of the primal religions. "There is a spirit of *harambee* (cooperation and sharing that characterize self-help groups of urban or rural women in Africa) that women strain themselves to promote."[75] Traditional African women understand spirituality as represented in AIC (African Instituted Churches) because here there is a space for freedom in prayers and spiritual expressions. "African spirituality seeks fullness of life here and now, even as it hopes we shall have it in the other dimension of life."[76] Any understanding of salvation or eschatology must be a present living *shalom* here and now for African communities. The Hebrew word *shalom* here refers to a reality greater than just peace as the absence of conflict. *Shalom* becomes wholeness, the welfare of the entire community as an expression of God's reality with the people. God becomes an active, power-giving spirit that empowers the people of God to combat the powers that threaten humanity through prayers, prophesies, and songs that speak a new world into existence. This shows itself in what Mercy Oduyoye calls "*Okyeso Nyame*"—the God who leaves no one out of the distribution of good things.[77] In the African understanding of Church, the people of God are fully gifted by God with spirit and power to bring new things into ex-

75. King, *Feminist Theologies from the Third World*, 370.
76. Ibid., 372.
77. Ibid., 374.

istence amidst the current reality. African women live in a way in which every part of their life is sacramental, and this worldview provides a deep sense of strength for the community of faith. All of life becomes spirit-filled or sacramental, an expression of worship and an opportunity for God's presence to be known and experienced. "African women's strength lies in the belief that the spirit-world is on the side of those who protect life and combat all that carries death in its wake."[78] African women operate from the reality that the interconnection with the spiritual world empowers them to cope with and combat horrible injustices in their current physical reality.

Speaking of rural faith communities in Africa, a larger picture of the definition of church must surface. Some move as far as to say that African religions must be understood as equivalent to African Christianity. Mercy Oduyoye believes that they are many churches, divided and "being church" in a number of ways all throughout Africa. One unified Church can only emerge if all expressions of church are validated in their representation of African Christianity based out of African culture. Each of these spirit-led representations of God must be acknowledged and vindicated in order to bring women into full personhood.

Part of the work of the church in African women's liberation theology is to stand and cry that inculturation is not sufficient. Inculturation is only worthy if the culture being reclaimed promotes justice and supports the life and dignity of African women.[79] African culture must first be redeemed toward women and their full personhood in order that any steps toward incorporating culture into the Church represent the vision of God's community. The church must become a body of inculturation and reconstruction, one that is both personal and ecclesial. As a body, it must reconstruct its dealings with management structures, financial policies, pastoral care, human resource development, research, family education, service, and witness. All of these are areas in which women are easily exploited and underrepresented within a patriarchal culture.

The Church in the Democratic Republic of the Congo

The Church for Congolese women must view itself as spirit-directed and shaped by the spirituality of women. Their experiences of suffering and injustice are ones that give them a unique insight into the workings and

78. Ibid., 375.

79. Kwok, *Hope Abundant*, 26.

nature of God as one standing with them and redeeming their suffering through worship. Women must be viewed as fully human and must work alongside men in spiritual practices and teachings that shape the Church. The Church must act as an agent to speak for those who have no voice in the Congo and advocate for peace in situations of violence. God's power must be channeled to direct the people of God against the forces that threaten humanity, forces like violence and sexual oppression of women. If the Congolese church becomes the representation of African religions, it will be able to shed colonialist and oppressive forces and live as a full representation of God's vision for the people of the Congo. This calls for a church that stands as more than inculturation but instead as one that understands all of life as sacramental and fully alive to the Spirit working in and through Congolese women.

Conclusion

The Church must address the current situation in the Congo. One voice, the liberation stream within theology, seeks to dismantle structures of sin and suffering as the praxis for theology. Here in writing on behalf of women in the Congo, the underlying hope is of one small step taking place toward a greater movement of translating the model of liberation theology onto a contemporary context of oppression. The hope is also that utilizing this example of sin contributes to a vision of what constructive global ecclesiology could look like. In addressing sin and the church as systematic aspects of liberation theology, areas of inculturation and the African worldview emerged as contextual issues. Likewise, working in harmony with African liberation theologians like Mercy Amba Oduyoye, indigenous theologians like Kwok Pui-Lan, and feminist theologians like Rebecca Chopp, it is clear that a future area of liberation theology is that of Congolese women.

As a sister in Christ gifted with privilege in my own context, my faith compels me to stand on their behalf and speak all I can about the reality of their experience of injustice. I continue to ask myself how the Church can do this, and in many ways it is a question I would rather avoid. Yet I do believe that one action the Church around the world must take is to stand in solidarity with women in Congo. We must advocate for their rights and do all we can from our own context to minimize their suffering. Any opportunity we have to empower them to speak on their behalf must be taken as an action of faithfulness to work toward creating God's just vision of the world. Their voices must be taken serious as norms and sources for the future of theology. And as a part of reclaiming the church, I affirm that, along with my Congolese sisters, we together must hold the Church accountable to being a community that lives the life of Christ, that preaches the reign and love of God and by its being and doing, serves God's people and God's purposes and presents itself as a sample of the *koinonia* (communion by intimate participation) approved of and by God, and in which God participates.[80]

Similarly, salvation must broaden to its individual and social implications, extending past the parameters of time and location, and providing both spiritual and material redemption. Any possibility of God's redeeming work only exists because of Christ on the Cross. Salvation as liberation for all, extending to households, families, communities, and neighborhoods emphasizes the global feminist construction of the interconnectivity of salvation. Life-giving resources must be an aspect of salvation, where freedom from bondage also comes with freedom into a new life of provision and abundance. The *Transforming Arms into Tools* program in Mozambique demonstrates that embodiment of salvation.

---

80. My paraphrase of Mercy Oduyoye's vision for the African church. Oduyoye, *Introducing African Women's Theology*, 89.

5

Constructive Global Ecclesiology

Peacemaking, Women in Leadership,
and Multiethnic Churches

Introduction

THE FINAL CHAPTER WILL address three more areas of constructive global ecclesiology: peacemaking, women in leadership, and multiethnic churches. Though many areas of ecclesiology could have been the focus, for the brevity of this work, three pivotal areas of practical theology will take precedence. The focus here will be an ecclesiology with a practical emphasis. These distinctives will represent the core values of Aquino, Kwok, and Oduyoye as representatives for other postcolonial and Third World theologies. These women would define the Church as a peacemaking body, demonstrating egalitarian leadership that elevates women in Church polity, and seeking to include ethnic diversity in its midst. If these values are absent, then the orthopraxy of such churches fails to embody what these women understand as the true Church. With this in mind, each of these distinctives will be defined and examined through a global lens, highlighting examples from across the world.

Peacemaking

In constructing a global ecclesiology, Oduyoye, Aquino, and Kwok all envision a world where the active work of building peace is an essential component in the theology of the Church. Christian communities must understand themselves as bodies that work to reconcile divided people groups, genders, social communities and those separated by violence. If we take reconciliation as one of the charges of the Church, true healing (*shalom*) takes places within self, with the environment, with the community, and with God. A female understanding of this must examine where women in the Christian Church must themselves be liberated to have true peace with self. This concept will be examined around a framework of the biblical vision of a peaceful community of faith, starting with the Prophets, ushered in through Jesus, and ending with the eschaton. Following this, women must also examine their own role as peace-building agents in the world. The role of women in working to heal communities devastated by violence has come to the surface in recent years, but this chapter seeks to explore how Christianity must empower women in their role as those who bring *shalom* by working to subvert patriarchy and the violence it implies. Beginning with the biblical narrative, this chapter will then move to a definition of peacemaking and a short discussion of the unique voice of women in any conversation regarding peace. A brief Quaker history will be examined, looking at women within the movement who worked for peacemaking such as Lucretia Mott and Margaret Fell, as well as modern-day examples of women as Christian leaders for liberation in violent communities. For the brevity of this chapter, two contemporary communities, Israel/Palestine and South Africa, will be examined in relation to the role of women and liberation toward peace. The intent is that such a construction will present a picture for why the true Church must stand as a peace Church.

Peacemaking in Feminism

Feminism presents a unique voice in the discussion of peacemaking. Women raise distinct issues in which the broader theological landscape must address. Mercy Oduyoye speaks of an overview of peace as a calling to a greater *shalom*, or wholeness of the entire community. "Peace and the well-being of the whole of creation is one agenda. The victims of war are victims of injustice and greed and they include human beings as well as the rest of creation. We cannot struggle for human rights in the midst of war, neither can we enjoy social and cultural developments when the conditions for peace are absent."[1] For women, peace comes when all oppressive actions are identified, such as wrongs done to creation, women, and all parts of humanity, be it wealthy or impoverished. The patriarchal structure of society and its institutions, including the church, must be identified as sources of perpetuating violence. From this framework, the themes of peace as woven throughout Scripture will be identified to ground the work of women in peacemaking.

The Biblical Narrative

Beginning with the Prophets, passages such as Amos 5:21—24 and Isaiah 58:6–7 are just two examples of many surrounding the narrative of God's people as creating a peaceful society for those within and outside of its boundaries. The initial discussion women bring to the narrative of peace in Scripture is that of not only locating the scenes of oppression as they appear throughout the entire patriarchal text but also showing how those are sinful acts committed against the will of God. From this, a peaceful ethic affirms the understanding of the Kingdom of God as the continuation of the prophetic tradition and Isaiah's vision of the reign of God.[2] The same God of the Magnificat is understood as a living God keeping hope alive for women in the face of poverty. This God is doing a new act to return dignity to those created in God's image through the community of God acting as Christ's Body in the world. This is continued as it is taught through Jesus in the Sermon on the Mount and represented in the famous portion of the beatitudes as "blessed are the peacemakers," a special form of communion with the divine that comes as a gift from God.[3] As the Spirit's healing and liberating power flowed through Jesus, he invited all into a deeper reality of the Kingdom, a reality that could be ushered into earth through justice-orientation actions. Luke 4:18–19 tells of Jesus's fulfillment of Isaiah's words in the Nazareth Manifesto, proclaiming that:

> The Spirit of the Lord is upon me,
> Because he has anointed me

1. Chetti and Joseph. *Ethical Issues,* 159.
2. I.e. Isa 2:4.
3. Matt 5:38–48.

To bring good news to the poor.

He has sent me to proclaim release to the captives

And recovery of sight to the blind,

To let the oppressed go free,

To proclaim the year of the Lord's favor.

Other words of Jesus such as "when you enter in a house, say 'peace be upon you'" as well as his words "go in peace and be cured of your affliction" to the woman hemorrhaging blood remind his followers that a lifestyle of healing and peace must be present in his followers wherever they go.[4] Jesus modeled peace through his submission to and ultimate triumph over the powers through the nonviolent atoning work of the Cross, as represented in his final act of forgiveness: "Father forgive them for they know not what they do."[5] Christ on the cross serves as a redemptive act through the fragile gift of a suffering servant of God who embodied the possibilities of a forgiving love. For women, Oduyoye argues, the Cross and Resurrection are twin events to be dually experienced in order to know the life of God and find true peace. "We risk sacrifice and cross, we struggle against evil and endure many scars, because armed with hope we already see life defeating death."[6] Only because of Christ can women risk to sacrifice for greater peace in society, for new life and justice has been made possible for them.

In Matthew 26:52—54, Tertullian believes that Christ disarms every soldier when he disarms Peter.[7] This is the hermeneutic of peace woven throughout the teachings and example of Christ for his followers. "Christ calls his children to bear his cross, not to crucify or kill others . . . Christ also urges them to flee the glory of this world, not to acquire it by warlike endeavors."[8] The ultimate metaphor in Revelation of the Lamb's War holds for the believer the truth of God overcoming as God over all Lords and God over of Kings.[9] Using the Lamb as a symbol for victory again identifies the lowest and the least as those being used for peace, overturning the structures of power and violence.

4. Luke 10:5; Mark 5:34.

5. Luke 23:34.

6. Oduyoye, *Introducing African Women's Theology*, 118.

7. Barclay, *Apology*, 428.

8. Ibid., 429.

9. Rev 17:14 (paraphrase mine).

CONSTRUCTIVE GLOBAL ECCLESIOLOGY

The narrative of peace woven throughout Scripture is one of a deep spirituality that trusts in God for true reconciliation and victory in the finality of all things. In the words of Robert Barclay, "There is nothing more contrary to human nature than refusing to defend oneself. But since this is so difficult for people, it is one of the most perfect points of Christian faith. It demands self-denial, and placing one's entire confidence in God."[10] Transforming faith is the invitation in following Christ: this involves trusting in the peace promised in John 14:27, a peace left with Christians by the power of the Spirit. In a more cosmic sense, there is a broader theme of reconciliation in Scripture between all of the world and God. The author of the epistle to Corinth speaks of this when God is told of "reconciling all things in [Godself]."[11] In an eschatological vision, all of the injustice in the world will be brought into the peaceful nature of God through the reconciling nature of the Cross by the eventual redemption of all things.

Peacemaking Principles

For this work, I will be distinctly using the term 'peacemaking' as opposed to 'pacifism' or 'peace studies.' Peacemaking implies an active stance where choices and involvement within any cultural context help to structure the reframing of a community away from violence and oppression. Ethicist Glen Stassen defines just peacemaking as more of an addition to the previous paradigms of either just war or pacifism in order to strengthen them and create a more convincing and legitimate alternative.[12] His definition of just peacemaking involves ten major principles of practice, which may be given different meaning in individualized contexts, but nevertheless serve as a valid starting point. Just peacemaking contains the following:

Initiatives:

1. Support nonviolent direct action.

2. Take independent initiatives to reduce threats.

3. Use cooperative conflict resolution.

4. Acknowledge responsibility for conflict and injustice and seek repentance and forgiveness.

10. Barclay, *Apology*, 434.

11. 2 Cor 5:19 (paraphrase mine).

12. Stassen, "Just Peacemaking as Hermeneutical Key," 171.

Justice:

5. Advance democracy, human rights, and religious liberty.

6. Foster just and sustainable economic development.

International Community:

7. Work with emerging cooperative forces in the international system.

8. Strengthen the United Nations and international efforts for cooperation and human rights.

9. Reduce offensive weapons and weapons trade.

10. Encourage grassroots peacemaking groups and voluntary associations.[13]

Peace, he believes, must be aligned with cooperative forces and international systems so that the greater world community can work with the individual nation in enacting peace, especially in the areas of economic stability and responsible governance. Stassen's intention is to create a paradigm for people of all faiths, but Lisa Sowell Cahill sees its mandate as especially strong for Christians worldwide. As a Christian woman, she advocates that these ten initiatives are intended to embody the proactive example of Jesus in present volatile situations around the globe rather than serve as an "eschatological ideal" abstractly taught but never understood until the Messianic apocalypse.[14] The biblical narrative is best lived out through communities that together seek to overturn the present world order through practical ideas such as fostering sustainable economic development and nonviolent reimagining of schools, churches, organizations, and governments. For the believer, this enactment of the peace of God as understood through Christ's establishment of the Kingdom is intended to actively step into the continuation of the Gospel story, rather than passively hope on the Lord's eventual eschatological reign.

It is also significant to note that praise for just peacemaking comes from its ability to meet needs left untouched by humanitarian aid, such as reducing weapons trade and working cooperatively between governmental forces (such as the UN or the African Union) and nongovernmental organizations. Martin L. Cook believes that in theory, just peacemaking's practices create self-sustaining units of communities working internally

---

13. Ibid., 177.
14. Ibid., 197.

toward creative, local solutions for lasting, transformative interventions.[15] "Just peacemaking's practices are indeed an essential augmentation to the short term ability of military forces to intervene and provide the stability that is the precondition for, but not the solution of, the underlying cultural, religious and economic conflict."[16] Essentially, what all these authors are arguing for is the strength and practicality of the just peacekeeping paradigm as it has been tested and observed in recent rebuilding of war-torn nations around the world.

Neal Blough, in his work from the Mennonite peacekeeping tradition, argues for the biblical imperative of peacemaking in light of globalization. He views the biblical models of salvation, especially looking at Old Testament themes from the stories of the Tower of Babel and the call of Abraham, as examples for how peacemaking is at the center of our understanding of salvation as God's people. "The salvation narrative originates as a response to a world that is not at peace, a world in which cultural, national and linguistic barriers are a source of separation and "non-communication" between families, peoples and nations."[17] Based on this, the Messiah came in many ways to bring *shalom* to all peoples and entrusted to his messianic community the "ministry of reconciliation." Likewise, ecclesial communities need to live out an integrated understanding of the Incarnation and the Trinity that sustains the practice of peacemaking in a violent world.[18] From here, Blough sees mission as the extension of that *shalom* to all peoples beyond the individual church community through highlighting movements of the Spirit in all areas of the world, but especially those plagued by war. The response of Abraham to the Babel narrative was the formation of a new people who will bless all people in the world, and Blough sees a peace-minded mission as one that does not desire to create conflict by imposing a worldview or faith but instead wants to bless and heal all nations.[19]

When peacemaking is looked at on the larger spiritual dimension, it interweaves theological with personal, social, and ecological spheres of life. In the words of Hizkias Assefa in his essay "Peace and Reconciliation as a Paradigm," he reconstructs peacemaking as a philosophy for all of Africa in this way:

15. Cook. "Just Peacemaking," 249.

16. Ibid., 250.

17. Blough, "From the Tower of Babel to the Peace of Jesus Christ," 11.

18. Ibid., 20.

19. Ibid., 29.

In typical peace negotiations, the parties in conflict come to the table armed with very self-centered cost-benefit calculations, ready to deny or defend their wrongdoings, determined to attribute total blame for the conflict to their opponents, and intent on extracting maximum concessions from their adversaries. In contrast, bringing the spiritual dimension into the peacemaking process can create access to the more deep-seated, affective base of the parties' behavior, enabling them to examine critically their own responsibility, confess their wrongdoings, be flexible with their demands, grant and ask for forgiveness when the need arises, and seek mutually beneficial solutions.[20]

Assefa addresses one of the key aspects that just peacemaking brings to the global stage in regards to conflict resolution, and that is the inward transformation of the Christ-centered person in working towards peace and the outward difference in attitudes and actions which follow. Movements towards peace in the Kingdom of God are not only following the "Way" of Jesus in presenting a better way to be in relationship with one another but also teach of an entirely better means of structuring communities in covenant with all people, communities of equality with Christ at the center.

Feminist Peacemaking

Much of the conversation regarding peacemaking for women starts with their own bodies. One of the primary ways in which women experience violence around the world is centered around the physical abuse and control of our bodies as women and the denial of basic rights over one's sexuality and sexual choice. "Violence and subjugation have been woven into institutionalized forms of religion whose patriarchal tenets have marginalized and domesticated the female and the feminine, shackling her and legitimizing violence against her."[21] Women found it difficult to persuade the church that the issue of violence against women is as much an issue of ecclesiology as it is a factor in political conflicts. "The ecclesial reality of the Church is intricately interwoven with its life as a moral community—it has to constantly test its authority to be the moral voice in the world against its ability to respond with courage and conviction to the voices of the excluded, the

---

20. Assefa and Wachira, eds., *Peacemaking and Democratisation in Africa*, 50–51.

21. Chetti and Joseph, *Ethical Issues*, 77.

voices from the margins."[22] Women often find themselves in daily ethical and moral choices they are called to make in their own lives but also in the lives of their families and community.

Peacemaking is a multifaceted enterprise for feminists and must be understood in its connection to the earth. Ecofeminists remind us that peace is a holistic enterprise, not one limited to persons who can speak for themselves. "Christian discipleship in our time, if it is to express love for God and for the earth, must be one of self-limitation, sacrifice and sharing so that the neighbors, all God's creatures, might flourish."[23] Sallie McFague believes that part of the discipleship process for Christians is working toward an equitable distribution of all of the earth's resources for the mutual flourishing of all of creation. This involves direct actions that better work toward stability and peace in our communities, and guiding a countercultural vision against the violence done to all bodies. Unlike other liberation theologies, ecological theology advocates for the understanding that North American Christians are the oppressors, and all of creation must be liberated from our domination. McFague calls for a Christianity that actively works on behalf of others in the work of justice that deals with the interplay of economics, ecology, and violence. There is a complex relationship between resources and the degradation of the environment and conflict and war, be it through scarcity conflicts or resource wars. Examples like the Gulf War, conflicts in North Africa, and Sierra Leone all represent conflicts centered on the distribution of environmental resources like oil, water, and minerals.

Women also speak uniquely to the role of language in shaping feminism. In a roundtable discussion of twelve women from Lesotho, Namibia, Scotland, South Africa, Uganda, and the United States, the theme of violence in our everyday lives emerged quickly. In their various languages, certain phrases with close English equivalents such as "battle," "kill," and "brain dead" came to light, speaking of how deeply anger and violence are embedded in the heart. Some of the women were even reluctant to say certain phrases in their mother tongues because they are so abusive, and English translations soften the impact, such as "I will beat you, go to hell with you."[24] Many of these women have known injustice and warfare firsthand and speak to the power of nonviolence beginning at the level of fam-

22. Ibid., 84.
23. McFague, *Life Abundant*, 23.
24. Phiri and Nadar, eds., *African Women, Religion, and Health*, 200.

ily. Speaking to the power of women united for peace, as will be discussed later in the context of South Africa, the women affirmed that "women bring important gifts to peacemaking . . . [they are] generally more compassionate and so societies expect them to try to achieve peace and unity. They are seen as striving for unity, especially in the family where the mother tries to bring everyone together without taking sides."[25] Though not all women are mothers, the roundtable affirmed that women have the advantage of society's expectation upon them as one who works to ease tensions and bring reconciliation into families. Kwok Pui-Lan, a voice highlighted within this work, summarizes this thinking well for Third World feminists:

> Peace is not the absence of war or conflict, but harmony, well-being and blissfulness because of just relationships. Peace is not a passive waiting for politicians and strategists to work out a solution for us, but passionate action in our local communities to empower to powerless, to strengthen the weak, and to restore what has gone wrong.[26]

This speaks to the unique manner in which Third World feminist descriptors of Church as a peacemaking body can, in fact, extend to the entire theological enterprise of ecclesiology and applies across geopolitical contexts and spaces.

Quaker Women and Peacemaking

"I am only too conscious that only a tiny fraction of Christians in the world accept the position which I hold and I feel humble about holding it in the face of the fact that the vast majority of Christians walk a different path from mine."[27] These words by the famous Quaker Rufus Jones speak to the rarity within Christendom of holding the position of pacifism. For the Quakers, a people founded on the "distinctive," a Quaker term for Church value, of equality of all persons, every person is an image-bearer of the Divine Light, or the presence of God. From this conviction, the Quakers became actively involved in the struggle for peace and justice for all people as bearers of God. Leading this struggle were Quaker women, who within

25. Ibid., 204.
26. Kwok, "Ecology and the Recycling of Christianity," in Barr, ed., *Constructive Christian Theology,* 270.
27. Trueblood, *The People Called Quakers,* 187.

this tradition could hold roles of leadership even before they were granted such rights in secular society. From its inception, Quaker women spoke of their own rights as well of the rights of African-Americans, American Indians, and all minorities as children of God. Here two of those Quaker women will be highlighted: Margaret Fell and Lucretia Mott.

Margaret Fell

Margaret Fell (1614—1702), often referred to as the "nursing mother of Quakerism," served as one of the original leaders of the Quaker movement and became a large advocate for the role of women. Through her marriage to George Fox, the two worked adamantly for the cause of conversions as well of social justice throughout England. Fell wrote the famous tract, "Women's Speaking Justified," an argument for women's ministry based on themes from the Bible, and for its time, one of the major works on women's religious leadership and rights. In this short work, she defines her case for equality of the genders on the basic treatise of spiritual equality in Quakerism. Her belief was that God created all people, therefore both women and men were capable of not only possessing the Inner Light but also of speaking, teaching, and prophesying for edification of the community of faith.

Fell is remembered as one who managed the Swarthmore Manor, her home, as a center of peace and hospitality. Her house served as a place to house ministers, runaway slaves, and any who needed a place to find refuge or respite.[28] Her works alongside her husband brought organization and structure to the entire Quaker movement, especially during times of state-sponsored persecution.

Margaret Fell serves as a wonderful example of early peacemaking through her work with the Quaker church. She wrote numerous tracts and worked to raise money and consciousness about those in prison for religious persecution or otherwise. George Fox recalls in his journal that Fell, his wife, "went to the King and told him what sad work there was in the city, and in the nation, and shewed him, that we were an innocent peaceable people."[29] Fell stood up to the king for the sake of the Quaker movement and the king's threats of imprisonment. Her words spoke the truth that a peaceful response in the face of any threats from the monarchy would be defining features of the Quaker movement. Margaret Fell became a

28. Ibid., 192.
29. Ibid., 194.

courageous voice for justice. In later years of Quakerism, the Friends often became a voice of justice on behalf of others. But at the genesis of its movement, when the continued existence of Quakerism was an open question, their call to justice was often on behalf of other Friends. With the example of Lucretia Mott comes a later Quaker with a deep commitment for justice on behalf of others.

Lucretia Mott

Lucretia Mott (1793—1880) devoted her life to the abolition of slavery, women's rights, school and prison reforms, temperance, peace, and religious tolerance. Mott became a Quaker minister, one of the only denominations allowing such a role for women, and she used her gift of preaching to speak to the Quaker distinctive of the equality of all people and the presence of the Divine light in every individual. Within the Quaker movement, she married James Mott and together the couple worked against the evil of slavery by giving speeches, founding women's abolitionist societies such as the Pennsylvania Anti-Slavery Society, and housing runaway slaves. Her own home became a stop on the Underground Railroad. Her founding of abolitionists societies was especially significant since other organizations within the antislavery movement failed to admit women. In her work for the antislavery movement, she advocated pacifism in advancing the movement based out of her Quaker convictions. She took the posture of boycotting any goods made or harvested by slaves, such as cotton and sugar cane, as a part of her peace testimony.

In 1837, Mott helped organize the First Anti-Slavery Convention of American Women, an event she worked on with her colleagues, the sisters Angelina and Sarah Grimké. Often she connected the causes of antislavery and feminism, to much criticism.[30] As she worked toward women's issues, Mott advocated for issues like equal pay for equal work as a part of her vision for both short-term and long-term reform. Years after the Anti-Slavery Convention, Mott channeled that energy into the first annual women's rights convention in 1845. One byproduct of this convention was a revision to the U.S. Declaration of Independence titled the Declaration of Sentiments. It boldly declared, "We hold these truths to be self-evident:

30. American National Biography Online, "Lucretia Mott."

That all men and women are created equal," leaving in its wake a host of controversy.[31]

Another action of Mott's, which continued her controversy, was the passage of the Fugitive Slave Act. This work was a part of her commitment to pacifism as well as to aid the plight of slaves toward equality for all. Mott spoke often on the value of all people and this position led her to advocate for women's entrance into higher education, equal property rights, and the ability to vote. Her work for all the disenfranchised—women, free blacks, slaves, and Indians—stemmed from her deep Quaker convictions of peace and equality.

Though the emphasis has been on female Quaker peacemakers, the distinctive of pacifism was significant for all members of the movement. As early as 1659, the Quakers saw value in being able to stand and say that they had not taken up arms when the Puritan Common was going under.[32] This established a heartbeat and legacy that was carried on until modern day. In the twentieth century, this aspect of the social reform legacy of the Quakers has set them apart from other churches and American society. "The Cold War, the arms race, apartheid, the pervasiveness of poverty, and the preponderance of oppressive regimes have forced Friends to seek, debate and agonize over what it means to be peacemakers . . . The constant challenge is for Friends to be effective Christian witnesses for peace."[33] Internationally, the Quakers supported nonviolent bodies such as the League of Nations, the International Court, the United Nations, and other various attempts to create world peace through diplomacy, arms control, or disarmament. More Friends have been imprisoned in any era since Fox and the early Quakers over the protest of rearmament.[34] On the domestic front, Friends work for peace through social programs, equal rights for minorities, and opposition of the draft.[35] The line between the testimonies of equality and peace amongst the Quakers is blurred to their interrelated understanding of how each distinctive shapes the other and vice versa.

31. Ibid.
32 Barbor and Frost, *The Quakers*, 46.
33. Ibid., 258.
34. Ibid., 268.
35. Ibid., 254.

Modern-Day Women Peacemakers

The call for women as peacemakers today is just as necessary as it was in the days of the start of the Quaker movement. The women's movement repeatedly has exposed the connections between male-ness and dominance, war, and violence. This does not imply that being male is in itself an evil, but the feminist critique examines the interplay between violence and oppression and male-led leadership. One wonders how the world would be different if women in partnership with men led nations and people. Within the Christian Church today, women are courageously leading the charge in creating peace in their communities in areas where the Church is growing: the Global South. Two examples, that of Israel/Palestine and South Africa, will be examined here.

Israel/Palestine and Peacemaking

As a Christian Palestinian woman living in Israel, Jean Zaru speaks of the social, political, economic, and religious structures of injustice that fill her everyday existence. She also resonates with the two previous examples because she is following in the Quaker footsteps of Margaret Fell and Lucretia Mott as a Friends woman working for social justice. Part of her embodiment of feminist peacemaking comes in a constant work to subvert the Israeli government as well as serve, love, and integrate her life with that of her Israeli neighbor. She sees the Quaker testimony of peace integrated into the Israeli context in three ways:

1. To refuse to take part in acts of war.
2. To strive to remove the causes of war.
3. To use the way of love open to us to promote peace and to heal wounds.[36]

Yet despite the violence she has witnessed firsthand, standing for peace is essential to her embodying the Christian witness. "All along, as Palestinians and as women, we were told to be peaceful. This was understood to mean being passive, being nice, allowing ourselves to be walked over."[37] The Israelis spoke about peace and yet the reality the Palestinians experi-

---

36. Zaru, *Occupied with Nonviolence*, 67.
37. King, *Feminist Theologies from the Third World*, 231.

enced was a peace achieved by pounding oppression into submission and crushing any protests against injustice. "The Israeli government thinks that by using more oppressive measures against us, we will give up our struggle and submit. But the Intifada has taught us not to relinquish the power to make our own decision about how we want our lives to be."[38] She speaks of the strength of nonviolence in offering respect and concern as well as defiance and noncooperation with injustice. "Put into a feminist perspective, nonviolence is the merging of our uncompromising rage at patriarchy's brutal destructiveness with a refusal to adopt its ways, a refusal to give in to despair or hate."[39]

For Zaru, nonviolence is highly practical. She uses the Arabic word *sumoud* to speak to the steadfast, nonviolent resistance. She speaks of how, on almost a daily basis, nonviolent demonstrations are taking place along the West Bank to protest the expansion of the wall and how in the process land is confiscated, and villages are split. Noncompliance with the military movement has also been an action led primarily by women, as they have looked to create their own products and boycott Israeli goods as often as possible. She tells the story of women in a Jalazone refugee camp in Ramallah who stood up to Israeli soldiers when they came to demolish their bread-baking business. The women told the soldiers that no matter what actions the soldiers took, the women would find a way to bake bread. This, Zaru believes, embodies *sumound*.[40]

Another aspect utilized with peacemaking in Zaru's context is that of *sulha*, or reconciliation. This idea takes on different connotations than the English term reconciliation because it also embodies a new relationship with it of equity and respect. She believes that the strength of this method comes from its offering respect and concern on the one hand while meeting injustice with noncooperation on the other.[41] The phrase used at the end of this process is the following: "You are in our home. You are one of us and we take it upon ourselves to help and protect the person who has done us wrong. Forgiveness is a gift from God."[42] After this, a meal is shared together as a commitment to friendship, a covenant meal signifying the

38. Ibid., 232.

39. Ibid., 233.

40. Zaru, *Occupied with Nonviolence*, 73.

41. Ibid., 79.

42. Ibid., 78.

new steps in relationship together and inhibiting the continued harboring of ill feelings.

Zaru believes that peace is consistently finding ways to deal creatively with inevitable conflict. Peace is the process of resolving conflicts in such a way that justice is done and relationship is restored. "Peace is not only the absence of war, but it is the absence of dire poverty and hunger. Peace is freedom from sickness and disease. It is employment and health . . . based on a deep sense of human equality and basic justice. Peace is when we have no fear to assemble, to worship, to work, to speak and publish the truth, even to the powerful."[43] This for the Palestinians means the establishment of rights based on laws, especially when laws are made and manipulated by the powerful to make life difficult for their Arab neighbors. Specifically for Zaru, her work advocates for the mutual recognition of both Israelis and Palestinians, a two-state solution, the right of return for Palestinian refugees, and equality for Palestinians living in Israel. She echoes these themes on the global scale, yet her intent is to live them out in her community and work to educate those she comes in contact with about their value.

South Africa and Peacemaking

South African women, from the years of Apartheid onward, have instigated nonviolent strategies to witness to the need for justice, equality, and peace. Two examples of that are the demonstration against the Pass laws on August 9, 1956, and the work of the Black Sash represent the power of women as a collective force for peacemaking actions. The Pass laws served as one of the most oppressive parts of the Apartheid system, limiting the travel and residence of those imposed upon. The Federation of South African Women organized a march on the Union buildings in September 1955 because they believed such laws threatened their homes and children.[44] Once passes were issued, women began burning passes, approximately 50,000 women in over 38 demonstrations at 30 different centers. The largest and most famous happened on August 9, 1956, at the Union Buildings in Pretoria, with an estimated 20,000 women participating. Susan Rakoczy recalls this event in saying "the women of South Africa knew their rights as human beings and so stood together in peace and solidarity . . . it was a wonderful sight."[45]

43. Ibid., 82.

44. Phiri and Nadar, *African Women, Religion and Health*, 197.

45. Ibid., 198.

This day is commemorated in South Africa as National Women's Day every year, a tale of the courage and conviction these women demonstrated. In the words of Mercy Oduyoye, "At least since 1956 when South African women hit the headlines with their protest against pass laws, they have never rested. They fight forced removals, they protest against the detention of their children. They continue to labor relentlessly for the birth of a South African that respects the humanity of all of God's children."[46]

From here, another event is remembered in South Africa's history, that of the Black Sash. This is a group of women who formed the Women's Defense of the Constitution League to protest the elimination of the common voter's role for the colored population. These women reacted through nonviolent actions, such as "silent, orderly stands and all-night vigils by women outside public buildings in the main urban centers."[47] The women wore black sashes as symbols of mourning and continued after the Separate Registration of Voters Act was passed to protest all of the effects of Apartheid.

Another significant aspect of peacemaking in South Africa came after Apartheid in the truth and reconciliation commission (TRC). This tool for restoring justice helped religious communities see their own complicity in the gross human rights violations of the Apartheid era. Through the means of memory, confession, guilt, and forgiveness for the interest of biblical reconciliation, the commission used the biblical idea of freedom from the past and also freedom for the future, for each other, and for God. One critique of the Truth and Reconciliation Commission was that it was too male. Most often, the women who appeared before the commission were mothers inquiring about the state of their children, husbands, and brothers. The commission spoke of itself as existing for a "gender-neutral truth," denying the role of gender as key in the political conflict. The apartheid regime impinged on the human dignity of women, specifically in the use of torture chambers.[48] Despite this critique, the TRC opted for a process of restorative justice driven by the narratives of the victims.

Deep inequality still exists in South Africa. Black women are the lowest-paid workforces in South Africa. They form 70 percent of the unemployed community. They form 60 percent of the church members, but are viewed by black men as the weaker, subordinate, non-thinking people. Roxanne Jordaan and Thoko Mpumlwana speak of the oppression against

46. Chetti and Joseph, *Ethical Issues*, 158.
47. Phiri and Nadar, *African Women, Religion, and Health*, 199.
48. Coward and Smith, eds., *Religion and Peacebuilding*, 254.

women in South Africa in their chapter in *Feminist Theologies from the Third World*. "With the rise of political violence in South Africa, more women have been raped by white troops in the townships and along the roadside than ever before." In response to these injustices, peace is made through black women becoming their own liberators, not through qualifications or training but through a lived reality. "Black feminist theology is preached in the bushes of Nyanga in Cape Town. Black feminist theology is lived in the streets of downtrodden Soweto. It is lived in the shacks and preached in the shacks throughout South Africa. Black women in South Africa are involved at the grassroots developmental level of a theology from both our intellectual capacity as well as from our inner strength and from our gut feelings."[49] From this they believe that black women's theology in South Africa does not differentiate itself from liberating political tendencies achieved through a peaceful means.

Patriarchy in South Africa must be dismantled because too often the focus has become only that of racial exploitation. "Apartheid has so affected our means of articulating perceptions of domination, subjugation, exploitation and repression that we cannot see the way gender discrimination has been sedimented into the fabric of our society."[50] The Church needs to better articulate a response to the particular injustices women have experienced under the apartheid regime. A deepening contemplative spirituality, in the quest for peace of mind and spirit and the quest for identity, is an important ministry that the Church can provide to women in Southern Africa. The brunt of the repressive laws aimed to control the black African population was borne by the women. Betty Govinden speaks of this phenomenon as the "feminization of poverty." As a result of the industrialization and urbanization, women became the primary income earners in South Africa.[51]

In response to such issues, Denise Ackerman wrote a memoir through the lens of feminist theology relating the healing praxis to the South African context. Her title comes from her study of the book of Joel, using the verse speaking of God repaying Judah for what the years of swarming locusts have destroyed. She speaks uniquely of her role as a white woman in Africa and the responsibility that comes with that skin tone. "So when I hear the term 'Africanisation' I understand it as an inclusive term, a political choice to be critically patriotic to Africa. It spells out commitment

---

49. King, *Feminist Theologies from the Third World*, 154.

50. Ibid., 286.

51. Ibid., 288.

to the freedom and dignity of all peoples in our country. It is also more. We live surrounded by great poverty and need. Africanisation means that we must do what we can about the want in our midst, acknowledging our responsibilities to each other as people who live and work, love and die in this place."[52] By using the medium of letters to those she loves deeply, she issues a challenge to embody a theology that will transform South Africa. She echoes of Dorothee Soelle and Jürgen Moltmann when she recalls that all true theology starts with pain but also comes to know God's delight. As a feminist theologian, she has seen the deep affects of a lack of strong advocacy for feminism in South Africa. She believes her family knew too well "how many South African women supported apartheid policies uncritically and had no qualms about benefiting from the cheap labour of their domestic helpers who were separated from their children and families. Sadly, women are no more immune than men to the seductions of power, to the abuse of privilege, or to the distortions of racism."[53] Doing theology from the core of women's experiences of oppression and with women's desire for justice became paramount for her. Her task of rethinking theology starting with women's experience for the sake of rebuilding a peace-centered Church is especially significant in her context because many of the trained ministers and theologians working on the taxpayers money and connected to the Dutch Reformed Church helped articulate and develop Apartheid theology. Theology as a peace-building enterprise must continue to challenge the dominant, oppressive, and often violent voices of the majority in order to allow a countercultural, liberating, and prophetic undercurrent to emerge.

The work of peacemaking serves as a mandate for the Church regardless of gender. Women in all contexts, be it the early Quakers or the modern-day violent communities of Palestine and South Africa, rise and stand for the ways exploitation must be countered in subversive actions. Issues of creation care, sexuality, and reconciliation all become interwoven pieces in the landscape of building peace when women enter the conversation. Through the narrative of Scripture, the biblical mandate emerges of a true healing (*shalom*) within self, with the environment, with the community, and with God. Any female grasp of this concept must continue to challenge the patriarchal framework of violence and continue telling the tales of women quietly and faithfully serving for peace throughout history

52. Ackermann, *After The Locusts*, 16.
53. Ibid., 32.

and today. Yet this mandate is not limited to women. The true Church must be a peace church, working to dismantle violent structures as well as seeking to reconcile divided peoples of every race, class, and social location. Peacemaking churches will be actively involved in countering community violence by doing the work resisting militarization, nuclear powers, and seeking to bring the Kingdom of God to earth.

As women become equal voices with men in church leadership, and the poor are given a place in the church as norms of power are overturned, then making peace becomes essential to ecclesiology. The Church must be in the struggle for justice and work toward peacemaking in all corners of the globe. The Church can only be as free as its most oppressed member, wherever they may be. This does not imply that all of these women support pacifism necessarily, but they all do believe that building peace in conflict-ridden communities and groups is the work of the Church. These three women understand the struggle for life as a collective struggle, and the Western church cannot disconnect itself from it.

Women in Leadership

Another ecclesial distinctive for Third World feminist theologians that is essential in critiquing Western Evangelicalism is the mandate for egalitarian ministry or mutuality in women and men serving as pastors, teachers, elders/deacons, biblical interpreters, and theologians. It is not surprising that out of feminist voices comes the imperative for women's experience and giftings of the Spirit be included in ecclesiology. These three women would understand the Church as failing to truly be the Church when it only represents a segment of its congregation.

Biblical Examples

The biblical basis for women in church leadership has been well-documented elsewhere, and this brief sketch will only serve to affirm the realities lived in the experiences of Maria Pilar Aquino, Kwok Pui-Lan, and Mercy Oduyoye. In Luke 8:2—3 and Luke 24:12, Joanna serves as the eyewitness and apostle, entrusted by Jesus to testify to the resurrection. Phoebe, spoken of in Romans 16, delivered the epistle to the Romans and served as a deaconess and patron of Paul. These two examples stand as women in leadership in harmony with men rather than lording over them or submitting under them. Other biblical examples as well as the theological vision of mutuality will be discussed further.

The baptism of the Spirit is characterized by an egalitarian nature. Elizabeth becomes a prototypical female example in this regard, immediately using the gifts of the Spirit for ministry by blessing Mary, her visitor.[54] God's saving and empowering work crosses both gender and ethnic boundaries in Church leadership. Galatians 3:28 reminds believers that "in Christ there is no longer male and female." The vision from the Corinthian congregation in 14:34—35 speaks to neither male nor female provoking disorder, indecency or impropriety. Acts 2:17–18 describes women as those the Spirit fills and uses to build up others. The Holy Spirit reorders the empowerment and call to ministry of male and female, young and old, wealthy and poor. Ecclesiological charismology extends to all members of the Body, including women, as numerous examples throughout Scripture demonstrate.

Theological Groundings

Constructive ecclesiology speaks of how Christians play a central role in sustaining the economy of sexual indifference. Women are understood theologically in economic terms, be it monetary, linguistic, sexual, and so forth, and such a modernist dilemma can be overcome by reconnecting theological rituals—such as baptism and Eucharist—with their "sensible transcendetals" of the raw materials of water and earth.[55] Women's bodies cannot be limited to economic exchange, understood as utilitarian tools in the patriarchal capitalistic enterprise. Instead, with connecting women with earthen elements as windows to the sacred and even understands this reimagining as helpful in the conversation of egalitarianism in the Church. This eco-feminist vision considers feminist experience and the female expressions of gender as aspects of the divine presence in the world.[56] Ideolo-

54. Luke 1:42–45. Young, *Renewing Christian Theology*, 57–61.

55. Armour, "Beyond Atheism and Theism," in Jones and Lakeland, eds., *Constructive Theology*, 51.

56. It is important to note here the expressions of gender that extend beyond the binary terms of female and male. The inclusion of women in Church leadership ought to extend to all expressions of gender within the Church, be it those who are intersex, transgender, genderqueer, and beyond. The elimination of patriarchy and male-driven, complementarian models of Church leadership extends the table of God's ministry to all persons.

gies of gender hierarchy may continue to remain deeply rooted in society, yet the Church can offer a different story.

God's embodiment in the entire world reflects the creative divine life that exists beyond gender. Embodiment does not imply sameness but instead evokes continuity and mutability. The embodied, relational God "weeps over a beloved people, a beloved earth, anguishes and builds, argues and responds, watches over creation like a mother eagle, and is steadfast as a rock."[57] This vision of God embodies the entirety of human experience through the Incarnation. This vision speaks against the classical doctrine of the incarnation, which emphasized Jesus's maleness as an essential aspect of the Incarnation. As Rita Nakashima Brock articulates it, "The doctrine that only a perfect male form can incarnate God fully and be salvific makes our individual lives in female bodies a prison against God and denies our actual, sensual, changing selves as the locus of divine activity."[58] Theology has too often supported structures of dominance and submission, building the theological argument that the headship of Christ over his body, the church is reflected in the headship of the husband over his wife. This thinking supported female submission in the Church and must be overcome so women can be welcomed into theological spaces as embodied equals, representing full personhood. New theological imagery must stress interdependence and mutuality, rather than a mere eliminating of gender with the replacement of androgyny.[59] The understanding of feminine inclusion in the Church must incorporate all peoples from the margins into full participation in Church life. Women must still present full human potential and provide an avenue for embodiment in theological discourse.

Such a mutuality of genders reflects God's character. "Trinitarian theology also highlights the perichoretic nature of divine relationality, which in turn provides a map for human communion."[60] This reflects Moltmann's theology as reflected in the section on political theology, as well as the vision of Miroslav Volf in *After Our Likeness: The Church as the Image of the Trinity*.[61] The implications for Volf from this assessment of the modality of

---

57. Ibid., 74.

58. Brock, "The Feminist Redemption of God," in Weidman, ed., *Christian Feminism*, 68.

59. Ruether presenting a helpful discussion of the inadequacies of androgyny for feminist theology in *Sexism and God-Talk*, 127–30.

60. Ibid., 320.

61. Volf, *After Our Likeness*.

persons of the Godhead are the reordering of ecclesial and interpersonal relationships that inspires mutuality. "The Trinity can be the paradigm for the human communion, however, because the Trinity represents the human communion's ground of possibility."[62] Volf understands that out of perichoretic mutuality comes true freedom, and this concept contains great potential for equal relationships within the Church. Volf builds upon feminist theology for his argument as well and states:

> I argue that the presence of Christ, which constitutes the church, is mediated not simply through the ordained ministers but through the whole congregation, that the whole congregation functions as *mater ecclesia* to the children engendered by the Holy Spirit, and that the whole congregation is called to engage in ministry and make decisions about leadership roles. I do not specifically address the ordination of women; I simply assume it.[63]

Rather than a house ruled by a patriarch, the Church best reflects the Trinity when it is a common people, gathered around the Eucharistic table, sharing hospitality with one another. This vision echoes that of feminist theologians Letty Russell and Elizabeth Shussler Fiorenza, as mentioned previously. This Trinitarian vision of women in leadership also critiques the individualistic notion of a separate self from the identity of the Church. The relational web of true ecclesiology promotes egalitarian relationships all throughout the Body. Egalitarianism must primarily champion women to positions of leadership in the church, yet also extend responsibility for the corporate life of the church to the entire community.

Third World Feminist Perspectives on Women in Leadership

Kwok Pui-Lan has written extensively on the value of feminist theology for the Church, particularly in the development of diversity in ecclesial spaces. She understands to even identify as an Asian women signifies the self-awareness of the construct of gender from a particular cultural vantage point that can either be viewed either as helpful or harmful to the growth of the Church. She identifies that being a woman is being an "Other" both in church ministry and in biblical scholarship. "With multiple subjectivity an Asian woman sees not only the fusion of horizons but also the rupture

62. Ibid., 80.
63. Ibid., 2.

of the order of things, not only the cogency of argument but also the arbitrariness of the construction of means, not only unity and coherence but also dissymmetry and fragmentation."[64] Women and their contributions to the Church, particularly from their cultural and ethnic vantage points, contain great potential for creative dialogues and multiple interpretations and readings of Scripture. These multiple marginalities force a rejection of dualistic or binary thinking that creates an "otherness" and forces construction forward, encouraging a multiple consciousness. Kwok advocates for women's ordination not so that they may have a fair share in power domination of church hierarchy over others but, instead because she affirms that women who are called by God should use their freedom and opportunity to exercise "power-with-others" to equip the whole church.[65]

Kwok utilizes the example of the Syrophoenician woman in Mark 7 as the example of Third World women in church ministry with its complex issues of the relationships between racial and ethnic divisions, the interactions of women and men, and of cultural imperialism and colonization in the Church still today.[66] She believes that Jesus's affirmation of this woman is one of many signs he gives of the legitimation of women's active roles in Church ministry. For the true inclusion of women into the life of the Church, the example of the Syrophoenician women represents the multiple marginality, which here is represented in gender, ethnicity, class and religious equality. Yet through her own words, this woman demonstrates to Jesus her great faith, and the theological argument is placed in the mouth of this woman to include both women and "Gentile sinners" in the movement of Jesus. "The story of the Syrophoenician woman makes women's contribution to one of the most crucial transitions in early Christian beginnings historically visible."[67] Kwok concludes that the story represents not a colonialist Jesus, coming to rescue the poor women on the margins but instead of a poor and lowly Jesus who is for the suffering women of Asia.

Maria Pilar Aquino writes of women's roles in Church ministry by describing the particular strengths that women bring to the Common Table. She creates the term "ora-praxis" (*oración* + praxis) as the prayer

---

64. Kwok, *Discovering the Bible in the Non-Biblical World*, 27.

65. Kwok, *Introducing Asian Feminist Theology*, 107.

66. Mark 7:24–30. Kwok cites biblical scholarship in saying, "referring to the woman as a 'dog' [in v. 27] represents not only the degradation of her as a Gentile but also opposition to women's role in the liturgical and theological life of the church." Wainwright, *Towards a Feminist Critical Reading of the Gospel according to Matthew*, 240.

67. Kwok, *Discovering the Bible*, 81.

combined with action that women understand as their role in the Church. "Women demonstrate such prayer in their families and in their communities through rituals, blessings, anointing the sick, preparing the dead for burial, preparing for the communal celebrations of family feasts, and for the feasts of our beloved saints such as Our Lady of Guadalupe and San Juan Diego."[68] This is not just merely social activism and private piety but an expression of women owning their ministry giftings wherever there is need in the name of God's mercy, peace, and justice.

Aquino believes that Latina theology understands the movement and inspiration of the Spirit in the Church as occurring through women and men. Women must cultivate the Christian faith through their cultural context, their understanding of the Christian tradition, and through their personal experiences with God as present in suffering, death, justice, and in the family and community. Liberationist and prophetic arguments for reordering the social order places women at the forefront of ecclesiology, ecumenicism and broader society. The Gospel story of Jesus, for Aquino, calls women to discipleship, liberation, and invites their own story to be used by God for the leading of the Church. She reminds that the majority of practicing Protestant and Roman Catholics are women in the Latin American context, and these women are the primary carriers of the ministry of the Church. Socioecclesial equality is likewise a guiding principle of Latina feminist theology because for Aquino ecclesial equality cannot be divorced from societal equality. "The consequences of inequality are lived only by [women], the "despised identities" of society, of the theological academy, and of churches."[69] Such a struggle for equality gives coherence to theology, praxis, and societal experiences.

Mercy Oduyoye similarly affirms women in Church leadership. In her work, *Hearing and Knowing*, Oduyoye reminds theologians that any conception of theological anthropology must integrate the feminist consciousness. "Women's experience should be an integral part of what goes into the definition of being human," and feminist theology therefore serves as a way of bringing the neglect of women by the church and by theology into the open.[70] This is her "second-generation" liberation theology, as she terms it.

68. Loya. "Latina Feminist Theologies," in Aponte and De La Torre, eds., *Handbook of Latina/o Theologies*, 233.

69. Aquino, "Latina Feminist Theology," in *A Reader in Latina Feminist Theology*, 153.

70. Oduyoye, *Hearing and Knowing*, 120.

This liberation theology now acknowledges the imbalance of the sexes and must therefore reframe Church practices and leadership. Even in a matriarchal society such as hers, women contained no real power and only found themselves valued in society in terms of their relationality to men: wives, mothers, daughters, and so forth. She reminds her readers that throughout the Church's history, women have been key renewalists and revivalists and they must continue to take this place today.

In many ways, Oduyoye describes women as "the other" or "the threatening other," sharing the language from other Third World feminist theologians. She boldly proclaims, "The women are very much concerned about the church, but the church is not so much concerned with women."[71] Ideas and language that legitimize the domestication and minimalization of women must be seriously challenged, and Oduyoye believes this can happen by integrating women into theological discourse. The role of women as central to growth in Christendom contains implications for soteriology, Christian ministry and ordination, and for considering theological anthropology in the contemporary global context.[72] Women must be viewed as integral part rather than "other" or opposite to be dealt with in order for humanity to best reflect God's image as well as for church leadership to best reflect God's nature.

Similarly, Oduyoye speaks of the value of integrating mythology and oral tradition from African religion into the sources for Christian theology, as has been discussed previously. When women's stories and experiences are included in theological discourse and women are welcomed in ministry leadership, theological work can move forward that better reflects true theological anthropology. Women's experiences of spirituality and observations from their lived realities must be understood as valuable starting points for theological reflection.

Overall, all three women emphasize feminine language and symbolism for the members of the Trinity in theological discourse. Oduyoye, for examples, pulls from the African tradition that utilizes a rich variety of female symbols for God, such as God as mother, and describes God with characteristics such as life, fruitfulness, and generational power. Each of these women advocates for broader integration of theological metaphor that truly reflect the language of Scripture and their continent's cultural traditions when speaking of the Divine.

71. Ibid., 135.
72. Young, *Renewing Christian Theology*, 101.

Women in Leadership: Constructive Examples

In embodying true gender inclusivity in the church, all persons now contain the potential to be gifted by the Holy Spirit for preaching, teaching, and other leadership roles. Examples of this include women as senior pastors, women as co-pastors alongside men, women as elders or deacons, women as biblical teachers, and women as denominational leaders. This egalitarian leadership ought to extend also to university and seminary spaces, with the Christian Church advocating for presidents and board members that equally represent both genders. The biblical vision of mutuality stresses that persons of all genders need one another in Church leadership. Perichoretic community highlights different roles in harmony together, interplaying off of one another's strengths and weaknesses. This contains a responsibility for the shepherding and care of the Church as well as the task of faithfully embodying the Gospel to the entire world to be shared by women and men. And because of this, now Christianity contains the true Spirit-initiated freedom to be experienced as good news for all creation, women and men together.

Multiethnic Churches

All three of these women also value intercultural faith communities and the role of intercultural dialogue. None of them believes that their particularized expressions are the "true church," only instead that they contribute aspects from their cultural experiences that the church has previously overlooked. Integration and conversation must be valued. Such valuing will also connect with standing with all who are marginalized and invite as many voices to the table as possible.

In order for this to be possible, the methods for doing theology in our churches today must change. Story now serves as a method for doing theology, and if that is the case, then all stories must be brought to the Sacramental Table and learned from and understood as holy. Story contains the capacity to broaden the cultural dialogue and invite experiences of spirituality in as well as cultural readings of Biblical narratives. Stories must extend across cultures and in any community, but especially in the globalized West, churches must create the space for all cultures and stories to enter in. This begins the process of valuing indigenous cultures and Spirit-led representations in the world over colonialist or exclusivist representations of Christianity. From this framework will be a discussion of the aspect of churches as multiethnic communities.

Theological Groundings

The vision of multiethnic churches is founded on what Maria Pilar Aquino, Kwok Pui-Lan, and Mercy Oduyoye call "intercultural theology." Aquino sees this as an alternative ethical-political project for advancing toward a new world of justice. The hope of another world being possible involves each of these feminist theologians believing that their own theologies or the schools of theology they most work within (Latina theology, Asian feminist theology, etc.) must be informed by other theologies from the margin. The strongest theological enterprise comes from a project where intercultural or multicultural dialogue exists to actively prevent kyriarchal Christianity from continuing a particularized branding of "orthodoxy" or "tradition."

The Church as a multiethnic community echoes the metaphor of Church as a colony of resident aliens in the world.[73] This exodus community understands themselves as strangers in a strange land together, living as aliens and exiles. As an alien community, the Church should be the space where all voices are included, particularly those of minorities as well as the majority. When diverse cultures and backgrounds are included in church communities, this is when the people of God are doing the ministry of God as reconcilers. Just as in Christ humanity has been reconciled to God, so now the chief task of the Church is to continue the ministry of reconciliation.[74]

For voices of the minority and the majority to come together, churches must acknowledge the reasons such exclusions have occurred in the past. This happens only when the Christian practice of confession is central to the liturgical practices of the Church. Recent racial examples such as the Truth and Reconciliation movement in South Africa, the Southern Baptist Convention's Resolution on Racial Reconciliation, and the recent practice of a large body of Japanese Christians confessing to a group of Korean Christians all serve as witness to the world of Christians acknowledging their sins of racism.[75] Those examples highlight this practice as a public

73. 1 Pet 2:11. This language is borrowed from Hauwerwas and Willimon, *Resident Aliens.*

74. 2 Cor 5:18.

75. For more on these examples, see Cannon et al. *Forgive Us.*

liturgical expression and witness to the larger community the difficult yet necessary steps being taken to integrate all voices into our churches.

Third World Feminist Perspectives on Multiethnic Churches

In Aquino's words, "Feminist theologies of liberation imagine and visualize a new world, and they use their interpretive resources (i.e. intercultural theology) to create religious languages that sustain every effort to establish the social conditions most compatible with that world of justice and liberation desired by God."[76] This is the only way that the future Church can begin to build a constructive global theology. Multiple voices must conduct a multidimensional, simultaneous process of doing theology in order to present a model strong enough to address and critique the concerns raised by the Western European Christian tradition now that imperialist, capitalist globalization has become normalized. As stated before, if part of the mission of the Gospel is to present a reality that our hope is in another world being possible here and now, then "the central concern of theology is making clear which historical acts bring salvation and which bring condemnation, which acts make God more present, and how that presence is actualized and made effective in them."[77] Aquino believes that we combat myopic theology by inviting as many voices to the table as possible. There is no homogenous identity of women and no unifying women's strategy for change, as evidenced for Aquino by the varieties of "mujerista theology" available. This principle for her extends beyond feminist concerns to racial and geographic ones, since the realities of globalization have made it so there is no one universal "Latina theology," and so forth. This principle is connected with globalization as pluralistic perspectives on theology become a critical systemic analysis of domination.

Aquino begins to construct multiethnic churches as what she calls "mestizo intercultural communities of justice and liberation." The common methodology is the historicity of the personal and communal reality that gives freedom to open hopeful possibilities and to deal courageously with limitations. "In conformity with our baptismal vocation, we are naming ourselves *as* church—not something to which we belong, but who *we are*."[78]

76. Aquino. *Feminist Intercultural Theology,* 21.

77. Ibid., 13.

78. Aquino. *A Reader in Latina Feminist Theology.* 149.

She characterizes these churches as having four major tasks in constructing an ecclesiology:

- Continuing to develop in a consistent and systemic way the various aspects involved in its theological foundations

- Continuing to claim our right to theological intellectual construction

- Deeply connecting theology and spirituality in feminist and intercultural terms

- Continuing our critical theological analyses of the impact of capitalist neoliberal globalization on everyday life.[79]

The church must include diverse voices in order to be the church according to Aquino's vision of ecclesiology. The ideas of these three women will now be expanded further as an intercultural ecclesiology begins to form.

For Kwok Pui-Lan, the vision becomes the inter-relationality of intercultural dialogue and relationships that are essential to faithful ecclesiology. "Feminist theology is not only multicultural, rooted in multiple communities and cultural contexts, but is also intercultural because these different cultures are not isolated but intertwined with one another as a result of colonialism, slavery and cultural hegemony of the West."[80] Kwok believes that these cultures must be constantly interacting in order for churches to avoid becoming myopic spaces. She stresses the inclusive metaphors in Scripture of the people of God and the Body of Christ as telling of how the Church serves as an intersection of contexts. The church can too often become a narrow, polarizing space, limiting its exposure to other cultural and ethnic perspectives. This can only occur, she proclaims, if the Church makes space within itself for the "other," the opposite, and for much of Western Evangelicalism, the neighboring minority communities.

Multicultural churches are built upon the theological value of aspects of the Gospel being accessible and uniquely understood through every culture. Culture becomes a lens for the Gospel, limited in its scope yet still providing particularized insights that highlight particular truths about God as well as particular sins within our midst. Kwok stresses that this is a demanding ecclesial task that requires much dialogue, struggle, and learning together. Such work, she tells, will "heighten our consciousness of

---

79. Ibid., 126.

80. Kwok. "Feminist Theology as Intercultural Discourse," in *Cambridge Companion to Feminist Theology*, ed. Parsons, 25.

the hermeneutical assumptions underlying Western Christian traditions."[81] Globalization presents intersectionality in our neighborhoods, and our churches must represent this diversity in order to continue faithfully representing the Church. As the Holy Spirit guides our Christian gatherings, what will form is a truer interpretation of Scripture and representations full of integrity of the Church as the community of "a great multitude . . . from every nation, from all tribes and people and languages."[82]

For Oduyoye, the Trinity serves as a model of unity in diversity for the community of faith. She paraphrases statements from the World Council of Churches, saying, "The Unity-in-diversity of the Trinity points to true community. God is One, yet has relationships among the three persons . . . Human communities are likewise to have unity, yet they must encompass diversity."[83] The Trinity serves as more than a metaphysical symbol of deity but also a model for diversity within the Church. She affirms that our human community must conform to the values of the Kingdom of God. She echoes the language of Ephesians: "Putting away falsehood, let every one speak the truth with their neighbor, for we are members one of another."[84] African Christianity understands a belonging to one another, with baptism and the Eucharist being practices that remind believers of our one, knit-together life in God. In African life, to eat from the same dish is to enter into vital relationship with one another, and Oduyoye believes that the work of Communion breaks down tribal and ethnic ties and creates a covenant stronger than blood through the life of Christ. "Because we Africans have our roots in the same soil, drink from the same river or recognize the same divinity, a bond is created that . . . imposes a responsibility to each other."[85] This unity as created and initiated by God is a practice of participating in the unifying life of God. Echoing the words of Acts 17:26, she boldly declares, "From one ancestor God made all nations to inhabit the whole earth," and because of this there is always an understanding of the family of God being a stronger tie than any earthly tie.

81. Kwok, *Discovering the Bible*, 68.

82. Rev 7:9.

83. Oduyoye, *Hearing and Knowing*, 142.

84. Eph. 4:25

85. Oduyoye, *Hearing and Knowing*, 111.

Multiethnic Churches: Constructive Examples

One particular work serves as helpful in the dialogue regarding the multi-ethnic nature of Evangelicalism. Soong-Chan Rah's seminal work, *The Next Evangelicalism*, attempts to begin the process of disentangling Western Evangelicalism from its cultural captivity.[86] Despite being a Western scholar in practical theology, Rah's Korean heritage gives him a vision for the future of the Evangelical church as not merely a color blind community but instead as a global, reconciling Body, faithfully confessing its past and ongoing racial sins. Through examining the intersecting Western lenses of racism, consumerism and individualism, Rah believes the Christian Church can better understand the true heart of the Gospel as dismantling all three of those structures of sin. "If the American church is able to look towards the future with a hope and a promise, then the sin of racism must be confessed and racial justice and racial reconciliation become a theological priority over and above the priority of producing a pragmatic paradigm of church growth."[87] Western phenomena such as Western cultural imperialism and the movement of megachurches have co-opted the true Church. Instead, Rah advocates for true ecclesiology learned from the African, Asian, and Latin American Christian communities in regards to suffering and celebration, holistic evangelism, and the adoption of a multicultural worldview, respectively. His project unabashedly advocates for multiethnic communities of faith as part of the solution for the future of Evangelicalism. "If we define a racially mixed congregation as one in which no one racial group is 80 percent or more of the congregation . . . for Christian congregations, which form 90 percent of congregations in the United States, the percentage that are racially mixed . . .[is only] five and a half."[88] Rah notes the shamefulness of this and how if any other institution lived by these standards, such as a government or higher education institute, there would be considerable outrage. His proposal is that the Christian Church has emphasized the church growth movement and single-ethnic ministries at the expense of the biblical values of racial reconciliation and justice. Too often, he laments, the church in the United States reflects a social reality rather than promoting a theological vision.

---

86. Rah. *The Next Evangelicalism*.

87. Ibid., 87.

88. Ibid., 85. Borrowed from DeYoung, et al. *United by Faith*, 2.

Pluralistically constituted identity and interrelationality are descriptors of global Christianity. The hybridity of Protestant and Catholic influences on church, as well as the economic globalization and political movements all influence the changing diversity within ecclesial spaces. In the current multicultural and multireligious context, biblical visions such as Ephesians 2 speak to an inclusivist ecclesiology. Passages such as Ephesians 2:14-17 burst with implications for overcoming ethnic and racial hostilities for a reconciliatory model. As discussed previously, *oikoumene* (Greek for "inhabited") forms the basis for "ecumene," the root of ecumenical and ecumenism. This vision of Church invites a multiethnic yet single unified global Church to develop across Christendom. "The postmodern and postcolonial situation . . . consists of not one center but of many, with communicative nodes and influences emerging from and extending in multiple directions simultaneously, bringing north, south, East and West into dynamic interaction in the Church."[89] The shift of the Christian center, as discussed previously, must imply an ecclesial mark of congregations representing multiple vantage points in their global theology as well as multiple ethnic groups within their congregations.

Conclusion

Peacemaking, women in leadership, and multiethnic churches are just three attributes of many that the constructive global ecclesiology seeks to include in its practical outworkings of theology. Feminist sisterhood understands the value of restructuring the entire enterprise of orthopraxy so that all on the margins are included in full participation in Church life. The Gospel compels the Body of Christ to be a reconciled people, representing all genders and including all ethnicities in its local communities. As long as the Church continues to ignore the work of building peace within its body and with surrounding neighborhoods, as long as it continues to exclude women in favor of patriarchal leadership, and as long as it remains a monolithic space built upon its white privilege, the Western Evangelical church will fail to represent Christ's true Church. Constructive global ecclesiology imagines an expansive space for ecclesial experiments, with the intentional inclusion of all at the Common Table.

89. Young, *Renewing Christian Theology*, 175.

Conclusion

Women seeking to dramatize the church in the round have sometimes discovered that so much of the furniture is fixed that to remove it demands the cooperation of the whole church.

—MERCY AMBA ODUYOYE[1]

PHENOMENA SUCH AS CAPITALISM, modernity, and colonialism are no longer distinct spaces and instead are now interwoven into society. Out of this reality comes the ability for different distinct methodologies within theology—strands such as liberation theology and evangelical theology—to interplay with one another. Liberation theology, which previously stood in stark contrast to traditions such as evangelical theology, now has more potential for being interwoven then ever before. These critiques seek to move the conversation of theology forward into the 21st century through intersectionality and dialogue.

The key term in the opening paragraph of this conclusion is *potential.* The reality of changing dynamics of Christianity in the West and in the Third World is far more complex and multifaceted than one manuscript can address. The decline of Christianity in the West and the rise of Christianity in the Third World are not limited to mere theological reasons, but cultural, political, and socioeconomic factors have much to do with that. Yet for the sake of this work, the thought experiment was addressed that quite possibly, theologians in the Third World now need to serve as teachers and guides for a fledgling Western Evangelicalism. Perhaps even despite persecution and injustice, the Third World church is incorporating different aspects of ecclesiology into its midst, aspects that western feminist such as Rosemary Ruether have been articulating for decades, but now the western

1. Oduyoye, "Re-imagining the World," 88.

Evangelical church may be poised to listen. Even further, if western Evangelicalism does not believe that it needs to listen to feminist theologians
from around the globe, it does not mean that their theological reflections
are any less true or any less important for the church today. This project is
not trying to belittle or oversimplify the complicated forces of globalization
and its interplay with contemporary Evangelicalism, but rather propose a
possibility as an attempt to move the theological conversation forward and
a *potentiality* that can help in new theological construction for the global
church.

Much has still to be addressed in the field of constructive global
ecclesiology. For the brevity of this project, five distinctives—Salvation,
Sin, Peacemaking, Women in Ministry and Multiethnic Churches—were
given primary focus, yet these do not adequately form a robust ecclesiology.
Theological anthropology and pneumatology, for example, will greatly form
this theological movement. Areas in worship such as a thorough treatment
of liturgy and the sacraments from a global perspective will help shape the
nature of this ecclesial discourse. Both in theology and in an ecclesiology
that informs practical theology, I believe the future of the Church will be
an expanding of its definition of these distinctives based on the inclusion of
voices from every corner of the globe. The constructivist framework invites
repositioning theology from nontraditional starting points in order to better expand on traditional themes and the creative imagination of the Body
still has much to envision.

For my own personal reflection, I do believe in the use of Third World
feminist ecclesiology to critique the Western Christian church. This is a
theological imperative, or one could also say a theological recommenda-
tion that should occur, but it is not an objective truth. Without this being
an absolute, it can serve as a framework for expanding theological ethics
and the field of practical theology going forth. Opponents of the perspective proposed in this work would see particularity as the direction of the
global church. Exclusivity and bounded sets will best inform theology in
the globalized, postmodern and post-Christendom world. Some would
also believe such an overlap of Third World feminist theologians informing Evangelicalism is an impossible or at least unhelpful project. I do not
see these separations as necessary or essential, and I believe that the more
that differing theological perspectives dialogue with one another, the more
robust global theology will be into the twenty-first century.

I believe more commonality exists between the future of Evangelicalism and the future of liberation theology than ever before. Liberation theology in its roots understood its movement as inexplicably connected with Marxist struggles against the totalitarian governments in Latin America of the late 1970s and early 1980s.[2] I believe this aspect is no longer the positioning of these emerging liberationist voices today, particularly of the three I highlighted here. This was the primary argument for Evangelicalism against liberation theology, and its substance no longer holds the weight of the past. Liberation theology also has valued Scripture as one of its starting points, partnered with the experiences of those on the margins, and this also serves as a space of commonality with Evangelicalism. Similarly, Evangelicalism is at a crucial point in its history where it is looking to expand its theological definitions of key tenets such as sin, salvation and so forth beyond the clutches of Western individualism. I believe that one strong example of how these two worlds could attempt to inform one another and attempt this dialogue was that of Orlando E. Costas with his works such as *Liberating News* and *Christ Outside the Gate*, speaking from his Puerto Rican perspective about those on the margins, yet primarily writing for the evangelical church.[3] I applaud his work, but the constructive feminist perspective seeks to push the conversation of global theology even further in order to be more representative. The more the Western Evangelical church can welcome critiques from its sisters and brothers in the margins around the world, the stronger and more representative its theology will be.

This work does not intend to be dismissive of the whole of Western theology as patriarchal and individualistic. However, both of those attributes appear strongly throughout the cannon of ecclesiology and more needs to be written from a communal and feminist perspective to represent true ecclesiology. This work stands of the should of wise men such as Karl Barth, Jurgen Moltmann, John Howard Yoder and others, and their contribution is not to be minimized. Voices such as Rosemary Ruether and other white feminist American theologians began this work, but now we stand at a moment in history when Third World Feminist theologians can continue that vision in teaching the Christian Church.

Much work has yet to be done. Oduyoye's quote above speaks to how difficult such change will be. Constructive feminist ecclesiology is a project of reframing the entire house of Christian theology. I affirm her assessment

2. For more on this, see Gutierrez, *A Theology of Liberation*; and Boff, *Ecclesiogenesis*.

3. Costas, *Liberating News*; and *Christ Outside the Gate*.

that this will take the entire church. And this will take a renewed posturing from many in theological spaces of privilege. But I believe there is no more important task for the entire church—for women and men, poor and wealthy, Third World and First World together. This is a global work of reframing theology, and this is a holy work.

Bibliography

Ackermann, Denise M. *After The Locusts*. Grand Rapids: Eerdmans, 2003.

Althaus-Reid, Marcella Maria, Ivan Petrella, and Luiz Carlos Susin, eds. *Another Possible World*. Reclaiming Liberation Theology. London: SCM, 2007.

American National Biography Online. "Lucretia Mott." Last modified Feb. 2000. http://www.anb.org/articles/15/15-0494.html.

Aponte, Edwin David, and Miguel A. De La Torre, eds. *Handbook of Latina/o Theologies*. St. Louis: Chalice, 2006.

Aquino, Maria Pilar. *Feminist Intercultural Theology: Latina Explorations for a Just World*. Maryknoll, NY: Orbis, 2007.

———. "Latin American Feminist Theology." *Journal of Feminist Studies in Religion* 14 (1998) 89–107.

———. *Our Cry for Life: Feminist Theology from Latin America*. 1993. Reprinted, Eugene, OR: Wipf & Stock, 2000.

———. "Perspectives on a Latina's Feminist Liberation Theology." In *Frontiers of Hispanic Theology*, edited by Allan Figueroa Deck, 23–48. Maryknoll, NY: Orbis, 1992.

———. "Theological Method in U.S. Latino/a Theology." In *From the Heart of Our People: Latino/a Explorations in Catholic Systematic Theology*, edited by Orlando O. Espin and Miguel H. Diaz, 6–48. Maryknoll, NY: Orbis, 1999.

———. "Towards A New World in the Power Of Wisdom." In *In the Power of Wisdom: Feminist Spiritualities of Struggle*, edited by Maria Pilar Aquino and Elisabeth Schüssler Fiorenza, 124–36. Concilium 2000/5. London: SCM, 2000.

Aquino, Maria Pilar, Daisy Machado, and Jeanette Rodriguez, eds. *A Reader in Latina Feminist Theology*. Austin: University of Texas Press, 2002.

Assefa, Hizkias, and George Wachira, eds. *Peacemaking and Democratisation in Africa: Theoretical Perspectives and Church Initiatives*. Nairobi: East African Educational Publishers, 2003.

Barbour, Hugh. *The Quakers in Puritan England*. New Haven: Yale University Press, 1964.

Barbour, Hugh, and J. William Frost. *The Quakers*. New York: Greenwood, 1988.

Barclay, Robert. *Apology*. Edited by Dean Freiday. 1678. Reprinted, Newberg, OR: Barclay, 2009.

Barr, William, ed. *Constructive Christian Theology in the Worldwide Church*. Grand Rapids: Eerdmans, 1997.

Barrett, David B., George T. Kurian, and Todd M. Johnson, eds. *World Christian Encyclopedia*. 2nd ed. New York: Oxford University Press, 2001.

Barth, Karl. *Church Dogmatics.* Vol. IV/3.2. Edinburgh: T. & T. Clark, 1962.
———. *Evangelical Theology: An Introduction.* 1963. Reprinted, Grand Rapids: Eerdmans, 1979.
Bartholomew, Craig, Robin Parry, and Andrew West, eds. *The Future of Evangelicalism: Issues and Prospects.* Leicester, UK: InterVarsity, 2003.
Bauckham, Richard. *The Theology of Jürgen Moltmann.* Edinburgh: T. & T. Clark, 1995.
BBC News. "Country Profile: Democratic Republic of the Congo." Last modified 13 Oct 2011. http://www.bbc.co.uk/news/world-africa-13283212.
———. "DR Congo: 48 Rapes Every Hour, US Study Finds." Last updated 12 May 2011. http://www.bbc.co.uk/news/world-africa-13367277.
———. "DR Congo Women March against Sexual Violence." Last updated 17 Oct. 2010. http://www.bbc.co.uk/news/world-africa-11562059.
———. "UN Classifies Rape a 'War Tactic.'" Last updated 20 June 2008. http://news.bbc.co.uk/2/hi/americas/7464462.stm.
———. "UN Was not Told about 'Mass Rapes.'" Last updated 25 Aug 2010. http://www.bbc.co.uk/news/world-africa-11092639.
Benson, Bruce Ellis, and Peter Goodwin Heltzel, eds. *Evangelicals and Empire.* Grand Rapids: Brazos, 2008.
Blough, Neal. "From the Tower of Babel to the Peace of Jesus Christ: Christological, Ecclesiological, and Missiological Foundations for Peacemaking." *The Mennonite Quarterly Review* 76 (2002) 7–33.
Boff, Leonardo. *Ecclesiogenesis: The Base Communities Reinvent the Church.* Translated by Robert R. Barr. Maryknoll, NY: Orbis, 1986.
Bonhoeffer, Dietrich. *Letters and Papers from Prison.* Rev. ed. Edited by Eberhard Bethge. New York: Macmillan, 1967.
Cannon, Mae Elise, Lisa Sharon Harper, Troy Jackson, and Soong-Chan Rah. *Forgive Us: Confessions of a Compromised Faith.* Grand Rapids: Zondervan, 2014.
Cavanaugh, William T. *Migrations of the Holy: God, State and the Political Meaning of the Church.* Grand Rapids: Eerdmans, 2011.
———. *Theopolitical Imagination.* New York: T. & T. Clark, 2002.
Cavanaugh, William T., Jeffrey W. Bailey, and Craig Hovey, eds. *An Eerdmans Reader in Contemporary Political Theology.* Grand Rapids: Eerdmans, 2012.
Chetti, Daniel, and M. P. Joseph. *Ethical Issues In the Struggles For Justice.* Kerala: Christava Sahitya Samiti Cross Junction, 1998.
Chopp, Rebecca. *The Praxis of Suffering: An Interpretation of Liberation and Political Theologies.* 1992. Reprinted, Eugene, OR: Wipf & Stock, 2007.
Cook, Martin L. "Just Peacemaking: Challenges of Humanitarian Intervention." *Journal of the Society of Christian Ethics* 23 (2003) 241–53.
Costas, Orlando E. *Christ Outside the Gate: Mission beyond Christendom.* 1982. Reprinted, Eugene, OR: Wipf & Stock, 2005.
———. *Liberating News: A Theology of Contextual Evangelization.* 1989. Reprinted, Eugene, OR: Wipf & Stock, 2002.
Coward, Harold and Gordon S. Smith, eds. *Religion and Peacebuilding.* SUNY Series in Religious Studies. Albany: SUNY Press, 2004.
DeYoung, Curtiss Paul, Michael O. Emerson, George Yancey, and Karen Chai Kim. *United by Faith: The Multiracial Congregation as an Answer to the Problem of Race.* New York: Oxford University Press, 2003.

Diocese of London. "Transforming Arms into Tools." http://www.almalink.org/transtool. htm.

Dulles, Avery Cardinal. *Models of the Church*. 1978. Reprinted, New York: Doubleday, 2002.

Dyrness, William A., and Veli-Matti Kärkkäinen, eds. *Global Dictionary of Theology*. Downers Grove, IL: InterVarsity, 2008.

Fitch, David. *The End of Evangelicalism?* Eugene, OR: Cascade Books, 2011.

Fox, George. *The Journal of George Fox*. Edited by Rufus M. Jones. New York: Capricorn, 1963.

———. "Letter to the Governor of Barbados." 1671. In *Faith and Practice*. Evangelical Friends Church Southwest, 2011.

Gillett, Richard W., *The New Globalization*. Cleveland: Pilgrim, 2005.

Gutierrez, Gustavo. *A Theology of Liberation: History, Politics, and Salvation*. Translated by Sister Caridad Inda and John Eagleson. Maryknoll, NY: Orbis, 1973.

Hamm, Thomas D. *The Transformation of American Quakerism: Orthodox Friends, 1800–1907*. Indianapolis: Indiana University Press, 1988.

Hardt, Michael, and Antonio Negri, *Empire*. Cambridge: Harvard University Press, 2000.

Hauwerwas, Stanley, and William Willimon. *Resident Aliens: Life in the Christian Colony*. Nashville: Abingdon, 1989.

Held, David, and Anthony McGrew. *Globalization/Anti-Globalization: Beyond the Great Divide*. Cambridge: Polity, 2007.

Horton, Michael. *Christless Christianity*. Grand Rapids: Baker, 2008.

Husbands, Mark, and Daniel J. Treier, eds. *The Community of the Word: Toward an Evangelical Ecclesiology*. Downers Grove, IL: InterVarsity, 2005.

Jenkins, Philip. *God's Continent: Christianity, Islam, and Europe's Religious Crisis*. Oxford: Oxford University Press, 2007.

———. *The New Faces of Christianity: Believing the Bible in the Global South*. New York: Oxford University Press, 2006.

———. *The Next Christendom: The Coming of Global Christianity*. 2nd ed. Oxford: Oxford University Press, 2007.

Jones, Serene, and Paul Lakeland, eds. *Constructive Theology: A Contemporary Approach to Classic Themes*. Minneapolis: Fortress, 2005.

Kelley, Thomas. *A Testament of Devotion*. New York: Harper, 1941.

King, Ursula. *Feminist Theologies from the Third World*. Maryknoll, NY: Orbis, 1994.

Küster, Volker. *The Many Faces of Jesus Christ*. Maryknoll, NY, Orbis, 1999.

Kwok Pui-Lan. "Chinese Non-Christian Perceptions of Christ." In *Any Room for Christ in Asia?*, edited by Leonardo Boff, Virgilio P. Elizondo, and Aloysius Pieris, 24–32. Concilium 1993/2. Maryknoll, NY: Orbis, 1993.

———. "Chinese Women and Protestant Christianity at the Turn of the Twentieth Century." In *Christianity in China: From the Eighteenth Century to the Present*, edited by Daniel Bays, 194–208. Stanford: Stanford University Press, 1999.

———. *Discovering the Bible in the Non-Biblical World*. Bible and Liberation Series. 1995. Reprinted, Eugene: Wipf & Stock, 2003.

———. "The Emergence of Asian Feminist Consciousness of Culture and Theology." In *We Dare to Dream: Doing Theology as Asian Women*, edited by Virginia Fabella and Sun Ai Park Lee, 92–100. 1990. Reprinted, Eugene, OR: Wipf & Stock, 2015.

———. "Feminist Theology as Intercultural Discourse." In *The Cambridge Companion to Feminist Theology*, edited by Susan Frank Parsons, 23–39. Cambridge Companions to Religion. Cambridge: Cambridge University Press, 2008.

———, ed. *Hope Abundant*. Maryknoll, NY: Orbis, 2010.

———. *Introducing Asian Feminist Theology*. Edinburgh: T. & T. Clark, 2000.

———. "Jesus the Native: Biblical Studies from a Postcolonial Perspective." In *Teaching the Bible: The Discourse and Politics of Biblical Pedagogy*, edited by Fernando F. Segovia and Mary Ann Tolbert, 69–85. Maryknoll, NY: Orbis, 1998.

———. "Mothers and Daughters, Writers and Fighters." In *Frontiers of Asian Christian Theology*, edited by R. S. Sugirtharajah, 147–55. Maryknoll, NY: Orbis, 1994.

———. "Racism and Ethnocentrism in Feminist Biblical Interpretation." In *Searching the Scriptures: A Feminist Introduction*, edited by Elizabeth Fiorenza, 1:101–16. New York: Crossroads, 1993.

———. "Unbinding Our Feet: Saving Brown Women and Feminist Religious Discourse." In *Postcolonialism, Feminism & Religious Discourse*, edited by Laura E. Donaldson and Kwok Pui-Lan, 62–81. New York: Routledge, 2002.

Kwok Pui-Lan, Rita Nakashima Brock, Jung Ha Kim, and Seung Ai Yang, eds. *Off the Menu: Asian and Asian North American Women's Religion and Theology*. Louisville: Westminster John Knox, 2007.

Kwok Pui-Lan, and Joerg Rieger. *Empire and the Christian Tradition*. Minneapolis: Fortress, 2007.

Lohfink, Gerhard. *Does God Need the Church?: Toward a Theology of the People of God*. Translated by Linda M. Maloney. Collegeville, MN: Liturgical, 1999.

McFague, Sallie. *The Body of God: An Ecological Theology*. Minneapolis, Fortress, 1993.

———. *Life Abundant: Rethinking Theology and Economy for a Planet in Peril*. Minneapolis: Fortress, 2001.

Min, Anselm Kyongsuk. *The Solidarity of Others in a Divided World: A Postmodern Theology after Postmodernism*. New York: T. & T. Clark, 2004.

Moe-Lobeda, Cynthia. *Healing A Broken World: Globalization and God*. Minneapolis: Fortress, 2002.

Moltmann, Jürgen. *The Church in the Power of the Spirit: A Contribution to Messianic Ecclesiology*. Translated by Margaret Kohl. 1975. Reprinted, Minneapolis: Fortress, 1993.

———. *Hope for the Church: Moltmann in Dialogue with Practical Theology*. Edited and translated by Theodore Runyon. Nashville: Abingdon, 1979.

———. *The Trinity and the Kingdom: The Doctrine of God*. Translated by Margaret Kohl. 1981. Reprinted, Minneapolis: Fortress, 1993.

———. *Theology of Hope: On the Ground and Implications of a Christian Eschatology*. Translated by James W. Leitch. London: SCM, 1967.

Müller-Fahrenholz, Geiko. *The Kingdom and the Power: The Theology of Jürgen Moltmann*. Minneapolis: Fortress, 2001.

Oduyoye, Mercy Amba. "Be a Women, and African Will Be Strong." In *Inheriting Our Mother's Gardens: Theology in a Third World Perspective*, edited by Letty Russell, Kwok Pui-Lan, Ada Maria Isasi-Diaz, and Katie Geneva Cannon, 35–45. Louisville: Westminster John Knox, 1988.

———. "Christian Feminism and African Culture: The "Hearth" of the Matter." In *The Future of Liberation Theology: Essays in Honor of Gustavo Gutierrez*, edited by Marc Ellis and Otto Maduro, 430–50. Maryknoll, NY: Orbis, 1989.

————. "Feminist Theology in an African Perspective." In *Paths of African Theology*, edited by Rosino Gibellini, 166–81. London: SCM, 1994.

————. *Hearing and Knowing: Theological Reflections on Christianity in Africa.* 1986. Reprinted, Eugene, OR: Wipf & Stock, 2009.

————. "The Impact of Women's Theology on the Development of Dialogue in EATWOT." In *Search for a New Just World Order: Challenges to Theology*, edited by K. C. Abraham, 89–111. Tagaytay, Philippines: Ecumenical Association of Third World Theologians, 1996.

————. *Introducing African Women's Theology.* Cleveland: Pilgrim, 2001.

————. "Liberation and the Development of Theology in Africa." In *The Ecumenical Movement Tomorrow: Suggestions for Approaches and Alternatives*, edited by Marc Reuver. Geneva: World Council of Churches, 1993.

————. "Re-imaging The World: A Global Perspective." *Church & Society* 84 (1994) 82–93.

————. "Spirituality of Resistance and Reconstruction." In *Women Resisting Violence: Spirituality for Life*, edited by Mary John Mananzan, 161–71. 1996. Reprinted, Eugene, OR: Wipf & Stock, 2004.

Olson, David T. *The American Church in Crisis.* Grand Rapids: Zondervan, 2008.

O'Mahony, Anthony, and Michel Kirwan, eds., *World Christianity: Politics, Theology and Dialogues.* London: Melisende, 2004.

Peters, Rebecca Todd. *In Search of the Good Life.* New York: Continuum, 2004.

————. *Solidarity Ethics.* Fortress, 2014.

Phillips, Timothy R., and Dennis L. Okholm. *A Family of Faith: An Introduction to Evangelical Christianity.* Grand Rapids: Baker Academic, 1996.

Phiri, Isabel Apawo and Sarojini Nadar, eds. *African Women, Religion and Health.* Maryknoll, NY: Orbis, 2006.

Rah, Soong Chan. *The Next Evangelicalism.* Downers Grove, IL: InterVarsity, 2009.

Rahner, Karl. "The Church and the Sacraments." In *Inquiries*. New York: Herder & Herder, 1964.

Rieger, Joerg. *Globalization and Theology.* Nashville: Abingdon, 2010.

Ruether, Rosemary Radford. *Sexism and God-Talk: Towards a Feminist Theology.* Boston: Beacon, 1983.

Russell, Letty M. *Church in the Round: Feminist Interpretation of the Church.* Louisville: Westminster John Knox, 1993.

Sanneh, Lamin. *Whose Religion Is Christianity? The Gospel beyond the West.* Grand Rapids: Eerdmans, 2003.

Schneider, John R.. *The Good of Affluence: Seeking God in a Culture of Wealth.* Grand Rapids: Eerdmans, 2002.

Schüssler Fiorenza, Elisabeth. *But She Said: Feminist Practices of Biblical Interpretation.* Boston: Beacon, 1993.

Smith, Hannah Whitehall. *The Christian's Secret to a Happy Life.* Westwood, NJ: Revell, 1883.

Sobrino, Jon. *No Salvation outside the Poor: Prophetic-Utopian Essays.* Maryknoll, NY: Orbis, 2008.

————. *The True Church and the Poor.* 1984. Reprinted, Eugene, OR: Wipf & Stock, 2004.

Spencer, Carole Dale. *Holiness: The Soul of Quakerism: An Historical Analysis of the Theology of Holiness in the Quaker Tradition.* Studies in Christian History and Thought. Eugene, OR: Wipf & Stock, 2007.

Stackhouse, John G., Jr., ed. *Evangelical Ecclesiology: Reality or Illusion?* Grand Rapids: Baker Academic, 2003.

Stansell, Ron. *Missions by the Spirit.* Newberg, OR: Barclay, 2009.

Stassen, Glen. "Just Peacemaking as Hermeneutical Key: The Need for International Cooperation in Preventing Terrorism." *Journal of the Society of Christian Ethics* 24 (2004) 171–91.

Tennent, Timothy C. *Theology in the Context of World Christianity.* Grand Rapids: Zondervan, 2007.

Trueblood, D. Elton. *The People Called Quakers.* Richmond, IN: Friends United, 1967.

Volf, Miroslav. *After Our Likeness: The Church as the Image of the Trinity.* Grand Rapids: Eerdmans, 1998.

Wainwright, Elaine Mary. *Towards a Feminist Critical Reading of the Gospel according to Matthew.* Beihefte zur Zeitschrift für die neutestamentliche Wissenschaft 60. Berlin: de Gruyter, 1991.

Watson, Natalie K. *Introducing Feminist Ecclesiology.* Introductions in Feminist Theology. 1996. Reprinted, Eugene, OR: Wipf & Stock, 2008.

Weidman, Judith L. ed. *Christian Feminism: Visions of a New Humanity.* San Francisco: Harper & Row, 1984.

Wright, N. T. "How Can the Bible Be Authoritative?" *Vox Evangelica* 21 (1991) 7–32.

———. *Surprised by Hope: Rethinking Heaven, the Resurrection and the Mission of the Church.* New York: Harper One, 2008.

Yoder, John Howard. *Body Politics.* Nashville: Discipleship Resources, 1992.

———. *The Politics of Jesus.* Anniversary ed. Grand Rapids: Eerdmans, 1994.

Young, Amos. *Renewing Christian Theology.* Waco: Baylor University Press, 2014.

Zaru, Jean. *Occupied with Nonviolence.* Minneapolis: Fortress, 2008.

Zizioulas, John. *Being as Communion.* Crestwood, NY: St. Vladimir's, 1997.

Made in the USA
Lexington, KY
15 December 2016